MASTERING
THE ART *of* BEADING

MASTERING THE ART *of* BEADING

GENEVIEVE A. STERBENZ

PHOTOGRAPHS BY **STEVEN MAYS**

CHRONICLE BOOKS

SAN FRANCISCO

This book is dedicated to four people who displayed extraordinary love, generosity, and support during this project. The words "thank you" don't begin to express my appreciation for what they've done for me or for the invaluable contribution they've made to this book. I am so very, truly grateful to:

Nancy Gilbert

Steven Mays

Marina Malchin

Frank Santopadre

Copyright © 2010 by Genevieve A. Sterbenz.

Photographs copyright © 2010 by Steven Mays Photography, New York.

Library of Congress Cataloging-in-Publication Data available.

ISBN: 978-0-8118-7160-0

Manufactured in China

Designed by Tracy Sunrize Johnson

Accu-Flex is a registered trademark of Fire Mountain Gems, Inc. Amazing Glaze is a registered trademark of SwimC, Inc. Corp. Artistic Wire is a registered trademark of Artistic Wire Ltd. Beacon Magna-Tac 809 Adhesive is a registered trademark of Beacon Chemical Co, Inc. Beadalon and Dandyline are registered trademarks of Wire and Cable Specialties, Inc. FireLine is a registered trademark of Pure Fishing, Inc. Fun Tak is a registered trademark of National Starch and Chemical Corp. Griffin is a registered trademark of Schinle Perlseiden GmbH Limited company (Ltd). GS Hypo Cement is a registered trademark of G-S Supplies, Inc Corp. Gudebrod is a registered trademark of Gudebrod, Inc. Jablonex is a registered trademark of Jablonex Group. Miyuki is a registered trademark of Miyuki Sawada Co., Ltd. Nymo is a registered trademark of Belding Heminway Compay Corp. Power Pro is a registered trademark of Innovative Textiles, Inc. Soft Flex is a registered trademark of Soft Flex Company, Michael G. Sherman, and Scott R. Clark. Swarovski is a registered trademark of Swarovski Aktiengesellschaft. Thread Heaven is a registered trademark of Hennen, Donna L. doing business as Adam Beadworks. Toho Treasures is a registered trademark of Toho, Co. Ltd. Tool Magic is a registered trademark of The Bead Factory Corp. Michaels the Arts and Crafts Store is a registered trademark of PNC Bank, Delaware, a Delaware Banking Corporation. Petals a Plenty is a registered trademark of DKM, Ltd. DBA Plaid Enterprises Corp. Jolee's is a registered trademark of EK Success, Inc.

10 9 8 7 6 5 4 3 2 1

Chronicle Books LLC
680 Second Street
San Francisco, California 94107
www.chroniclebooks.com

TABLE *of* CONTENTS

INTRODUCTION

Mastering the Art of Beading is an illustrated encyclopedia of techniques and original designs, but it is also a comprehensive reference guide to the art and craft of beading. I have written this book to gather together in one volume all of the information I have gained through years of first-hand experience as I learned and practiced this inspiring and incredibly enjoyable craft.

When I first learned to bead, I searched for information that would help me produce pieces of beaded jewelry that I would be proud to wear or give as gifts. I quickly discovered that there was no single source that included all I wanted to know or that could explain in simple terms the subtle and often intricate maneuvers that I needed to understand if I were to improve my work or advance to the next level in my beading. I found that some books provided dependable technical information but did not venture past the basics. Others were packed with projects but lacked sufficiently detailed illustrations and photographs to support the text, visuals that would have helped me across the gaps in my own knowledge. Many, many books were beautiful and inspiring, featuring lavish photos and even including some charts and diagrams, but these illustrations related specifically to the projects featured in the books. Of course, there were the rare and authoritative few that featured exactly what I was looking for: accurate information, charts, and diagrams. These were so consistently helpful that I continue to refer to them today.

Over the years, I have continued my search and added countless new books to my library. I continued to bead with ever-increasing interest, searching for and working with any new products and tools that came onto the market, keeping those that improved my work and putting the others away in a drawer. I researched new techniques and expanded my base of knowledge and experience. I attended bead fairs and consulted with beading experts and friends who were beaders, listening for any bit of advice that would add to my knowledge and help me hone my skills. My confidence and passion for beading continued to grow, and I became a better beader and a better designer. I took a relentless trial-and-error approach to my work, often beading until the early-morning hours just to figure out why something wasn't working—even though it was "supposed to" according to something I had read. Little by little, I came to trust my intuition and rely on my skills, and I began to develop innovative approaches of my own that, while admittedly quirky, actually worked time after time, until they became new habits. I also changed the sequence of some working methods and developed effective shortcuts that helped me achieve the results I sought without compromising my standards, which made me a more confident and happier beader.

Nonetheless, the world of beading is vast and expanding every day, and although I would have loved to fit everything I have discovered, practiced, and learned into this one volume, it was not possible. However, what is here is as thorough, clear, and inspiring a resource as you could ever hope to find. In truth, it is the resource I would have wanted for myself, the one I've searched for since my first year of beading.

As you immerse yourself in your beading, you may find that a few words about this book's organization will help you to use it more effectively. *Mastering the Art of Beading* is a big book. It begins with the ILLUSTRATED GLOSSARY, a section that visually identifies all of the tools and materials you'll need while beading. Additionally, it clearly explains the purpose and function of each cited item. Through its pairing of visual and written information, you'll be able to identify any supplies that you need or that you are considering purchasing, and you will be able to navigate your way around any bead store with ease.

Central to the work is THE COLLECTION, a section that is divided into five parts, each dedicated to one jewelry-making category: necklaces, bracelets, earrings, rings, and hair jewelry. There are forty original, elegant, fun, and inspiring projects to choose among (plus ten bonus projects online at www.chroniclebooks.com/beading). Each project is introduced by a full-color photograph and a short description, followed by lists of the materials and tools that you will need. From there, you can follow the step-by-step directions, which are supported by over six hundred close-up photographs of all of the projects' essential details. Additional hints and design tips accompany every project to alert you to unique circumstances.

Following THE COLLECTION is TECHNIQUES, a section that includes more than ninety distinct and essential techniques that demystify and simplify ways to bead. It also showcases three hundred step-by-step photographs and easy-to-follow directions. Overall, I have drawn heavily on my firsthand experience, as well as my research, offering approaches that I tested again and again until only the most straightforward and workable directions remained. I know that the more direct the route is to learning a new technique, the sooner you will be able to apply that technique in making beaded pieces of your own design. For extra help, I also include a handy table of contents (see pages 266–267) of all the techniques and applications that are featured in the book, which will make it easy to locate information as you are working.

Concluding *Mastering the Art of Beading* is SOURCES AND RESOURCES, a section that provides an annotated, up-to-date guide to the very best places (whether retail or online) to buy jewelry-making supplies. As every beader knows, there is no end to the pursuit of the perfect bead, the most efficient tool or innovative technique; nor is there ever enough time to transform all the beads we have collected in vials and partitioned boxes into the pieces we imagine.

Even after spending countless hours designing, beading, researching, testing, writing about my beading experiences, and sharing my project designs, I realize that there is so much more to know and so many more designs that I want to begin. I am not alone in this pursuit, and I hope that *Mastering the Art of Beading* becomes the trusted guide and resource you'll reach for each time you spread out your beads, ready your thread or wire, and begin beading a piece of jewelry. I believe that the collaboration between author and reader throughout the pages of this book will enhance your skills and inspire you to follow your creative heart, so that each piece of beaded jewelry you make will bring you satisfaction and inspire you to the next creative level.

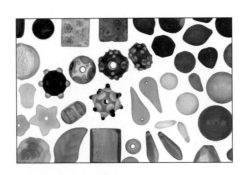

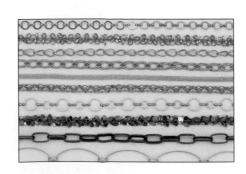

ILLUSTRATED GLOSSARY

BEADS

SEED BEADS

Used in on- and off-loom bead weaving and beaded embroidery, as spacer beads, for simple stringing, and many other purposes, **seed beads** are tiny glass beads. They are available in many shapes, sizes, colors, and finishes. The most uniform and highest-quality seed beads come from the Czech Republic and Japan, although seed beads are also manufactured in France, China, India, and Taiwan. They're sold in packages, tubes, vials, and hanks, usually labeled with their country of origin.

"Seed bead" can refer to the general category of small beads or to the popular, slightly flattened donut shape typical of seed beads. Also known as **rocailles** (French for "rock" or "pebble"), these round beads' shape differs depending on their manufacturer. Czech round seed beads are rounder than Japanese round seed beads, which are square or angular in comparison. Rocailles are also available in a style called true-cut or one-cut. They have one flat facet so they reflect more light. Those that come in size 13/0 are called "Charlottes." In sizes other than 13/0, they are referred to only as "true-cut."

Seed beads come in a number of other shapes: triangle or tri-cut, square or cube, hex or hex-cut, bugle, and fringe or drop beads. Triangle beads are three-dimensional triangles with slightly rounded sides. Hex beads are six-sided cylinders. Bugle beads are skinny, long tubes and may be smooth or twisted; they are available in many lengths. Fringe beads earned their name because they're often used to create beaded fringes on hems. They are tiny teardrop- or egg-shaped beads. Their hole is placed not in the center, but at the narrowest part of the bead; this is called "head-drilled."

Cylinder beads are another type of small glass bead and can be used in all the ways that seed beads are. Most are made in Japan. Brand names include Miyuki Delicas and Toho Treasures. Matsuno is another well-known manufacturer. These short tubes, which look just like crimp tubes, are renowned for their uniformity and extra-large holes, making them perfect for tight weaving stitches such as the peyote stitch.

Both seed and cylinder beads are sized in the same way, notated either by a /0 or an ° symbol, as in "11/0" or "11°" (pronounced "eleven aught" or just "number eleven"). **Aught** refers to how many beads can fit into a given unit of measurement—in this case, an inch. Upon its conception, this sizing system worked well: a size 6/0 seed bead meant that six beads would fit in an inch. As bead manufacturing practices and new technologies evolved, the beads became more precisely cut and uniform, but the sizing system remained the same. If you review the chart that follows, you'll see that this system is no longer very precise. Please note that the numbers listed are approximations. Still, many beaders use it as a general guideline. The most important thing to remember with seed beads is that the lower the number, the larger the bead.

AUGHT SIZE	MILLIMETERS DIAMETER	BEADS PER 1 IN/30.5CM	ACTUAL SIZE
6/0	3.3	10	●
8/0	2.5	13	●
9/0	2.2	15	●
10/0	2.0	16	●
11/0	1.8	20	●
12/0	1.7	22	●
13/0	1.5	24	●
14/0	1.4	25	●
15/0	1.3	27	●

CYLINDER BEADS

11/0 (JAPANESE)	1.7	22	●
11/0 (CZECH)	1.8	20	●

Seed beads range in sizes from 1/0 to 24/0, but you'll typically see only 6/0, 8/0, and 10/0 to 15/0. Cylinder bead sizes are more limited, but you can find 8/0, 10/0, 11/0, and 15/0. Keep in mind that all sizes of beads are not created equal. For example, a Czech 11/0 has a larger diameter but a smaller hole than a Japanese 11/0. Each bead manufacturer has a slightly different sizing system.

The lack of standardization between manufacturers raises another issue: how do you know how much to buy? Czech seed beads come in hanks, typically twelve strands of 20 in/51 cm each. But, depending on the manufacturer, hanks may be sold with fewer strands, or shorter strands. Retailers either sell the hanks as is or break them up and sell the beads by the gram, packaging them in bags or vials. Japanese seed bead are always sold by the gram, rarely by the hank. Some beads are sold in 5-gram bags, or 10-gram vials, but sometimes the smallest amount available is a 40-gram bag. The problem is that a gram doesn't determine bead count, a gram is a metric unit that measures weight. Different bead-making methods mean that a Czech 11/0 bead might not weigh the same as a Japanese 11/0 bead, thus changing the number of beads in a gram. Because it can be so difficult to determine how many beads you're getting, most Web sites will provide an approximate bead count for each size and shape of seed bead specific to their particular packaging.

Seed and cylinder beads can be clear, colored, transparent, translucent, or opaque. They're also treated with various finishes, some applied inside the bead hole. In these color-lined beads, color is adhered inside the hole of a clear glass bead. In silver-lined, gold-lined, and copper-lined beads, foil is adhered inside the hole, making both clear and colored beads glow from the inside. Finishes applied to the outside of beads include AB (aurora borealis), iris, and rainbow (iridescent coatings), matte (frosted or velvety appearance), satin (low luster), pearl (applied to opaque beads), ceylon (a pearl coating applied to semitransparent beads), luster (shiny coating), painted, metallic, and galvanized.

Painted finishes are not permanent and tend to rub off and fade in sunlight—particularly if they are pink, purple, or fuchsia. The very reflective finish, usually zinc-based, used on metallic and galvanized beads is baked onto the beads and rubs off easily. Some beads are plated with a thin coating of real 24K gold, sterling silver, copper, bronze, titanium, nickel, or hematite, and these finishes are permanent. If you intend to use beads for a piece—a bracelet, for instance— that will constantly rub against your skin, be sure that their coating is permanent. Prior to starting your beading, soak the beads overnight in alcohol, acetone, or bleach. If they're fine in the morning, and the finish is still intact, they'll be fine for your piece.

SEED BEADS

A :: Japanese opaque luster pearl blue seed beads

B :: Czech opaque red and orange seed beads

C :: Czech clear color-lined hot pink seed beads

D–E :: Czech transparent red and coral seed beads

F :: Czech transparent baby pink AB seed beads

G :: Japanese transparent matte green seed beads

H :: Chinese painted metallic pink seed beads

I :: Czech silver-lined gold seed beads

J :: Czech metallic blue bugle beads

K :: Japanese silver-lined crystal triangle beads

L :: Japanese silver-lined gold cylinder beads

M :: Japanese hematite cylinder beads

N :: Japanese galvanized silver cylinder beads

O :: Japanese 24K gold true-cut seed beads

GLASS BEADS

Glass beads are the largest and most varied category of beads. They are the most plentiful in bead stores and are generally inexpensive. Excluding seed beads, glass beads are usually sized in 1 mm increments, from 2 mm dia. to 20 mm dia. The most popular types of glass beads include the following:

Pressed-glass beads are made by pressing molten glass into molds and they're known for their whimsical shapes and textures: flowers, leaves, fruit, and animals. The highest-quality beads are made in the Czech Republic and Germany. This handmade bead-making method is also used to produce popular druk beads, which are perfectly round, seamless beads. They come in practically every shape and color imaginable, but be sure to look for ones without seams, which indicate the beads were poorly made.

Fire-polished glass beads are an excellent, less expensive alternative to full-lead crystal beads. These faceted beads are available in the same shapes and sizes that Austrian crystals come in but are made from glass and contain no lead. Fire-polished beads do not have sharp edges or clearly defined facets, but they do come in gorgeous colors and finishes. After they are machine cut, the beads are placed in a kiln, which melts and softens the facets. Look for high-quality Czech fire-polished beads from companies like Jablonex.

Lampwork beads are made by hand. Glass is melted with a flame torch before the beads are shaped. Because they are created around a mandrel, their holes tend to be larger than those of manufactured beads. They are also more expensive. They can be plain—simple round or oval beads in bright colors—or elaborately decorated—with raised decorations such as bumps ("bumpies," or dots of glass) and flowers. High-quality lampwork beads' bumpies are widest where they are attached to the bead. Glass dots with a narrow base will break off easily. Other handmade glass beads include foil-lined, dichroic, millefiori, hand-blown cane beads, Venetian-style beads, and artist-crafted beads.

Cubic zirconia (CZ) diamond look-alike beads have brilliant sparkle and color, much like full-lead crystal beads, but they're made in a laboratory from a crystalline form of zirconium dioxide. Though they're not made from glass, Web sites typically place CZ beads in the glass category, so look for them there. Despite these beads' beauty, they tend to be less durable than full-lead crystal beads. Wire wraps tend to grind away their thin sides. Drop them once, and they'll shatter.

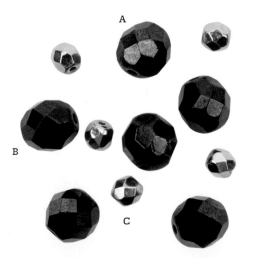

FIRE-POLISHED GLASS BEADS

A :: Metallic green Czech fire-polished round beads

B :: Metallic aubergine Czech fire-polished round beads

C :: Gold Czech fire-polished round beads

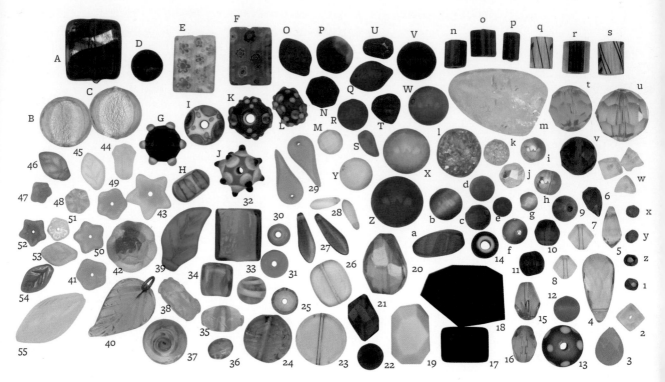

GLASS BEADS

A :: Fuchsia German foil-lined lampwork flat rounded square

B :: Pink foil-lined lampwork coin

C :: Blue foil-lined lampwork coin

D :: Deep purple foil-lined lampwork round bead

E :: Blue millefiori flat rounded rectangle (or tablet)

F :: Orange millefiori flat rounded rectangle (or tablet)

G :: Blue bumpy lampwork rondelle

H :: White with blue and green geometric dots lampwork rondelle

I :: White with fuchsia and blue geometric ringed dots lampwork rondelle

J :: Blue with white and brown bumpy lampwork round bead

K :: Orange flowers lampwork rondelle

L :: Orange flowers lampwork rondelle

M :: Light green faceted fire-polished round bead

N :: Red faceted fire-polished round bead

O :: Red Czech pressed-glass lemon

P :: Variegated Czech pressed-glass fruit

Q :: Orange Czech pressed-glass lemon

R :: Orange Czech pressed-glass orange

S :: Yellow Czech pressed-glass leaf

T :: Red Czech pressed-glass leaf

U :: Red Czech pressed-glass tulip

V :: Red round glass bead

W :: Salmon round glass bead

X :: Pink round glass bead

Y :: Light green glass round bead

Z :: Bubblegum pink Czech druk bead

a :: Pink cat's-eye four-sided oval

b :: Pink cat's-eye round bead

c :: Orange faceted cat's-eye round bead

d :: Orange cat's-eye round glass bead

e :: Orange cat's-eye round bead

f :: Blue cat's-eye round bead with rhinestones

g :: Blue faceted cat's-eye round bead

h :: Green metallic side-coated round bead

i :: Blue metallic side-coated round bead

j :: Crystal AB fire-polished round bead

k :: Crystal AB German pressed-glass quilted coin

l :: Peach crackle glass bead

m :: Crystal crackle nugget

n-p :: Purple striped hex-cut glass beads

q-s :: Pink and black glass cane beads

t :: Blue faceted round glass bead

u :: Pink faceted round glass bead

v :: Lavender faceted round glass bead

w :: Light blue glass chips

x-y :: Lavender metallic Czech fire-polished round beads

z, 1 :: Teal metallic Czech fire-polished round beads

2 :: Pink glass cube

3 :: Lavender faceted glass flat briolette

4 :: Pink faceted glass flat briolette

5 :: Pink faceted glass briolette

6 :: Purple faceted glass briolette

7 :: Lime green glass flat diamond

8 :: Pale green glass flat diamond

9 :: Pink and green variegated glass round bead

10 :: Orange variegated glass round bead

11 :: Hot pink glass round bead

12 :: Green matte glass round bead

13 :: Green matte white-lined glass round bead

14 :: Orange glass pony bead

15 :: Yellow faceted glass drop

16 :: Green faceted glass oval

17 :: Opaque purple glass flat rounded rectangle (or tablet)

18 :: Garnet faceted glass nugget

19 :: Opaque light blue faceted glass nugget

20 :: Pink AB Czech fire-polished nugget

21 :: Purple faceted glass irregular flat oval

22 :: Garnet faceted glass coin

23 :: Light blue glass coin

24 :: Aqua blue lampwork flat coin

25 :: Aqua blue glass spacer disc

26 :: Pink part-frosted glass flat rounded rectangle (or tablet)

27 :: Pink glass dagger beads

28 :: Light pink AB glass dagger beads

29 :: Lime green glass paddle beads

30 :: Opaque green glass rondelle

31 :: Aqua blue glass spacer disc

32 :: Turquoise lampwork flat rectangle

33 :: Blue and white lampwork round bead

34 :: Blue and green lampwork flat square

35 :: Green stripe lampwork rolled oval

36 :: Blue lampwork oval

37 :: Blue and clear lampwork round bead

38 :: Green and aqua lampwork wheel

39 :: Aqua blue German pressed-glass leaf

40 :: Aqua blue lampwork leaf

41 :: Lime green Czech pressed-glass flower

42 :: Pink and clear frosted German pressed-glass rose

43 :: Light blue Czech pressed-glass flower

44 :: Yellow AB Czech pressed-glass tulips

45 :: Yellow AB Czech pressed-glass leaf

46 :: Green Czech pressed-glass leaf

47 :: Mustard yellow Czech pressed-glass button flower

48 :: Pink German pressed-glass flower

49 :: Aqua blue Czech pressed-glass flower

50 :: Blue frosted Czech pressed-glass flower

51 :: Yellow AB Czech pressed-glass flower

52 :: Olive green Czech pressed-glass flower

53 :: Pink matte Czech pressed-glass leaf

54 :: Aqua blue AB Czech pressed-glass leaf

55 :: Venetian-style hand-blown glass oval

CRYSTALS

Crystal has multiple meanings in the beading world. It can refer to the naturally forming semi-precious clear stone quartz crystal (also called rock crystal). It can also refer to machine-cut faceted beads that are made of glass, or to leaded-glass beads such as Austrian or Czech crystals. It can be a color reference, too, meaning "clear."

When purchasing authentic crystal, look for beads that are made from leaded glass (also called lead crystal). The addition of lead is what changes glass into crystal. Full-lead crystal must contain at least 24 percent lead, and well-known companies such as Swarovski use around 32 percent. Glass alone has a specific refractive index, which means that even when it is cut into a faceted bead, the light passing through it will be reflected only a certain amount. Adding lead oxide to molten glass to produce lead crystal raises the refractive index, giving lead-crystal beads much more sparkle and shine than glass. It also makes them weightier than glass beads of the same size. It should be noted that the added lead is stabilized within the glass, so crystal beads aren't toxic. For more information, read the health and safety sections of each company's Web site.

Austrian crystal has become synonymous with Swarovski crystal. Manufactured in Wattens, Austria, Swarovski is known for its high-quality full-lead crystal beads. In the late 1800s, Daniel Swarovski was the first to perfect machine-cut facets that are microscopically identical in size and shape; the sharp-edged facets of Swarovski beads produce maximum sparkle. Swarovski was also the first to duplicate gemstone colors in his crystals. While Swarovski crystals are still the best known, other companies such as Preciosa Crystal, in the Czech Republic, have developed new innovations and technologies of their own. Today there is very little difference, cost- or quality-wise, between the two.

Other countries such as China and Japan make lead-crystal beads as well. Unfortunately, quality control of Chinese crystals is less standardized, and it's more difficult to authenticate the lead percentage, even if it's listed on the packaging. Japanese crystals, while high quality, have less-precise facets than Austrian or Czech crystals. Still, these crystal beads are beautiful and much less expensive, so don't count them out, especially for a design that requires a lot of beads.

Crystals come in many shapes, sizes, and colors and some are available with specialized coatings permanently applied to the surface area of the bead. These change both its color—sometimes subtly, sometimes boldly—and the way it reflects light. The most common coating is called aurora borealis, for the northern lights, abbreviated as AB. This extremely thin iridescent coating creates a subtle rainbow effect. Other coatings include matte finish, vitrail, satin, glacier blue, and dorado.

AUSTRIAN CRYSTAL

A–G :: Round crystals

H :: Donut

I–O :: Rondelles

P–Y :: Bicones

Z, a–d :: Cubes

e–f :: Cubes with AB finish

g :: Square ring (no bead hole)

h :: Crystal cosmic bead (also called cosmic freeform diamond or faceted crystal nugget)

i :: Butterfly

j :: Marguerite flower (also called Margarita flower)

k :: Round ring (no bead hole)

l–o :: Briolettes

p :: Flat briolette

q :: Twist (also called faceted-coin)

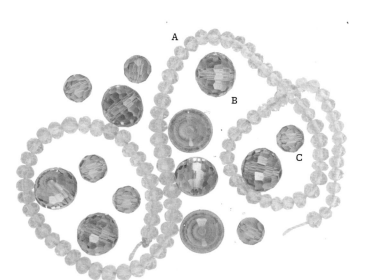

CHINESE CRYSTAL

A :: Rondelles

B :: Multifaceted hexagon-cut round beads

C :: Hexagon-cut round beads

RHINESTONES

Rhinestones are faceted glass or crystal, but sometimes plastic, that imitate sparkling diamonds and colorful gemstones. Rhinestones are often backed with silver, gold, or colored foil to enhance their sparkle and color. Just as with beads, full-lead crystal rhinestones will give you the most brilliance and gemstone-like color. Swarovski makes crystal **flat-back rhinestones** in many colors, ranging in size from SS5 to SS48 (1.9 mm to 11 mm in diameter). They also make **pointed-back jewels with sew-on settings** in twenty-one colors, eight shapes, and twelve sizes (available at M&J Trimming; see "Sources and Resources"), which are excellent focal beads and rival the look of precious stones. Sew-on settings with open backs and four holes in the setting can easily be used with beading wire or other stringing material. **Rhinestone chain, buttons, charms,** and **costume jewelry** (whole pieces or parts) are also excellent sources of rhinestones to feature in your beading designs.

RHINESTONES

A–C :: Rhinestone buttons

D–E :: Rhinestone earrings

F :: Flat-back rhinestones

G :: Rhinestone chain

H :: Rhinestone beads with shanks

I–K :: Rhinestone pins

L–M :: Rhinestone earrings

N :: Rhinestone charm

O–P :: Pointed-back rhinestones with settings

PEARLS

Pearls are created when an irritant, such as a grain of sand, gets inside a mollusk, such as a saltwater oyster or a freshwater mussel. Layers of nacre (the iridescent coating seen inside shells, also known as mother-of-pearl) are added around the irritating particle. After years of layering, a pearl is produced. This laborious process makes naturally occurring pearls rare and expensive. **Cultured pearls** are less expensive. Instead of waiting for nature to introduce an irritant, humans do. Variously shaped beads are added as irritants, which result in variously shaped pearls. Saltwater oysters can produce only a few cultured pearls each, while freshwater mussels can produce as many as fifty each, making freshwater cultured pearls less expensive still. Cultured pearls typically come in white and cream, and sometimes have a pink, peach, or lilac hue. They are usually bleached (with light) and/or dyed and are graded, although this grading system is not standardized. Generally speaking, the more layers of nacre, the more luminous the luster and the rounder the pearl, and the higher the grade it will receive, such as A, AA, or AAA. A grade-D cultured pearl will have more wrinkles or ridges and less consistent luster or color. Other, even less expensive but very high-quality options are **glass** and **crystal pearls.** Multiple layers of a pearlescent coating are added over glass or crystal (such as Swarovski crystal pearls). They are available in a wide variety of shapes and colors, and new technologies have made them resistant to flaking, peeling, and chipping.

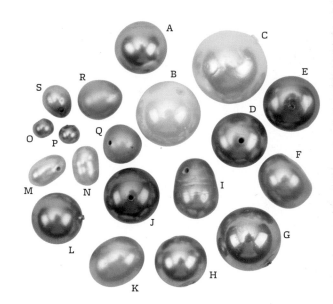

POPULAR PEARL SHAPES

A– C, G–H, L, O–P :: Round

D–F, J :: Button (round with one flat side; drilled through short center)

I, S :: Top-drilled potato (can be bottom-drilled too)

K, Q, R :: Potato (drilled on short or long dimension)

M–N :: Head-drilled rice (egg or oval shaped; usually drilled on long dimension)

SHAPES NOT FEATURED IN PHOTO:

Teardrop :: Resembles potato but with well-defined point

Coin :: Flat round disc

Stick :: Long and narrow, resembling a stick; may be long-drilled, top-drilled, or center-drilled

Keishi or petal :: Freeform cup or petal shape

SHELLS

PLASTIC BEADS

Natural materials, such as wood, horn, seeds, and shells, have long been used to create beads. Beads made from **shells** are extremely common and available in most bead stores. Typically you'll find pretty, but ordinary, whole shells with holes drilled in them for stringing, as well as exotic shells such as the iridescent ocean-colored paua shells. Beads made from mother-of-pearl are the most readily available and can be dyed in soft pastels or vibrant bright colors and shaped into coins, ovals, squares, donuts, chips, and even intricately carved flowers.

Plastic beads are often considered the ugly ducklings of the bead world—cheap, poor-quality substitutes for glass and stone. But don't overlook them. They come in so many styles, shapes, and brilliant colors and add only a fraction of the weight of glass or stone to your jewelry designs. They blend in beautifully with other types of beads and can offset the overall cost. New plastic beads are usually made from acrylic and are available as glitter and miracle beads, crackle beads, faceted beads that mimic crystal, vacuum beads, beads inlaid with rhinestones and resin that look like frosted glass. High-quality plastic beads do not have seams.

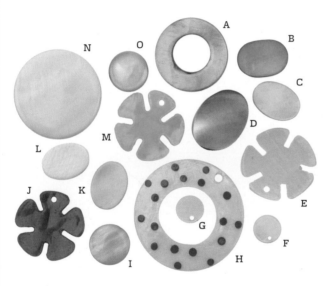

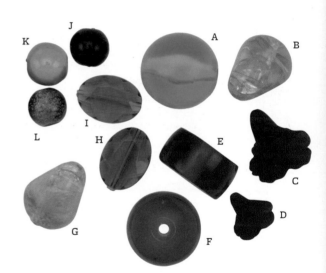

SHELLS

A :: Dyed mother-of-pearl donut

B, C, K, L :: Dyed mother-of-pearl flat oval

D :: Brown lip shell flat oval

E, J, M :: Dyed capiz shell five-petal flower

F–G :: Dyed mother-of-pearl top-drilled coin

H :: Hand-painted capiz donut

I, O :: Dyed mother-of-pearl coin

N :: Synthetic mother-of-pearl coin

PLASTIC BEADS

A :: Round resin bead

B :: Acrylic crackle drop

C–D :: Vintage Lucite flowers

E–F :: Resin wheels

G :: Acrylic crackle drop

H–I :: Faceted acrylic flat ovals

J–K :: Round miracle beads

L :: Glitter acrylic bead

Plastic beads made from Bakelite and Lucite are considered vintage and are among the most collected and prized plastic beads. The term **vintage** can mean the beads are old—many have been out of production for decades—although new bead companies bought out the old inventory of Bakelite and Lucite manufacturers and currently sell them as vintage. Other bead companies purchased old bead molds and use the old Bakelite and Lucite recipes to create new beads, which are also sold as "vintage."

CERAMIC BEADS

Ceramic and **porcelain beads** are made from clay that is glazed and fired in a kiln. They are the oldest types of beads, have a nice weight, and can be found in styles ranging from ultra-modern to ones that resemble ancient pottery. Ceramic and porcelain can be shaped and molded into flowers or animals, sculpted with three-dimensional details, or painted with intricate scenes. You can even buy "blank" white porcelain beads and paint and decorate them yourself. You can also use polymer clay to make your own beads. Although it is technically a plastic, this clay is available in tons of colors and can be shaped or sculpted and baked in a regular household oven, making it easier to use than ceramic or porcelain.

CERAMIC ROSE WITH IRIDESCENT GLAZE

METAL BEADS

Metal beads are among the most versatile. Large ones, or grouped sets, can become a focal point and resemble pieces made by a metalsmith; small ones, such as **spacer beads,** can be used as accents. They come in precious metals, including gold and silver, and base metals, such as brass, copper, and aluminum, as well as a variety of gold, silver, and copper tones and metal finishes, including antiqued beads, which are pitted or darkened to look aged. Whether they are plain round beads or elaborate **filigree beads** with lacy open wirework, most metal beads—especially ones made from precious metals—are hollow to reduce weight and cost. (See Metals, page 46, for more information.)

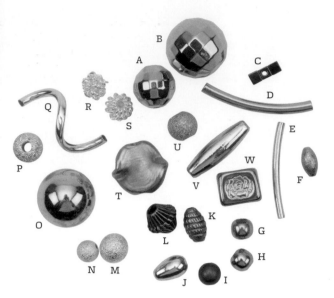

METAL BEADS

A–B :: Faceted round gold beads (also called disco beads)

C :: Hematite cubes

D–E :: Gold-plated and sterling silver curved tubes

F :: Brushed gold oval

G–I :: Gold, silver, and antique copper hollow round beads

J :: Silver-plated hollow teardrop

K :: Antique silver corrugated oval

L :: Antique gold corrugated bicone

M–N :: Bright silver laser-finished round beads (also called stardust beads)

O :: Gold-plated solid round bead

P :: Sterling silver laser-finished round beads (also called stardust beads)

Q :: Sterling silver twisted tube

R–S :: Silver-plated coiled-wire round beads

T :: Matte gold German metal twisted coin

U :: Gold-filled laser-finished round beads (also called stardust beads)

V :: Silver-plated long oval

W :: Gold-plated embossed cube

METAL SPACERS

A, E :: Gold-plated corrugated round beads

B, F :: Hollow brass- and silver-plated round beads

C–D :: Antique silver and gold-plated daisy spacer (also called a dotted rondelle)

G :: Silver-plated disc

H :: Antique gold corrugated flower saucer

I :: Sterling silver Austrian crystal rhinestone rondelle

J :: Gold-plated disc

K :: Gold-plated ridged tube

L :: Antique gold corrugated saucer

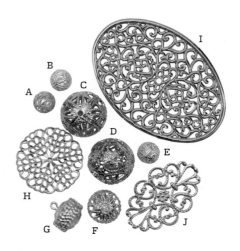

FILIGREE BEADS

....

A, B, E :: Silver-plated filigree round beads

C–D :: Gold-plated filigree round beads

F–G :: Silver-plated filigree charm beads

H–J :: Silver-plated round and oval filigree components

Precious and **semiprecious stones** are made from rocks, minerals in the earth that are harvested for their beauty or rarity and cut and polished by artisans. Only four gems are considered precious stones: diamond, ruby, sapphire, and emerald. These gemstones are so prized and expensive that they are rarely drilled with holes and turned into beads. They are typically showcased in precious-metal settings so that no part of them is wasted.

In the beading world, you will deal almost exclusively with semiprecious stones. This category incorporates all natural rock minerals, and some organic minerals such as cultured pearls and coral, except for "big four." Important semiprecious stones include amethyst, aquamarine, turquoise, peridot, topaz, opal, and lapis lazuli. Goldstone is included in the photo, but it is technically not one since it's made from glass with tiny copper flecks. It's included in this section because it's not treated like glass; it's shaped, cut, and drilled just as semiprecious stones are.

Before purchasing semiprecious stones, inspect them carefully. Stones get shopworn and facets and edges can chip or crack. If you notice one flawed stone on a strand, ask about removing it or lowering the strand's price. Store employees are usually happy to negotiate, and you might be able to conceal small flaws within your jewelry designs, making the strand worth buying.

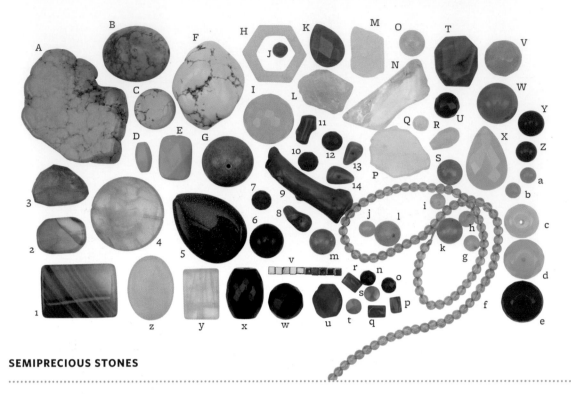

SEMIPRECIOUS STONES

A :: Stabilized and dyed turquoise slab

B :: Turquoise oval

C :: Turquoise coin

D :: Turquoise oval

E :: Faceted turquoise flat rounded rectangle

F :: Stabilized and dyed turquoise nugget

G :: Rhodonite round bead

H :: New jade hexagon-shaped donut

I :: Faceted new jade round bead

J :: Faceted dyed jade round bead

K :: Faceted dyed jade flat briolette

L :: Rough-cut rose quartz nugget

M :: Rough-cut quartz crystal nugget

N :: Quartz crystal flat irregular fancy briolette

O :: Rose quartz round bead

P :: Rose quartz chip

Q :: Faceted rose quartz rondelle

R :: Faceted rose quartz teardrop

S :: Faceted cherry quartz round bead

T :: Irregular faceted cherry quartz nugget

U :: Faceted dyed quartz round bead

V :: Faceted dyed quartz round bead

W :: Dyed quartz round bead

X :: Faceted dyed quartz flat briolette

Y :: Dyed quartz round bead

Z :: Dyed jade round bead

a–b :: Red aventurine round beads

c–e :: Faceted dyed quartz rondelles

f :: Peridot round beads

g–m :: Olive jade round beads

n–o :: Faceted carnelian round beads

p–r :: Carnelian flat rectangles

s–t :: Faceted carnelian coins

u :: Faceted carnelian nugget

v :: Hematite cubes

w :: Faceted onyx round bead

x :: Faceted onyx barrel

y :: Fluorite flat rectangle

z :: Jade flat oval

1 :: Agate flat rectangle

2 :: Agate flat oval

3 :: Amber nugget

4 :: Hematoid quartz coin

5 :: Goldstone flat briolette

6 :: Carnelian round bead

7, 10, 12 :: Faceted dyed coral round beads

8, 11, 13–14 :: Dyed coral chips

9 :: Dyed coral stick bead

BEAD SHAPES

Here are some common **bead shapes** you should be familiar with.

A :: Faceted flat briolette

B :: Briolette (head-drilled)

C :: Teardrop (or briolette)

D :: Rough-cut nugget

E :: Nugget

F :: Faceted pipe

G :: Cylinder (or tube)

H :: Faceted long diamond
(or long bicone)

I :: Dagger

J :: Rondelle

K :: Rice

L :: Oval

M :: Potato

N :: Rondelle

O :: Rondelle

P :: Faceted barrel

Q :: Round

R :: Faceted round (small)

S :: Faceted round (large)

T :: Heart

U :: Faceted flat melon

V :: Flat oval

W :: Bicone

X :: Flat diamond

Y :: Flower

Z :: Faceted twisted coin

a :: Twisted coin

b :: Faceted coin

c :: Chips

d :: Donut

e :: Paddle

f :: Oval

g :: Flower

h :: Saucer

i :: Faceted wheel

j :: Coin drop

k :: Flat square

l :: Flat rounded square

m :: Flat rounded rectangle
(or tablet)

n :: Square ring (no bead hole)

o :: Cube

p :: Octagon

q :: Barrel

BEAD SIZE CHART

Beads are usually measured in millimeters. As expected, the higher the number, the larger the bead. The exception to this are seed beads, where the lower the number, the larger the bead. A size 10/0 seed bead is approximately the same width as a 2 mm round bead. The following are common bead sizes.

ROUND BEADS

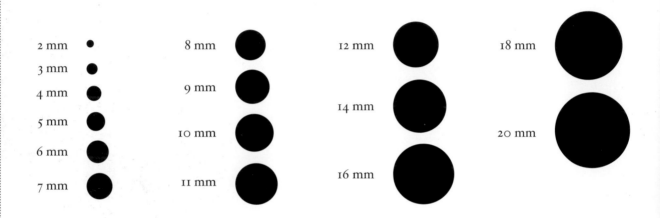

OVAL BEADS

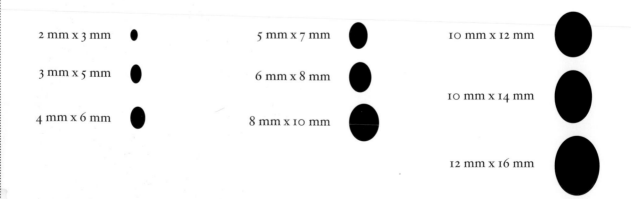

JEWELRY LENGTHS CHART

NECKLACES

Collar: 12–13 in/30.5–33 cm

Choker: 14–16 in/35.5–38 cm

Princess: 17–19 in/43–48 cm

Matinee: 20–24 in/51–61 cm

Opera: 28–35 in/71–89 cm

Rope: 40–45 in/102–114 cm

Lariat (no clasp): 48 in/122 cm and up

BRACELETS

Small Bracelet: 6.5–7 in/16.5–18 cm

Medium Bracelet: 7–8 in/18–20 cm

Large Bracelet: 8–9 in/20–23 cm

Small Ankle Bracelet: 9 in/23 cm

Medium Ankle Bracelet: 10 in/25.5 cm

Large Ankle Bracelet: 11 in/28 cm

TOOLS AND EQUIPMENT

The more beads you collect, the more different types of **storage** you will need. Small vials, little boxes (such as the ones shown), and shallow bead trays are best for storing and accessing small beads, seed beads, and crystals. Bead boxes with deeper compartments should be used for larger beads. Clear plastic containers or metal containers with clear tops make identifying your beads easier. Most clear plastic bead boxes are made from modular plastic or acrylic and will crack if dropped. Soft, opaque plastic bead boxes are a safer option, but you can't see into them.

It is very easy to drop and lose beads while working with them. Cover your work surface with a **bead cloth** such as a dish towel, a hand towel, or a piece of flannel or brushed cotton prior to beginning your work. Or use a **bead mat,** a rubberized or flocked mat available at bead and craft stores, to prevent runaway beads. It is also a good idea to place an area rug or towel under your work chair if you don't have carpeting.

Clips and **clamps** are good to have on hand to temporarily secure the ends of stringing materials and prevent beads from falling off them as you work. Choose ones that won't dent or damage your stringing material or wire. Alternately, cover their sharp edges with masking tape, or place scraps of fabric between the clip and stringing material.

The more you bead, the more findings you'll collect, too. Keep jump rings, crimp beads, and clasps categorized in secure storage boxes. Check out bead and craft stores for all the different storage options.

A **polishing cloth** is the last tool you need to finish your jewelry pieces. Use this dry microfiber cloth to remove any grease, dust, and fingerprints. You can also purchase polishing cloths that are coated with cleaner to remove tarnish from your sterling pieces. Read manufacturer's instructions to ensure that you don't use a cloth that could strip off gold or silver plating.

MEASURING TOOLS

You'll need a **ruler** and **measuring tape** to measure stringing materials, wire, and beaded strands as you work. You'll also want to have **calipers** that measure beads and findings in millimeters. You can also use calipers to estimate the size of items sold online before you buy them.

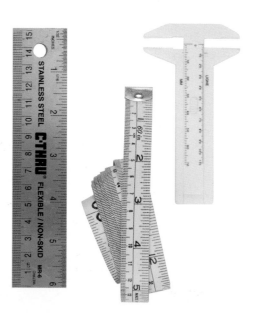

A **bead design board** helps you lay out beads for single and multistrand necklaces and bracelets before you string them. Bead boards like the one shown here have multiple grooves that are molded into the plastic and a flocked surface that keeps beads in place. They are also marked with inches so you can track the length of your pieces.

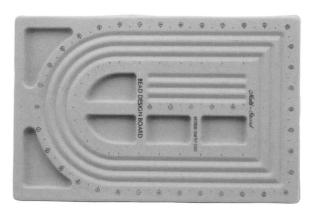

A **ring mandrel** is a long, tapered rod, usually made of plastic or metal, that has markings along its length that indicate ring sizes. Mandrels are used to size ring bands and to size and shape wire. They are very useful in making wire-wrapped ring bands and adjusting the size of coiled wire.

If you don't need specific ring sizes, many household items, including pens, markers, dowels, and prescription bottles, make excellent mandrels for wirework. As long as they are rigid and smooth, these objects can help you make consistently sized loops, coils, and rings.

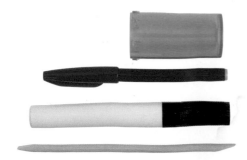

NEEDLES *and* RELATED TOOLS

English beading needles are long (longer than sewing needles), flexible needles with very small eyes. They are used with fine stringing material, such as thread, as well as with most beads. Their especially small eye makes them perfect for stringing seed beads or other beads with small holes and doing on- and off-loom bead weaving. They are available in sizes #10 (the thickest, with the largest eye) through #16 (the thinnest, with the smallest eye) and need to be coordinated with the right size beading thread and seed bead. There is an approximate correlation between needle sizes and seed bead sizes. A size #10 or # 11 needle can be used with 11/0 seed beads, but see the chart on page 40 for more information. English beading needles vary in length from 1¼ in/3 cm to 3 in/7.6cm.

If you have trouble threading a needle's eye, a **threading tool** can help you. **Sharps needles** (not shown) are short and stiff and can be used with buttons and some beads, but they are mostly used to create hand-beaded embroidery on fabric.

Twisted wire needles are long and flexible, made of steel or brass, and, because of their large eyes, are easy to thread. Use them with soft stringing materials other than thread; the eye collapses as it moves through the bead hole. They are available in fine, medium, and heavy gauges to coordinate with the size and weight of your beads. You can shorten them with wire cutters if you like.

Don't use them with seed beads (their eyes are too big). Note, too, that certain techniques, such as off-loom bead weaving, require a much stiffer needle, such as an English beading needle.

To thread wide stringing materials such as ribbon, you'll need a **twisted wire needle with a large eye,** like the one shown below. As the needle is threaded through the bead hole, the eye collapses. Another option is to use a **big-eye needle** (not shown), which is really two thin needles soldered together at both ends. The space between the two needles is the eye, which extends for almost the entire length of the needle. To thread it, pry the two needles apart in the center with another needle or tweezers, and then thread the ribbon through.

MASTERING THE ART *of* BEADING

Beeswax and **thread conditioner** are used to condition beading thread. Beeswax makes thread stronger and stiffer (to maintain tension), keeps out moisture, and prevents tangles. It also makes thread sticky, which attracts dirt. Thread conditioner, such as Thread Heaven, sold in small containers, is a synthetic alternative to beeswax that also strengthens thread and wards off tangles but is less sticky than wax.

Bead scoops allow you to pick up large quantities of small beads like seed beads with ease. You can also use a simple household teaspoon, but the scoops' flat bottoms contain beads best.

A **bead reamer** enables you to smooth away sharp or rough areas inside bead holes. It also allows you to enlarge the hole in some beads. The ones featured are manual tools whose ends are coated with crushed diamonds: insert them in a bead hole and twist to file away interior excess. Use them only on soft semiprecious stones and pearls. They tend to chip and crack glass and crystal beads.

Needle files and **emery cloth** are used to smooth rough wire ends after they've been cut. Both are available in hardware stores and jewelry supply stores. When deburring wire ends, first use a needle file, and then use increasing grades (indicating coarseness) of emery cloth to smooth and polish. Emery cloth looks and works like sandpaper, but it is coated with a fine-grain rock and mineral mixture meant for use in hand metalworking.

If you are just beginning to bead, it is not necessary to purchase all of the following pliers. However, you will need a good pair of chain-nose pliers and an additional pair of either long chain-nose pliers or bent-nose pliers to open and close jump rings and chain links. You also need round-nose pliers to make any kind of loop. After that, if there's room in your budget, crimping pliers are an excellent investment.

Chain-nose pliers are extremely versatile pliers ideal for gripping and bending wire, crimping, wire wrapping, opening jump rings, and closing findings such as clamshells. They have a short needle nose and a flat closing surface. They come in many sizes. Some have serrated edges, but stick to the smooth-edged variety so you do not end up with unsightly marks and dents in your wirework. Some varieties have an edge for cutting wire, but they don't make very clean cuts. Some beaders prefer **flat-nose pliers** (not shown). Their rectangular jaws and square nose function much like those of chain-nose pliers and are good for grasping, bending wire, and closing jump rings.

Long chain-nose pliers and **needle-nose pliers** have flat, long jaws that taper to a point. The inside surface of the jaws is smooth, not serrated. These narrow-tipped pliers are better for fine details and tight spaces than ordinary chain-nose pliers.

Bent-nose pliers are a version of chain-nose pliers that bend partway down their nose. They give you a different angle and good leverage to reach tight places. They are extremely good at opening and closing jump rings. Do not use bent-nose pliers with a serrated edge for gripping materials—they will dent and scratch your wirework, especially soft metals such as silver and gold.

Round-nose pliers have smooth, cylindrical, tapered jaws that allow you to create wire loops of various sizes, depending upon where the wire is placed on the pliers' jaws. When a wire is wrapped around the tip, the resulting loop is small. When the wire is placed farther back on the jaws (toward the joint), the loop is large. Gripping with round-nose pliers tends to dent wire; use chain-nose, needle-nose, or bent-nose pliers instead.

Nylon-jaw pliers have nylon jaws. Since nylon is softer than metal, you can use them to shape and manipulate wire without scratching, denting, or chipping it. They can be used to remove kinks in wire and to work-harden wire and findings (see page 303). They are available with square, pointed, round, and half-round/half-flat jaws to suit all types of wirework.

Crimping pliers are used on crimp beads to secure stringing materials such as beading wire. They have two chambers: one turns the crimp bead into a kidney shape and the other folds the bead in half, creating a fine, rounded finished product. Regular crimping pliers are best suited for 2 mm dia. crimp beads, but other sizes are available. **Micro crimping pliers** are best for 1 mm x 1 mm crimps, while **mighty crimping pliers** are best for 3 mm x 3 mm crimps. **Euro crimping pliers** are a unique tool with three chambers instead of the usual two, allowing them to be used with a larger range of crimp bead sizes: 2 mm x 1 mm, 2 mm x 1.5 mm, and 2 mm x 2 mm crimps.

Magic crimping pliers are highly specialized pliers designed to turn 2 x 2 mm sterling-silver or gold-filled crimp tubes into round beads. Their secret is the ball-shaped mold that is hollowed out in their jaws. Always use the recommended size crimp tube and .018 in/0.46 mm dia. or .019 in/0.48 mm dia. beading wire.

Split-ring pliers (not shown) are used to open split rings, which are used in place of jump rings. If you don't use split rings often, they are not a must-have.

CUTTERS, TWEEZERS, *and* AWLS

You can get by with one good pair of wire cutters that cuts medium and small gauges. When buying cutters, read the manufacturer's instructions so you'll know exactly what they're capable of cutting.

These wire cutters are called **nippers.** They are best suited for cutting nylon-coated beading wire in narrow diameters and fine dead-soft wire, gauges 26 to 30. They are able to make clean, close, flush cuts in narrow places.

Wire cutters or **side cutters** can cut nylon-coated beading wire and dead-soft wire, gauges 18 to 24. They do not make a flush cut, so you will need to file and smooth wire ends.

Flush cutters are specialized wire cutters that produce perfectly flush wire ends on one side.

Heavy-duty chain cutters are useful for cutting thick chain links and dead-soft wire, gauges 12 to 16. You might not use them often, but you'll really appreciate having them when you do need them.

Memory wire cutters can cut the especially rigid memory wire and other hard wires with ease. Memory wire should never be cut with any other kind of wire cutters. If you do, you will hurt your hands and damage your pliers.

Having various sizes of good, sharp **scissors** on hand will help you make clean cuts on your soft stringing materials. A large pair can be used to cut ribbon or cord. A medium pair will help you cut materials that are hard to negotiate or reach, and a small pair can be used to trim away small threads close to your beadwork.

A **heat gun** is used to melt embossing powder. It generates heat but does not blow out air. This tool is excellent, but not a strict necessity, for use with Amazing Glaze.

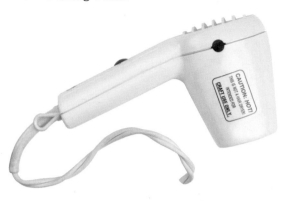

Tweezers with pointed ends are great for grabbing tiny beads and other small materials. They are also essential in tying successful knots. They will help you grasp short threads and cord ends, and you can use them to slide a loosely made knot along a strand to position it properly against a bead before you pull the knot tight. (Specific beading tools, such as a knotting awl and the specialty knotting tool, are excellent for knot tying as well, but if you have tweezers on hand, they'll work just as well.)

Amazing Glaze is a clear, dimensional embossing powder that is typically used with rubber stamps. Use it to create a hard, glossy, glasslike surface over collages, photos, or beads in recessed pendants.

STRINGING MATERIALS

BEADING WIRE

Nylon-coated beading wire, or simply **beading wire**, is a stringing material and is not to be confused with wire (see page 43). It is durable, strong and flexible, made from twisted stands of stainless steel coated with nylon. Available in many different diameters, beading wire is an excellent stringing material for all kinds of beads, especially heavier ones. Depending on the manufacturer, the packaging may list its diameter in millimeters, inches, or both. Typically, the larger the diameter, the stronger the stringing material, but strand number also determines its strength. It is available with as few as three strands and as many as forty-nine. Beading wire with three strands is made up of three twisted stainless-steel strands coated with nylon. Beading wire with forty-nine strands has seven bundles of seven twisted strands each. The higher the strand number, the stronger, more flexible, and abrasion-resistant the wire and the better its drape and resistance to kinking. Beading wire with nineteen or more strands is so supple it can be knotted. When selecting a beading wire, choose one that will fill the bead hole, in order to cut down on excess abrasion, but remember that if multiple strands need to be fed through the same crimp tube to finish them, you may want to choose a beading wire with a narrower diameter and a higher strand count.

Tigertail, although still a brand name, is now also used as a generic term for nylon-coated beading wire. Other popular brands include Beadalon, Soft Flex, Acculon, and Accu-Flex. All are available in fashion colors, different finishes, and metals, such as sterling silver, gold- and silver-plated, brass, and plain stainless steel.

Crimp beads are the best way to secure all beading wire to findings.

COORDINATING NYLON-COATED BEADING WIRE WITH CRIMP BEADS

The following is just a guideline. Please experiment to see what works best for you.

BEADING WIRE	CRIMP BEAD SIZE
.010-.013 in/0.25-0.33 mm	1
.015-.021 in/ 0.38-0.53 mm	2
.024 in/0.61 mm	2, 3
.026 in/0.66 mm	3, 4
.030 in/0.76 mm	4
.036 in/0.90 mm	4

CORD

Generally speaking, the difference between **cord** and thread is that cord is thicker and is usually woven. Another difference is that cord is used when you intend the stringing material to be seen. Soft, woven strands of silk, nylon, or satin will enhance your designs, but these materials are prone to stretching and fraying. Typically, this problem is solved by coating the strands with thread conditioner or beeswax, as you would do with beading thread. But would you condition visible cords? Never. They'd look just awful. Consequently, certain cords have some limitations on the types of beads to use with them. Cords are available in a wide variety of colors and diverse materials and are worth using to showcase your favorite beads.

Silk beading cord (shown below) is a strong and durable stringing material made up of tight, twisted strands of silk. It is traditionally used in knotted pearl necklaces but can be used with other lightweight glass beads or semi-precious stones as well. It doesn't stretch much but is biodegradable. **Nylon beading cord** (not shown) is stronger and more durable than silk, and better brands won't stretch. It can be used with the same types of beads. Both options are sold on spools or on cards with twisted wire needles already attached to the cord. These cords are sized by number, which corresponds

to their width in diameter. Unfortunately, both measurements aren't always listed, so note that the lower the number, the smaller the width of the cord. You will typically find size #2, which is approximately 0.45 mm/.017 in dia. up to size #16, which is approximately 1.05 mm/.041 in dia. Popular brands include Gudebrod and Griffin.

Satin cord, with its silky, shiny surface, is another soft stringing material worth using to highlight your bead designs. It is good for knotting or stringing large beads in light or medium weights with smooth bead holes; beads with sharp edges or rough bead hole interiors will fray it. It comes in many colors and three thicknesses: 1 mm (bugtail), 1.5 mm (mousetail), and 2 mm (rattail).

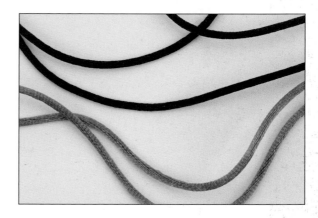

Suede lace, rubber tubing, and **nylon thread-wrapped chain** are additional options to use as stringing materials. Suede and leather are available from bead suppliers and are available in many colors. They work very well with medium and heavy beads made from any type of material but look especially beautiful with wood, clay, or stone beads. Rubber tubing is a modern and industrial stringing material now available in bright, fun colors. It can be used with beads made from most materials and in any weight or size. Nylon thread-wrapped chain is a softer alternative to metal chain and is available in different colors and sizes. It too has no bead restrictions. You may also be interested in other common stringing materials made from imitation leather (pleather) and suede, cotton, linen, flax, hemp, sinew, and twine (not shown). Stringing cords made from natural fibers can be strong. Ones made from hemp are particularly hearty and fray resistant. However, the qualities in these natural materials can vary wildly so take care when pairing them with beads that may wear them down. Web sites offer lots of information about the particular cords they sell and their capabilities.

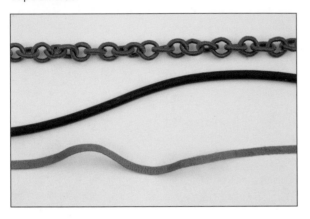

Transite, illusion cord, clear nylon cord, and **monofilament** are all some of the names for clear, 100 percent nylon stringing material. They are so versatile that they work equally well when they are visible in your designs, like typical cords, or hidden within the beads.

Monofilament (fishing line) is an inexpensive single-thread strand that can be used to temporarily string beads. Don't use it in finished jewelry pieces—it doesn't stand up over time. Nylon cords made for jewelry making have been treated to withstand UV rays. Fishing line is not treated and will eventually become brittle.

Some clear, nylon cords and threads are not single strands (monofilaments) but woven strands, making them much stronger and even better suited for beads with sharp edges or abrasive bead holes. All nylon cords and threads will not fray or stretch which makes them suitable for use with most beads.

When strung, clear nylon stringing materials are practically invisible, making them perfect for illusion or floating designs, clear or pale beads, especially Austrian crystal, and for projects in which you don't want to see the stringing material. Nylon cord can be secured with knots or crimp beads so it can be attached to findings in the same manner as other soft stringing materials, as well as nylon-coated beading wire. It is available in various diameters, but choose one that fills the bead hole in order to reduce abrasion, unless you need to make multiple passes through the same bead holes.

Elastic stringing cord looks like monofilament but stretches like elastic. It's produced specifically for jewelry making, doesn't fray, won't crack or harden over time, and is best suited for light- to medium-weight beads. It comes in several colors, but the most popular is clear. It is available in diameters from .5 mm to 2 mm. All sizes can be secured with two single overhand knots and a drop of cyanoacrylate glue or crystal cement between them. Sizes 1.0 mm and larger can also be secured with a crimp bead.

You can use **ribbons** to create a clasp, weave through chain, and embellish jewelry with bows. Ribbon is also an excellent stringing material—choose lightweight ribbons made from organdy or organza in widths narrower than 1/2 in/1.2 cm and beads with larger holes and smooth interiors.

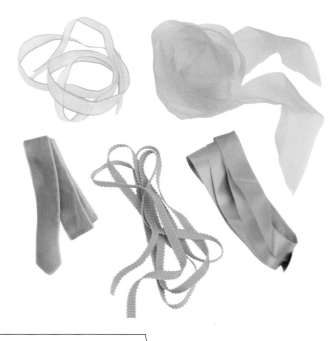

Use **beading thread** in projects where the stringing material can be hidden completely by the beads. Thread is typically prone to stretching and fraying and always needs to be conditioned to help prevent this, but you don't want the unsightly waxed threads to ever show. Beading thread is most commonly used with seed or cylinder beads for on- and off-loom bead weaving, but certain types work for regular stringing as well. Choosing a beading thread is a personal preference. Some beaders swear by one type or another. It is wise to experiment with a few of them to see what you like best.

Nylon beading thread is strong and durable, but not suitable for regular stringing, except perhaps for light seed beads. Its strength is mostly gained by the multiple passes made through the same

beads during bead weaving. Although some brands use unique sizing systems, it's commonly available in weights 00, 0, A, AA, B, C, D, E, EE, F, FF, and FFF. (00 is the thinnest thread, requiring the lightest beads; FFF is the thickest and can accommodate heavier beads.) Nylon is a much better material for beading than natural fibers such as silk and cotton, because it is strong and sturdy, resists fraying and abrasion, and doesn't degrade. Nymo, a common brand of nylon thread, is a flat, untwisted monofilament that resembles dental floss; you must prestretch and condition it prior to use. Other popular brands include Super-lon nylon thread, which has almost no stretch but does require conditioning. Superlon size AA is equivalent to Nymo's size B and size D is slightly thicker than Nymo size D. Silamide is a twisted, two-ply, prewaxed nylon thread whose size A is equivalent to Nymo's size D. All of these nylon threads come in a wide variety of colors.

Also available are braided nylon or polyethylene threads, which are suitable for weaving and stringing, because they can handle beads heavier than seed beads and those with rough edges or sharp holes like crystals. They are often fray-resistant, don't stretch, rarely tangle, and are waterproof. They are sized by diameter, just as nylon-coated beading wire is, and are packaged similarly. Popular brands include Fire Line, Dandyline, and Power Pro. The downside to these threads is that they are available in extremely limited colors, usually black and white or clear. Beading Web sites will make needle size recommendations for each diameter thread size. These threads require wire cutters to cut them, not scissors.

COORDINATING THREADS, NEEDLES *and* SEED BEADS

Coordinating all these materials can be confusing. Keep these important points in mind:

:: Beading needles have eyes that are the same diameter as the rest of the needle so there is no need to account for additional "eye" room.

:: Needle sizes roughly correlate to bead sizes—a size #10 or #11 needle will work well with 11/0 beads.

:: If your bead weaving stitch requires multiple passes through the same bead, you may want to choose a narrower needle than the ones recommended below.

THREAD SIZE	NEEDLE SIZE	BEAD SIZE
0,00,000 (smallest)	#13, #15	15/0
A or 0	#13	14/0
A or 0	#12	13/0
A or B	#11	12/0
A or B	#10	11/0
B or D	#10	10/0
D, E, or F	#10	9/0
E, F, or FF (largest)	#10	8/0

Generally:

:: Thread size AA and smaller can be used with bead sizes 15/0 and smaller and a size #15 needle.

:: Thread size B and smaller can be used with bead sizes 15/0 and larger and a size #13 needle.

:: Thread size D and smaller can be used with bead sizes 15/0 and larger and a size #10 or #12 needle.

CHAIN

Premade lengths of **chain** are readily available from bead suppliers. They are typically divided by metal type: gold, gold-filled, gold-plated, sterling silver, silver-plated, brass, copper, gunmetal, steel, and aluminum. They come in all types of gauges, from fine chain to heavy, chunky links, and in all kinds of finishes, from matte and antiqued to highly polished. You can purchase chain with small beads already attached between each link, chain in all kinds of fun colors, and rhinestone chains in gold or silver settings. Chain available in stores is generally sold by the foot/30.5 cm, but online it is sold in different increments depending on the company.

Chains with open links provide useful spaces to attach other beaded components along the strand, such as wrapped-wire loops, and their ends can easily be secured to clasps using findings like jump rings. Fine-link chains can be used like a stringing material, sliding beads directly on, and their ends can be secured to clasps if you attach end connectors directly to them. (See the Jewelry Findings section of the Glossary, page 48, and

Watercolors necklace, www.chroniclebooks .com/beading for specific information.) Chain comes in a wide variety of link styles and it's helpful to be familiar with them so you can iden- tify the styles you like. The following is a list of types of chain and their defining characteristics:

Ball chain: round balls replace open links and have bar links between them.

Bar chain: small, open, round links separated by solid, elongated, straight, or curved bar links.

Beading chain: fine, tubular links small enough to fit through bead holes. Use crimps to secure beads in place.

Box chain: tiny cubes joined together.

Cable chain: uniform round or oval-shaped links where alternating links are rotated 90 degrees. This three-dimensional chain does not lie flat.

Curb chain: uniform oval links twisted 85 degrees and flattened. The links appear interwoven and the chain lies flat.

Diamond cut: links that lie flat have diamond- shaped flat facets cut into the face of the link. Facets are highly polished and reflect more light.

Fancy chain: ornate links of filigree or decorative shapes other than round or oval.

Figaro chain: links lie flat and have a distinctive pattern: one long link followed by a series of shorter links.

Figure 8 chain: oval links connected by smaller, twisted, figure-8 links.

Flat link: means links are flat (made of square wire or hammered flat, for example), not that the chain lies flat.

Omega chain: rounded metal plates set side by side forming a smooth, flexible tube rigid enough to retain its ring shape when worn.

Oval chain: large or small oval-shaped links, usu- ally flat in the curb chain style.

Rollo chain: uniform, round links in the cable-link style.

Rope: oval links braided together and twisted in a spiral.

Round chain: large or small round links, usually flat in the curb chain style.

Singapore: a twisted curb chain with flat, dia- mond-cut, interwoven links.

Snake chain: round wavy, cylindrical links set side by side forming a flexible tube with a smooth, scaly texture like snake skin.

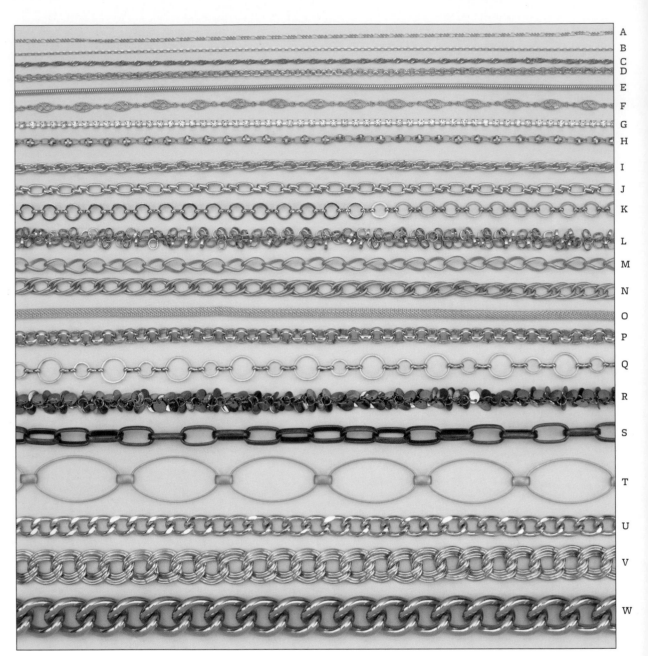

A
B
C
D
E
F
G
H
I
J
K
L
M
N
O
P
Q
R
S
T
U
V
W

CHANS

A :: Fine Figaro	I :: Rope	Q :: Large and small circle link
B :: Diamond cut cable	J :: Fancy curb	R :: Paddle
C :: Singapore	K :: Circle	S :: Rectangular cable link
D :: Rollo	L :: Hoop	T :: Large flat oval link
E :: Snake	M :: Twisted cable	U :: Diamond cut curb
F :: Fancy	N :: Double curb chain	V :: Double curb flat-link chain with grooved wire
G :: Rhinestone	O :: Round hollow mesh	
H :: Cable link with beads	P :: Rollo	W :: Curb

WIRE

Wire, not to be confused with beading wire (see page 36), is an essential element in jewelry making and is available in many metals, finishes, sizes, shapes and levels of hardness. Wires need to be malleable enough for you to shape and manipulate without breaking, but strong enough to become sturdy components in your designs. Wires used in jewelry making are made from both precious and base metals. The most common wires you'll need for all types of wirework include gold and gold-filled, fine and sterling silver, copper, brass and gold-, silver-, copper-, and bronze-plated craft wires. See page 46 for more information.

Wire size is determined by the wire's thickness. In the U.S., its thickness is measured in inches—or, more accurately, in microinches. A microinch is one millionth of an inch. These incredibly small increments prompted the creation of a simplified standardized system: American Wire Gauge (AWG). A wire's thickness is represented by its **gauge** number. The smaller the gauge, the thicker the wire; 16- to 22-gauge wires are generally

considered thick. The higher the gauge, the thinner the wire; 24- to 30-gauge wires are considered thin. When purchasing other findings made with wire, such as headpins and jump rings, you'll notice that their size (length, width, and so forth) is listed in addition to their gauge. In European countries, gauge is not used; instead wire thickness is measured and noted in millimeters.

Wire is available in different **shapes,** including round, half-round, square, triangular, and twisted, which can be seen in cross-section. **Round wire** is most widely available, especially in base metals. It's very versatile and great for beginning beaders. You're likely to find other wire shapes in precious metals only. **Half-round wire** works especially well for making ring bands because its flat side is comfortable against the finger. **Square wire** grips stones and cabochons better than round wire does. Once you have developed good wirework skills, these shaped wires are worth trying.

WIRE SHAPES

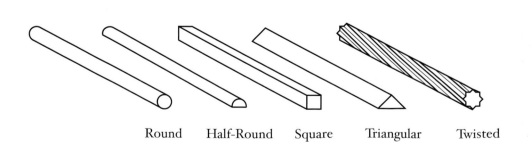

Round   Half-Round   Square   Triangular   Twisted

AWG	DIAMETER IN INCHES	DIAMETER IN MILLIMETERS	SOLD IN EUROPE AS	ACTUAL SIZE
1	0.2893	7.348		
2	0.2576	6.544		
3	0.2294	5.827		
4	0.2043	5.189		
5	0.1819	4.621		
6	0.1620	4.115		
7	0.1443	3.665		
8	0.1285	3.264		
9	0.1144	2.906		
10	0.1019	2.588		
11	0.0907	2.305		
12	0.0808	2.053		
13	0.0720	1.828		
14	0.0641	1.628		
15	0.0571	1.450		
16	0.0508	1.291		
17	0.0453	1.150		
18	0.0403	1.024	1 mm	
19	0.0359	0.912		
20	0.0320	0.812	.8 mm	
21	0.0285	0.723		
22	0.0253	0.644	.6 mm	
23	0.0226	0.573		
24	0.0201	0.511	.5 mm	
25	0.0179	0.455		
26	0.0159	0.405	.4 mm	
27	0.0142	0.361		
28	0.0126	0.321	.3 mm	
29	0.0113	0.286		
30	0.0100	0.255	.25 mm	
31	0.00893	0.227		
32	0.00795	0.202	.2 mm	
33	0.00708	0.180		
34	0.00630	0.160		
35	0.00561	0.143		
36	0.00500	0.127		

Wire temper describes how hard or soft wire is. For the cold wirework used in this book, you need to know about four common tempers: dead-soft, soft, half-hard, and full-hard. **Dead-soft wire** is very malleable and can be shaped with your hands, even in low gauges. It's ideal for all kinds of wrapping and coiling. It has not been hardened and can be manipulated for a long time before it becomes brittle or breaks. **Soft wire** is a good alternative. **Half-hard wire** is ideal for jewelry components that require structure and need to maintain their shape under stress, such as earring wires, ring bands, jump rings, and eye pins. **Full-hard wire** is harder than half-hard wire and is good for sturdy jewelry elements, but it's much more difficult to work with. I recommend you stick with half-hard wire, work-hardening as needed to increase its stiffness (see page 303).

Colored wires such as Artistic Wire and Parawire are permanently colored copper wires that resist tarnish, chipping, and peeling. Regardless, it's best to work with nylon pliers. They're available in many different gauges and brilliant colors, making them very inspiring design elements.

Niobium, a completely hypoallergenic, tarnish-resistant base metal, is often anodized (given an oxidized coating) into six vivid signature colors: pink, purple, dark blue, teal, green, and gold. **Plastic-coated wire** covers a base-metal wire with a brightly colored plastic sheath. Geared toward children's jewelry, it wraps and coils beautifully and can be used in adult designs as well. (See the Lime Wire bracelet, page 117.)

Memory wire is tempered stainless-steel wire with a springlike shape. Even after it's been stretched, it snaps back into its original coil. It resists most corrosion and tarnish and is available in gold or silver tones and three sizes: necklace, bracelet, and ring. It is extremely hard and rigid and should be cut only with memory-wire cutters.

METALS

Metals used in jewelry making are divided into two categories: **precious metals** and **base metals**. Gold, silver, platinum, and the platinum group metals (iridium, palladium, ruthenium, rhodium, and osmium) are precious metals. Metals other than these are base metals.

Precious metals are softer than base metals and, in their purest forms, too soft for jewelry making. Mixtures of different metals, called alloys, give softer metals strength and durability. Both precious and base metals are used to make beads, wire, chain, and findings.

Metals are defined by their purity, also referred to as fineness or parts per thousand. If a metal is 999 fine, it's 99.9 percent pure. The greater the purity, the higher the price. Knowing this will help you identify what you are buying.

Platinum is a rare white metal, 95 percent pure and hypoallergenic. It is available in beads, findings, chain, and wire.

Palladium is a white-silver metal that is hypoallergenic and tarnish resistant. When palladium replaces some of the copper in sterling silver, it produces a metal resembling white gold that is five times more tarnish resistant than sterling. Palladium sterling silver is available in beads and findings.

Rhodium is a whitish-gray metal that looks like platinum when electroplated onto gold, sterling silver, and base metals. It enhances shine, is hypoallergenic, and is less expensive than platinum. Rhodium is available in beads, chain, and findings.

Gold wire, findings, chain, and beads are available in 10 karats to 24 karats and in yellow, white, and pink varieties. Gold's purity is measured in karats, denoted as k or kt in the US. (Fineness is used outside the US.) Fine, solid or 24kt gold is 100 percent pure (1000 fine). 18kt gold is 75 percent pure (750 fine) or eighteen parts pure gold; the rest is an alloy that gives the gold more strength and durability. The more pure, the softer the gold and the deeper and richer the color. 14kt gold is 58.3 percent pure (585 fine); 10kt gold is 41.6 percent pure (416 fine). Gold less than 10kt is known as gold tone, but not gold. Gold is hypoallergenic, easy to work with, but expensive.

Different alloys added to pure gold can create new varieties. **Yellow gold** is made by adding silver, copper, and zinc. **White gold** made using nickel is very inexpensive, but nickel is a known allergen. Gold mixed with platinum, iridium, or palladium creates hypoallergenic white gold, but the whitest gold results from plating gold with rhodium. **Rose or pink gold** combines gold with copper.

Gold filled wire, beads, chain, and findings look like fine gold but are less expensive. Made by permanently bonding a thick layer of 10kt to 18kt gold to a brass base metal, gold filled items are hypoallergenic and the gold will not wear off or tarnish.

Vermeil beads, chain, and findings are made by plating at least 10kt gold onto sterling silver. It has a thicker layer of gold than standard plating, but not as thick as gold filled. Vermeil has the richness and shine of gold that won't wear off or tarnish.

Fine silver is 99.9 percent pure and doesn't tarnish easily. Wire made from fine silver is slightly softer than dead-soft sterling silver wire. Not quite durable enough for beads and findings, fine silver is readily available in many gauges and shapes of wire.

Sterling silver is an alloy made from 92.5 percent silver and 7.5 percent copper. Copper strengthens the silver, making it harder, stronger, and easier to work with than fine silver. Sterling does oxidize, creating tarnish that needs polishing on a regular basis. Sterling is abundantly available in wire, beads, chain, and findings and is hypoallergenic.

Silver filled wire, beads, chain, and findings permanently bond a thick layer of sterling silver over a base metal. Silver filled items are hypoallergenic and the silver will not wear off or tarnish.

Gold and silver finished, color, or washed means a nonstandardized thickness of gold or silver is electroplated to a base metal. This layer is thinner than gold and silver filled but thicker than gold-and silver-plated.

Gold- and silver-plated beads, findings, chain and wire have a very thin standardized layer of precious metals plated onto the surface of a base metal. Plating is not durable and the finish often chips off or wears away. Plated items are the least expensive.

Copper is a base metal with a pink-gold color that tarnishes, but it can be polished back to its original appearance. It is extremely durable and malleable so it is often plated with other metals to make wires, such as sterling silver with a copper core. Hypoallergenic, copper wire, beads, findings, and chain are readily available.

Brass is a base metal alloy made from 70 percent copper and 30 percent zinc. It resembles yellow gold and is used to make wire beads, chain, and findings.

Bronze is a base metal alloy made from 85 percent copper and 15 percent zinc or tin. It has a rich warm orange-red color and is used to make wire, beads, chain, and findings.

Nickel is a silvery-white base metal that is commonly used in jewelry making because it is inexpensive and resists oxidation. It is also the metal that most people are allergic to, so use caution. (Look for items labeled "nickel free" if you can.)

Pewter is a base metal alloy of 85 percent to 90 percent tin with the balance consisting of copper, antimony, and lead, but lead free pewter is available. Pewter has an appealing antiqued silver-gray color and is often used to make beads and jewelry findings.

Stainless steel is a silver-gray base metal alloy made of steel and chromium. It is extremely strong, durable, and rust and corrosion resistant. Stainless is available in wire, beads, chain, and findings and is hypoallergenic.

JEWELRY FINDINGS

These are the large category of components, typically made of metal, that are used to construct jewelry. Findings such as clasps, headpins, crimp beads, bead caps, and jump rings enable you to turn beaded strands into pieces of jewelry. See Metals, page 46, for more information on the variety of metals used in findings.

CLASPS

Spring rings are one of the most commonly used clasps, especially on necklaces. They are readily available, the larger ones are strong enough to secure heavy beads, and they come in a variety of sizes and finishes. The clasp will stay closed until you push down on the lever, which slides the small inner ring along the large outer one.

Lobster clasps are one of the most frequently used clasps because they are readily available, are strong enough to secure heavy beads, and are sold in many sizes and finishes. They look just like lobster claws and have a spring in the arm. The spring keeps the clasp closed until you push down on the lever, which makes it one of the more secure clasps.

Toggle clasps are made up of two pieces: a bar portion and a ring portion. (The ring can be shaped like a heart, flower, or anything else, as long as it's open in the center.) One portion is attached to each end of a bracelet or necklace; then the bar portion is fed through the ring to secure it. Toggle clasps should be used with medium to lightweight beads and are not as secure as clasps that lock closed.

S-hook clasps are shaped like an S. They can be plain or ornate and are available in many sizes and finishes. These clasps work particularly well on heavy necklaces. Jump rings are attached to the ends of a beaded strand, and then one jump ring is threaded onto each opening of the S-hook clasp. Bend one wire end against the middle of the clasp to trap the jump ring and beaded strand inside. On the opposite side, bend the wire end in but leave enough space to take the necklace on and off. The weight of the beads keeps the strand secure within the loops of the clasp.

Barrel clasps consist of two textured portions that screw together to form a barrel shape. They are attached via an eye loop on either end to the strands of a necklace or bracelet. They are secure clasps that can be used with medium-weight beads.

Magnetic clasps have very strong magnets that make putting your jewelry on and taking it off easy. If the clasp catches on something, it will come undone, so you may want to invest in a safety chain. Also, as you attach a magnetic clasp, it will stick to your metal tools, such as pliers. Caution: If you are pregnant or have a pacemaker, do not use magnetic clasps.

Box clasps are composed of two pieces. One piece is the housing, or box, which has an opening into which a metal wedge is fitted. The wedge opens within the housing, and the clasp stays closed. Pushing down on an exterior lever squeezes together the two flat pieces of the wedge, so that you can slide it out of its housing. Box clasps should be used with medium- to lightweight beads and are not as secure as clasps that lock closed.

Multistrand clasps are designed with multiple loops on each side to secure multiple beaded strands. By attaching one strand to each loop, you can keep strands evenly spaced. You can also add spacer bars along the length of the beaded strands to keep them separate throughout the design. Most multistrand clasps have one, two, or three loops.

Multistrand tube bar clasps have multiple loops on each side to secure multiple beaded strands. They are sturdier than regular multistrand clasps and have as few as two loops and as many as seven. Most have a twist-and-lock mechanism, some have a magnet closure, and others provide the extra security of built-in end locks.

Decorative **buttons** also make beautiful clasps. They are often seen with a beaded loop closure, but you can also attach lobster clasps secured to multiple strands to the button's shank. Then the button can be worn in front as part of the design while more utilitarian elements remain hidden.

ENDS *and* **CONNECTORS**

End caps can be both a generic and a specific term. Generically, it refers to the category of metal caps that finish stringing materials, such as the ones featured here with connector loops, as well as ones without loops, such as cone ends and bullet ends. Even bead caps can be called end caps. Specifically, they are a sturdy metal cap with a connector loop and are glued onto the end of soft stringing material. They are sometimes called **end cap connectors.** They are available in different sizes, metals, and finishes.

Cone ends are hollow findings shaped like cones. They are used to conceal the gathered ends of multiple beaded strands to give multistrand necklaces or bracelets a neat appearance. They are available in different sizes, metals, and finishes and can be fancy or plain.

Bullet ends are hollow findings shaped like bullets, and they also give multistrand necklaces or bracelets a neat look and come in various sizes, metals, and finishes.

Bead caps are convex metal findings placed on the top and bottom of a bead during the stringing process to give the beads a decorative appearance. They can be plain or ornate, solid or filigree, and they come in many sizes to fit round and oval beads. They can be found in many metals and finishes.

Coil ends or **spring ends** (or **coil** or **spring end connectors**) are used to secure soft stringing materials such as satin cord or leather. Multiple coils of wire are finished with an eye loop to attach a clasp or other findings. The coil is slipped over the glued end of the stringing material and is secured in place using chain-nose pliers. Coil ends are available in different sizes, metals, and finishes. Making your own is very simple.

Foldover crimp ends or **foldover crimp end connectors** are used to secure the ends of soft stringing materials or fine chain. Their tall metal sides are wrapped around the ends, trapping the stringing material inside. A clasp or other finding can then be attached to the connector loop. They are available in many sizes, metals, and finishes.

Clamp ends or **clamp end connectors** are metal wedges that are used to secure ribbon ends. Along one open edge of the clamp is a row of teeth that pierce the ribbon and keep it in place. Squeeze the two open ends closed along its entire bottom edge using pliers. At the opposite end is a loop to connect a clasp or other finding. Clamp ends come in different sizes, metals, and finishes.

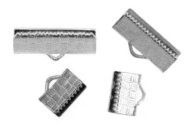

Rhinestone chain ends or **rhinestone chain end connectors** are used to secure rhinestone chain to a connector loop. The last rhinestone on the chain is placed in the connector and the side prongs are bent in toward the stone to secure the chain. They are available in various sizes, metals, and finishes.

Multistrand end bars or **end bar connectors** work the same way as multistrand clasps, but you'll need to add a clasp. End bars are available with only a few or many loops (see the Renaissance bracelet, page 121, which uses end bars with thirteen loops).

Connectors are decorative metal findings with two or more loops, so they can be attached to other beaded elements, chain, wire, or stringing materials. They can be found in different sizes, metals, and finishes and can be plain (made entirely of metal) or ornate (with enamel or rhinestone elements). They can be used in necklaces, bracelets, earrings, rings, and hair jewelry.

Spacer bars or **separator bars** are flat findings with multiple holes that separate beaded strands in a multistrand piece. Add them while stringing your beads; you'll need to use several throughout the piece, each at the same point on the strands, to keep the strands evenly spaced and help them to lie flat. Spacer bars can be plain or ornate; they are most readily found in metal but can also be made of bone, leather, and wood.

Clamshells, also known as bead tips or knot cups, are metal findings shaped like clamshells that conceal knots at the end of stringing materials. A clamshell has a hole in its bottom hinge for the stringing material. It goes around the finished knot and closes at the bottom to form a round bead with a connector hook.

Bead tips refers to the category of metal findings (sometimes also known as **knot covers** or **knot cups**) that conceal the knots at the ends of stringing material, including clamshells, knot cups, and the bead tip shown here. All bead tips have a hook or loop to attach them to other findings. They are available in many sizes, metals, and finishes. This particular bead tip has a hole at its base for the stringing material. It goes around the finished knot and closes at the side to form a round bead with a connector loop.

Knot cups are the category of findings that conceal knots at the end of stringing materials. It can also mean this specific finding featured here. A knot cup has a hole in the bottom of its "cup," which resembles half a round bead, and a hook to attach it to a clasp or other finding. The stringing material is threaded through the hole, and the knot sits in the cup, which hides it.

MASTERING THE ART *of* BEADING

Jump rings are strong wire rings, usually round or oval, used to connect or fasten findings and stringing materials together. They are available in different sizes, gauges, metals, and finishes and can be easily opened and closed using pliers. Another alternative is **split rings,** which function in the same way but look like little key rings. Other elements are fed into the coil and slid along the wire until they reach the ring's center. Split rings can't accidentally be pulled open like jump rings but are bulky and a bit harder to use. If you intend to use split rings, buy a pair of split ring pliers. **Closed jump rings** are soldered shut, which makes them safer and stronger, but they can't be opened or closed.

HEADPINS *and* EYEPINS

Headpins, sometimes known as flat-head pins, look very much like sewing pins but have a blunt end. Thread beads onto the dull end, and the flat head at the opposite end will keep the beads on the wire. They come in a wide variety of metals, gauges, and lengths. Once they have been beaded, they can be attached to earrings, bracelets, and necklaces to create drops or dangles.

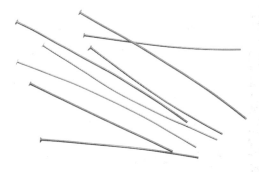

Headpins with ball ends, sometimes known as ball headpins, ball pins, or fancy headpins, look just like regular headpins, but, instead of a flat head at one end, they have a ball that keeps beads on the wire. The ball end looks like a small round bead, usually in gold or silver, and thus ball headpins can be a more elegant alternative to regular headpins. They come in a wide variety of metals, gauges, and lengths. Also available are headpins with paddle ends (not shown) and headpins with rhinestone, crystal, or jeweled ends.

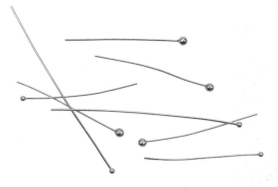

Eyepins are sold in many metals, gauges, and lengths, but they are very simple to make yourself. They have an eye loop at the end that keeps the beads on the wire. The eye loop sits below the beads, and other beaded elements can be attached to it to make drops or dangles.

CRIMP BEADS *and* TUBES

Both of these findings are used to secure nylon-coated beading wire ends and are available in base and precious metals. **Crimp beads** are round, soft metal beads with large holes that look very similar to round metal spacer beads. You can typically find crimp beads in sizes 1, 2, and 3, usually indicating diameters of 1 mm, 2 mm, or 3 mm, depending on the manufacturer. **Crimp tubes** are soft metal tubes that have two dimensions: width and length. Sometimes they will be labeled only as, for example, size 2, or you may find them labeled as 2 mm x 1 mm or 2 mm x 2 mm. Each manufacturer is different, and size 2 doesn't always mean 2 mm. So make sure to check. The longer the tube, the more secure the beading wire will be, so tubes are particularly good to use with heavy beads.

Crimp covers look like small, hollow, round beads that are open on one side. They are fitted around crimp beads or crimp tubes and closed to conceal those elements' utilitarian look, replacing it with the look of a round metal bead. They are available in most metals and finishes, with decorative textures such as ridges, or with laser-finished surfaces (stardust beads).

Scrimp Beads are used in place of crimp beads or tubes and are secured to beading wire with a screw and special screwdriver. They are available in different metals, finishes, and shapes. Round and oval Scrimps can be used with beading wire up to .024 in diameter, and bullet-shaped Scrimps can be used with beading wire up to .018 in diameter.

Silicone-lined **Smart Beads** look just like gold or silver round beads and are available in various shapes and textures. Their special inner lining allows them to hold beads in place by firmly gripping chain, wire, beading wire, transite, ribbon, and cord.

PROTECTORS

Wire guardians are rigid, metal, horseshoe-shaped findings that protect and conceal stringing materials from undue wear and abrasion. They are used in the same way and for the same purpose that French bullion wire (see below) is used. You can find them in sterling, gold-filled, copper, and silver- or gold-plated brass and in a few different sizes. Be sure to check the manufacturer's guidelines to choose the right size of guardian and to pair it with the correct size of beading wire.

French bullion wire, French coil, gimp, or **bullion** is a hollow tube of tightly coiled fine wire. It is sold in gold- or silver-plated varieties, in sizes fine, medium, heavy, and extra heavy. It is used to protect soft stringing material from fraying when it is attached to metal components.

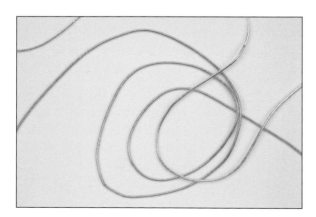

PENDANTS

Any **pendant** with a recessed portion can hold beads, photos, collages, and much more. Pendants can be used as necklace elements, attached to a ring form, or turned into a brooch with the addition of a pin back.

BAILS

Bails are used to turn beads into pendants so they can be attached to a necklace or bracelet. You can make your own bails using beaded strands or wire, but you can also purchase them from bead stores. They can be plain or ornate and are available with their "pegs" (the metal pieces that are inserted into the bead) in different positions so they can be used with head-drilled or top-drilled beads of various shapes and sizes.

STRINGING MATERIAL	SUGGESTED FINISHING TECHNIQUES	NEEDLE REQUIREMENTS	BEAD SUGGESTIONS	NOTES
BEADING WIRE	Crimp beads, crimp tubes, Magic crimping pliers, Scrimp Beads, loop with bead or button clasp	No needle necessary	Works with all bead types	See **nylon-coated beading wire** in the glossary. Heavier beads require beading wire with larger diameter and high number of strands.
WIRE	Wrap, twist, loop, Scrimp Beads	No needle necessary	Works with all bead types	See glossary for more information
MEMORY WIRE	Wire loop, end bead, cap or cone (glued)	No needle necessary	Works with all bead types	See glossary for more information
MONOFILAMENT/ TRANSITE	Knot, crimp beads, crimp tubes	No needle necessary on thicker diameters. Use a twisted wire needle or make a faux needle on finer strands.	Light- to medium-weight beads. Avoid beads with rough bead holes which can cause fraying.	Choose a size that fills the bead hole unless multiple passes through the same beads are necessary
ELASTIC CORD	Knot, crimp beads, crimp tubes	Use big eye, twisted wire, or faux needle	Light- to medium-weight beads. Avoid beads with rough bead holes that can cause fraying.	Choose a size that fills the bead hole
BEADING THREAD	Clamshells, knot cups, bead tips, loop with bead or button clasp	English beading needle	Seed and cylinder beads	See glossary entry and section on peyote stitch for more information

STRINGING MATERIAL	SUGGESTED FINISHING TECHNIQUES	NEEDLE REQUIREMENTS	BEAD SUGGESTIONS	NOTES
SILK CORD	Clamshells, knot cups, coil ends, loop with bead or button clasp	Twisted wire needle	Light- to medium-weight beads with smooth bead holes	See glossary entry and knotted necklace information
SATIN CORD	Fold over crimp ends, end caps, coil ends	Use big eye, twisted wire or faux needle	Light- to medium-weight beads	Avoid beads with rough bead holes, which can cause fraying
LEATHER, SUEDE, AND RUBBER TUBING	End caps, fold over crimp ends, coil ends	No needle necessary	Works with all bead types	See glossary entry
RIBBON	Clamp ends, fold over crimp ends, end caps	Use big eye or twisted wire needle with collapsible eye	Light- to medium-weight beads	Avoid beads with rough bead holes, which can cause fraying
CHAIN	Coil ends, fold over crimp ends, rhinestone crimp ends	No needle necessary	Works with all bead types	See glossary entry

OTHER FINDINGS

Making hair jewelry requires attaching beads to **hair findings,** or base elements such as combs, barrettes, and bobby pins. Many items can be found in drugstores, but wider varieties are available in bead stores, some specifically designed with beading discs or wire loops to make beading them easier.

Ring findings are available in bead stores and make creating beaded rings simple and easy. Some forms come with beading discs, loops, holes, or platforms to aid in attaching your beads. Ring-size memory wire is another option, which lets you string beads directly onto wire. Plain bands in metal or faceted shell, for example, can also be purchased. These bands can be attached directly to beads, beaded decorative pendants, and beaded wire loop domes.

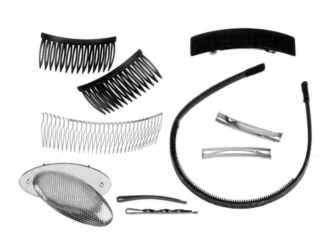

You can buy many kinds of **earring findings** in bead stores. Typical styles include hoops, posts, leverback, kidney, clip-on, screw-on, and fish hooks (also known as French wires). They can be embellished or plain and are available in many metals and finishes. Be certain they are made from a high-quality metal that won't cause an allergic reaction. Plated and sterling silver, gold, niobium, and surgical steel are all good choices.

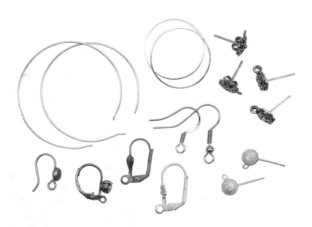

GLUES AND ADHESIVES

Jewelry making requires many types of glues and adhesives, each with a specific purpose and application. Be sure to follow the manufacturer's directions and pay close attention to any safety precautions listed. Glues such as cyanoacrylate, permanent adhesive, and epoxy are toxic and/or flammable, as is cyanoacrylate solvent, so use them with caution.

High-tack white glue is perfect for preventing fabric, ribbon, cord, or thread from fraying. This glue dries clear and is flexible.

Beacon Magna-Tac 809 Permanent Adhesive bonds fabric, lace, beads, glass, metal, wood, and leather. It has a consistency like that of rubber cement, which makes it very easy to use—it stays where you put it, and it dries clear.

Cyanoacrylate liquid and **gel instant glues** are essential for beading. Liquid glue works well for filling in spaces because it expands as it cures: for example, you can let glue run down a wire and into a bead hole to keep the bead in position. Gel glue is better suited to gluing uneven surfaces or broken beads together; it's also used when precision is needed, because the gel doesn't run. Both types bond swiftly, so plan your design ahead of time and work quickly.

Cyanoacrylate solvent When you inevitably get cyanoacrylate on your hands, work surface, and all over your beads, this cyanoacrylate solvent comes to the rescue. Not only does it allow you to safely pry apart your glued fingers, but you can also remove the glue that got on your beads and is now clouding up their finish. Test the solvent first in an inconspicuous place. It can remove some metal finishes, but it works wonders on crystal and glass beads.

GS Hypo Cement has a very fine built-in needle-like tip that allows you to apply it with great precision. It should be used on nonporous surfaces such as glass, ceramic, and plastic beads. It works well on knots, dries clear, and sets in ten to fifteen minutes. It is always wise to let your pieces cure for longer, though.

Five-minute two-part epoxy can be found in all hardware and home stores, as well as through craft and bead suppliers. Simply squeeze equal portions of the resin and the catalyst from each chamber onto an aluminum-covered piece of cardboard. Mix them together with a toothpick to activate the glue. This epoxy bonds within five minutes, which gives you some time to work (more time than cyanoacrylate does). It works best on nonporous surfaces, especially metal. It is extremely strong and is water and solvent resistant.

Clear nail polish is used to secure small knots and is probably something you already have on hand. It tends to flake and won't hold like glue, but for small, delicate projects it works well and is easy to use. It can also be used to make a faux needle on soft stringing material: brush the polish over the end, which, once dry, should be sufficiently stiff to thread on your beads. Simply trim away the needle when you're done.

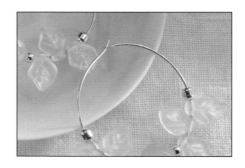

THE COLLECTION

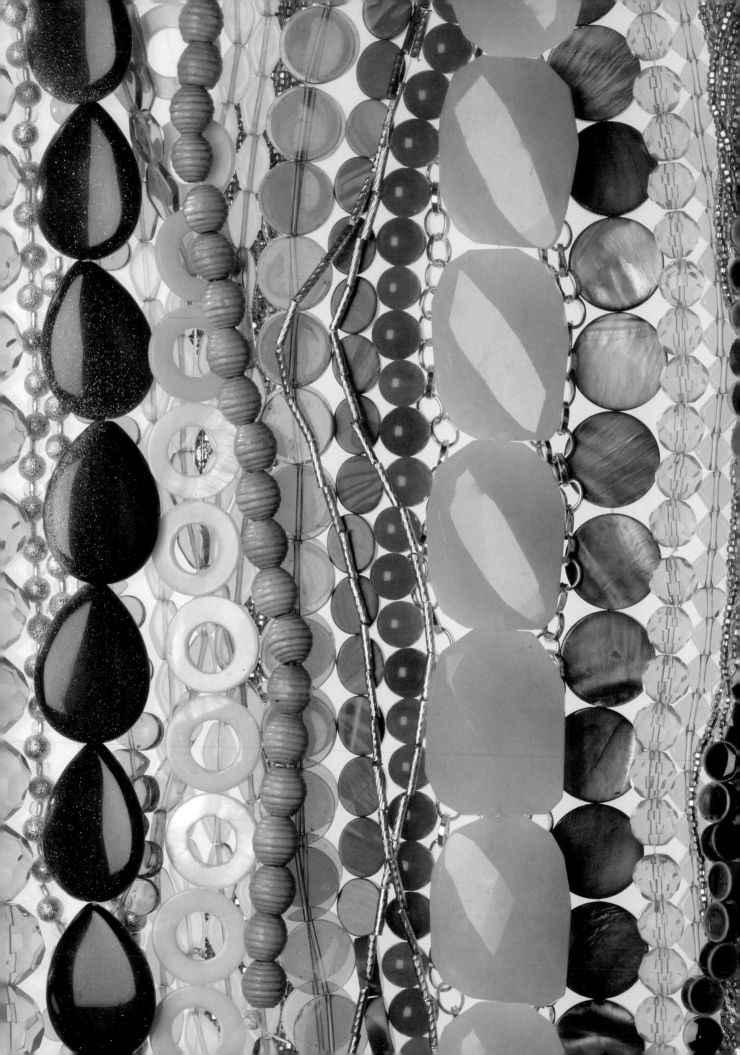

NECKLACES

LADIES WHO LUNCH

Fashion-forward and sexy, this modern update on the classic single-strand necklace combines perfectly round beads in Tiffany blue (each the size of a gumball!) and a show-stopping clasp that tempts you to flaunt the back of the necklace. Actually, the necklace can be worn in many ways, depending upon your mood and the occasion. For a demure display of glamour, move the disco ball of glittering rhinestones to the back. For a bit of show-off chic, slide the trio of sterling silver findings to the front, allowing the gleaming jewels to rest on your collarbone.

MATERIALS

28 opaque round glass beads, aqua blue, 14 mm dia.

2 rondelles with crystal rhinestones, silver, 11 mm dia. × 9 mm long

2 round spacer beads, silver, 2.5 mm dia.

French bullion wire, sterling silver, medium

2 crimp tubes, silver, size 2

2 crimp bead covers, silver, size 3

1 round ball clasp with crystal rhinestones and screw closure, silver, 15 mm dia.

Beading wire, bright stainless steel, .013 in/ 0.32 mm dia.

TOOLS

Ruler

Wire cutters

Crimping pliers

Chain-nose pliers

FINISHED SIZE

18 in/46 cm

DIRECTIONS

1 :: Use wire cutters to cut two ¼-in/6-mm lengths of French bullion wire. Set these aside. Use wire cutters to cut one 22-in/56-cm length of beading wire.

2 :: Thread one crimp tube, one of the lengths of French bullion wire and the clasp onto one end of the beading wire.

3 :: Attach the beading wire to the clasp using crimping pliers. (See "How to Secure a Crimp Tube with Crimping Pliers," page 274, and "How to Cover and Protect Stringing Material," page 272.)

4 :: Use chain-nose pliers to conceal the crimp tube with a crimp cover. (See "How to Use a Crimp Cover," page 277.)

5 :: Thread on one rondelle, one spacer, and a few blue beads, hiding the end of the beading wire inside the beads. String on the remaining blue beads. Finish by adding one spacer and one rondelle.

6 :: Thread on the remaining crimp tube and the remaining length of French bullion wire. Thread the beading wire through the opposite side of the clasp.

7 :: Attach the end of the beading wire to the opposite side of the clasp using crimping pliers. (See "How to Secure a Crimp Tube with Crimping Pliers," page 274.) Hide the end of the beading wire inside the last beads. Use chain-nose pliers to conceal the crimp tube with the remaining crimp cover.

• • • • **TIP** • • • •

Before you attach the second beading wire end to the clasp, hold the wire and let its opposite end hang down so it can untwist. The beading wire should be as straight as possible before you attach the clasp.

COCO

Wrapped in sophisticated style, the Coco necklace makes clever use of a careful selection of gold-link chains—a twisted cable link, a cable link with beads, and a fine Figaro—that flow like molten rivulets through the strand of rough-cut chunks of rosy-pink quartz. Threaded onto the necklace as the beads are being strung, the chains add a warm glow of color to an otherwise pale and monochromatic palette. The substantial clasp secures the necklace at the back, and a delicate chain cascades freely as a counterpoint.

MATERIALS

16 rough-cut rose quartz nuggets, approximately 15 mm wide × 20 mm long × 14 mm thick

3 ft/91 cm twisted cable-link chain, matte gold, links 7 mm wide × 10 mm long

4 ft/122 cm cable-link chain with beads, matte gold, links 3 mm wide × 8 mm long

2 ft/61 cm fine Figaro chain, gold, links 1.5 mm wide × 2 mm long and 1 mm long

2 crimp tubes, gold, size 2

1 jump ring, gold, 18 gauge, 7 mm dia.

1 lobster-claw clasp, gold, 12 mm wide × 22 mm long

Beading wire, satin gold, .018 in/0.45 mm dia.

TOOLS

Ruler

Wire cutters

Crimping pliers

Chain cutters

Chain-nose pliers

Bent-nose pliers

FINISHED SIZE

16 in–22 in/40.5 cm–56 cm (adjustable)

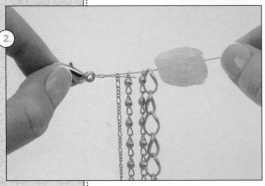

DIRECTIONS

1 :: Use wire cutters to cut an 18-in/46-cm length of beading wire. Attach the beading wire to the lobster clasp using a crimp tube and crimping pliers. (See "How to Secure a Crimp Tube with Crimping Pliers," page 274.)

2 :: Use chain cutters to cut the twisted cable-link chain into a 1-ft/30.5-cm and a 2-ft/61-cm length. Set the 1-ft/30.5-cm length aside. Use chain cutters to cut the cable-link chain with beads into two 2-ft/61-cm lengths. Insert the beading wire end into the last links on the Figaro chain, both cable-link chains with beads, and the 2-ft/61-cm twisted cable-link chain. Thread on one quartz nugget. Hide the end of the beading wire inside the bead.

3 :: Slide the chain ends and the nugget up the wire and against the crimp tube. Wrap all four lengths of chain around the outside of the nugget. When the chains meet the bottom bead hole, insert the beading wire end through one link in each chain.

4 :: Thread on another nugget.

5 :: Wrap the chains around the opposite side of the nugget. Insert the beading wire end through one link in each chain.

6 :: Bring the chains around to the opposite side. Continue to thread on the remaining nuggets, following them with the four lengths of chain (alternating sides each time) and threading the beading wire through each length.

7 :: Use a crimp tube and crimping pliers to attach the end of the beading wire to the jump ring. (See "How to Secure a Crimp Tube with Crimping Pliers," page 274.) Hide the end of the beading wire inside the last beads. Trim away excess wire.

8 :: Use chain cutters to cut the remaining 1-ft/30.5-cm length of twisted cable-link chain into two 6-in/15-cm lengths. Set one aside to use in another project. Use both pliers to open the jump ring. (See "How to Open and Close a Jump Ring," page 309.) Insert one end of the jump ring through the last link on one end of the chain. Close the jump ring. The lobster clasp can be secured to any link along this chain in order to wear the necklace.

TIPS

Remember: It is better to use too much chain when wrapping the nuggets than too little. Not leaving enough slack will make the necklace hang incorrectly and can place too much stress on the beading wire, possibly causing it to break.

If you love the look of chain, you can add more than four lengths. And if you leave more slack in the chain, it will drip off the nuggets, making the necklace very dramatic. Experiment with different styles and finishes of chain, such as the vintage look of antique silver, the sweet pink tones of copper, or the cheerful yellows of brass.

COUNTRY GARDEN

As sweet and dainty as a nosegay of just-picked flowers, this little garden of vintage Lucite and pressed-glass beads makes a perfect accessory. Although many separate elements—flowers with beaded stamens and sprays of delicate buds and leaves—make up its arrangement, the piece is airy and surprisingly lightweight, making it comfortable to wear. As versatile as they are appealing, the flowers are attached at opposite ends of lengths of silver chain that are accented at regular intervals with pearls in watermelon pink, bringing the main colorway (which just means color palette) around to the back of the necklace and unifying its design.

MATERIALS

6 Lucite trumpet flowers, bright rose, 10 mm dia. × 30 mm long

12 Lucite flowers in various sizes, bright rose:

> 6 large: 16 mm dia. × 12 mm long
>
> 6 small: 11 mm dia. × 8 mm long

9 rose quartz heart-shaped beads, pale pink, center-drilled in two sizes:

> 3 large: 14 mm wide × 14 mm long × 9 mm thick
>
> 6 small: 10 mm wide × 10 mm long × 6 mm thick

2 jade heart-shaped beads, soft mint green, center-drilled, 12 mm wide × 12 mm long × 4 mm thick

20 German pressed-glass leaves, frosted celadon, 8 mm wide × 11 mm long × 2 mm thick

6 Austrian crystal rondelles in various colors, 8 mm dia. × 6 mm long:

> 2 watermelon pink
>
> 2 grass green
>
> 2 pale yellow

3 faceted rose quartz briolettes, light pink, 7 mm dia. × 12 mm long

2 Austrian crystal briolettes, light pink, 7 mm dia. × 12 mm long

12 faceted round jade beads, mint green, 6 mm dia.

9 round glass pearls, watermelon pink, 6 mm dia.

1 Austrian crystal rondelle, pink, 6 mm dia. × 3 mm thick

2 Czech crystal wheels, fuchsia, 6 mm dia. × mm thick

2 glass discs, fuchsia, 6 mm dia. × 2 mm thick

2 glass briolettes, light pink, 5 mm dia. × 9 mm long

6 freshwater pearls, cream, 4 mm dia. × 7 mm long

6 round glass pearls, ivory, 2 mm dia.

18 opaque seed beads, yellow pearl, size 11/0

16 headpins with 1 mm ball end, silver, 24 gauge, 2 in/5 cm long

1 ft/30.5 cm cable-link chain (with splits in the links), sterling silver, links 4 mm × 5 mm

4 jump rings, sterling silver, 18 gauge, 5 mm dia.

1 clasp with floral detail, sterling silver, 8 mm wide × 14 mm long × 5 mm thick

Silver wire, dead-soft, 20 gauge

Silver wire, dead-soft, 24 gauge

Silver wire, dead-soft, 28 gauge

TOOLS

Ruler

Wire cutters

2 pairs chain-nose pliers

Round-nose pliers

FINISHED SIZE

22 in/56 cm

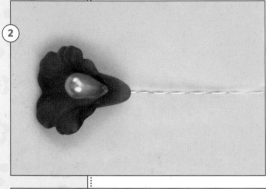

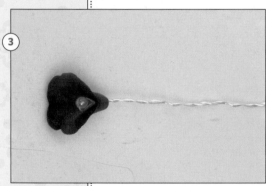

DIRECTIONS

1 :: To add stamens to the trumpet flowers, use wire cutters to cut three 6-in/15-cm lengths of 28-gauge wire. Slide a yellow seed bead to the midpoint of one length. Bring the wire ends together and twist them to secure the bead. (See "How to Make Beaded, Twisted Wire," page 336.) Repeat these steps to add seed beads to the remaining two lengths of wire. Coming from the top, thread all three twisted wires through the center of one trumpet flower. After they exit the bottom of the flower, twist the wire ends together. Repeat with the other five trumpet flowers.

2 :: To add freshwater pearl centers to the large Lucite flowers, use wire cutters to cut one 5-in/12-cm length of 28-gauge wire. Insert the wire end through one freshwater pearl, sliding the pearl to the wire's midpoint. Bring the wire ends together and twist them to secure the pearl. Coming from the top, insert the wire ends through one large flower bead and twist the wire ends to secure them. Repeat with the other five large Lucite flowers.

3 :: To add pearl centers to the six small Lucite flowers, use 4-in/10-cm lengths of 28-gauge wire, the small pearls, and the same technique as described for the large Lucite flowers.

4 :: Thread the large and small rose quartz heart-shaped beads, jade heart-shaped beads, rose quartz briolettes, and faceted light pink briolettes onto headpins. Set these aside. Add twisted wire stems to the remaining beads, with the exception of the watermelon-pink pearls. Use 5-in/12-cm lengths of twisted 28-gauge wire and the same technique as described for the Lucite flowers.

5 :: Use wire cutters to cut a 9-in/23-cm length of 20-gauge wire and an 18-in/46-cm length of 24-gauge wire. Beginning 2 in/5 cm from one end, wind the 24-gauge wrapping wire around the 20-gauge foundation wire; tightly wrap a 2-in-/5-cm-long segment, working toward the center. (See "How to Wrap Thin Wire," page 304.)

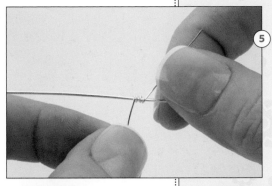

6 :: Position the wire ends from a small Lucite flower on the foundation wire after the 2 in/5 cm of 24-gauge wrapped-wire ends. Wind the flower wire ends around the foundation wire.

7 :: Positioning each bead next to the one before it, wrap the headpin end of a small pink heart and then the wire ends of one leaf around the foundation wire.

8 :: Wind the 24-gauge wrapping wire around the foundation wire, trapping the bead wires inside to secure them in place.

9 :: In this fashion, continue adding the remaining beads with twisted wires or headpins and securing them to the foundation wire by wrapping them with the 24-gauge wire.

(continued page 76)

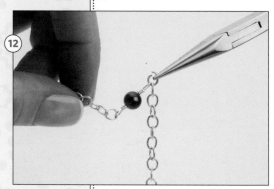

10 :: Make an eye loop on one wrapped-wire end using round-nose pliers. Trim away any excess wrapping wire that still covers the foundation wire end after it crosses the wire stem at the base of the loop. Then wrap the now bare foundation wire end around the base of the eye loop to make a wrapped-wire loop. (See "How to Make a Wrapped-Wire Loop on Both Ends Using Wire," page 317.)

11 :: Repeat step 7 on the opposite end. Bend the flower cluster into shape as desired.

12 :: Cut seven 1-in/2.5-cm lengths of cable-link chain. Set these aside. Cut nine 4-in/10-cm lengths of 24-gauge wire. Pair one length of wire with one watermelon-pink pearl and make wrapped-wire loops on both ends. (See "How to Make a Wrapped-Wire Loop on Both Ends Using Wire," page 317.) Repeat this step to add wrapped-wire loops to the remaining eight pink pearls. To make the shorter length of chain, connect four of the pearls with wrapped-wire loops to one another by attaching three 1-in/2.5-cm lengths of chain between them. To do this, open an end link on a length of chain and insert it into a wrapped-wire loop on one pink pearl. Close the link. Repeat this step to attach a length of chain to the wrapped-wire loop on the opposite side. Repeat these steps to complete the chain. Set this aside. To make the longer length of chain, connect the other five pearls with wrapped-wire loops by attaching four 1-in/2.5-cm lengths of chain between them in the same fashion as described above.

13 :: Open one jump ring. (See "How to Open and Close a Jump Ring," page 309.) Insert one end into one wrapped-wire loop on the longer side flower cluster and the wrapped-wire loop end of one pink pearl on the shorter length of chain. Close the jump ring. Repeat this step to add the other length of chain to the opposite side.

14 :: Open one jump ring. Insert one end into the loop on one half of the clasp and the wrapped-wire loop on the end pink pearl. Close the jump ring. Repeat this step to attach the remaining chain to the clasp.

TIPS

Because these beads are secured with wire, the floral cluster and the flowers themselves can be shaped and molded. You can gently move the flowers to cover spots of bare wire, shape their stems, and twist their wires to cluster them together.

If your chain does not have split links that can be opened and closed, use jump rings to attach the wrapped-wire loops on the pink pearls to the lengths of chain. Or see "How to Join Wrapped-Wire Loops without Using a Connector," page 320, and attach the wrapped-wire loops directly to the chain's links.

This flower cluster was purposefully designed to be fuller and longer on one side. It is intentionally off center. The pearl chain attached to the side with fewer beads is longer. Of course, if you prefer a symmetrical design, you can simply add an equal number of beads to the right and left sides of the midpoint and use equal lengths of chain.

BALI HA'I

Bold color and strong radial lines establish the modern design of this bamboo coral necklace, but it is the polished luster of the twig-shaped segments and their rich red and orange colors that create its style. Its elements harvested from tropical waters, possibly in the South Pacific, the Bali Ha'i necklace will become a prized signature piece among your jewelry. Be certain to handle this necklace with extra care, as bamboo coral is an organic material that can break.

MATERIALS

1 dyed sea bamboo coral stick bead, red, 13 mm dia. × 9 cm long

14 dyed sea bamboo coral stick beads, red, ranging from 6 mm dia. × 4.5 cm long to 11 mm dia. × 7 cm long

54 polished coral chips, red, approximately 8 mm wide × 12 mm long × 4 mm thick

Cable-link chain (with splits in the links), gold, links 4 mm wide × 7 mm long

2 clamshells, gold, 4 mm dia.

2 crimp tubes, gold, size 2

1 headpin with 1 mm ball end, gold, 22 gauge, 2 in/5 cm long

1 jump ring, gold, 18 gauge, 7 mm dia.

Toggle clasp, gold, ring 16 mm dia.; toggle 26 mm long × 2 mm dia.

Beading wire, bright stainless steel, .013 in/0.32 mm dia.

TOOLS

Ruler

Wire cutters

Crimping pliers

2 pairs chain-nose pliers

Chain cutters

Round-nose pliers

Masking tape (optional)

FINISHED SIZE

18 in/46 cm

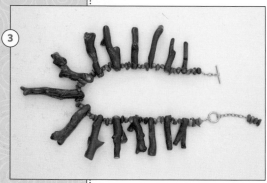

DIRECTIONS

1 :: Use wire cutters to cut a 22-in/56-cm length of beading wire. Thread one end of the wire through a clamshell, a crimp tube, and the loop at the base of the ring portion of the toggle clasp. See "How to Use a Clamshell to Cover a Crimp Tube or Bead," page 283, to secure the wire to the clasp.

2 :: String on four coral chips and one of the two shortest stick beads, hiding the cut end of the wire in the beads.

3 :: Following the beading layout, string on six more stick beads in graduated sizes, placing three chips after each one. At the necklace's midpoint, string on the largest stick bead. Follow with the seven remaining stick beads in decreasing sizes, remembering to place three chips after each stick. Finish the strand by stringing on four chips.

4 :: Use chain cutters to cut one 1-in/2.5-cm length and one 1½-in/4-cm length of chain. Set the longer chain aside. See "How to Use a Clamshell to Cover a Crimp Tube or Bead," page 283, to secure the beaded strand to an end link on the shorter chain. Treat the link the same as the loop on the toggle clasp in step 1. Trim away excess beading wire and then tuck the wire tail into the last few beads. Use chain-nose pliers to open the last link on the opposite end of the shorter chain. Insert one end of the opened link into the loop at the base of the second half of the toggle clasp. Close the link to secure it.

5 :: Thread four chips onto the headpin.

6 :: Use chain-nose and round-nose pliers to make a wrapped-wire loop, and attach it to an end link of the unused length of chain. (See "How to Make a Wrapped-Wire Loop Using a Headpin," page 316.)

7 :: Open the jump ring. (See "How to Open and Close a Jump Ring," page 309.) Insert one end of it through both the last link on the opposite end of the chain from step 6 and the round portion of the toggle clasp. Close the jump ring.

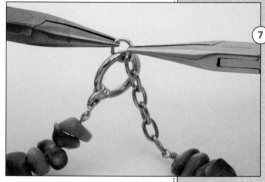

● ● ● ● TIP ● ● ●

The natural curves and branchlike qualities of the coral stick beads cause them to lie in unique ways when worn. Before you begin making this necklace, string the stick beads onto a length of scrap beading wire and place it around your neck. Use small pieces of masking tape to mark the beads that should be flipped over while you work. This prep work will make wearing the necklace comfortable and will help you to create a beautiful design.

SUN-KISSED

Inspired by the illusion-style necklace, in which beads are fixed in particular stations along the strand material so they appear to float, Sun-Kissed staggers beads in warm, sun-drenched tones—Indian red, persimmon, orange, and gold—across four delicate strands that tangle to create a scattering of organic shapes.

MATERIALS

8 German metal twisted coins, 22K gold plated, 15 mm dia. × 3 mm thick

9 faceted carnelian nuggets, persimmon, in sizes ranging from 10–12 mm wide × 11 –12 mm long × 5 mm thick

5 round glass beads, variegated orange, 8 mm dia.

6 Austrian crystal briolettes, citrine, 7 mm dia. × 13 mm long

8 faceted carnelian coins, melon, 6 mm dia. × 2 mm thick

4 faceted round glass beads, champagne, 7 mm dia.

8 faceted round glass beads, champagne, 5 mm wide × 6 mm long

11 Austrian crystal bicones, tomato red, 4 mm

15 Austrian crystal bicones, Indian red, 4 mm

5 peridot round beads, green, 3 mm dia.

46 seed beads, metallic gold, size 11/0

90 crimp beads, gold, size 2

4 German metal oval jump rings, 22K gold plated, 18 gauge, 5 mm wide × 8 mm long

1 German metal clasp for strands with floral detail, 22K gold plated, 16 mm wide × 27 mm long

Beading wire, satin gold, .018 in/0.46 mm

TOOLS

Beading cloth

Ruler

Wire cutters

2 pairs chain-nose pliers

FINISHED SIZE

24 in/61 cm

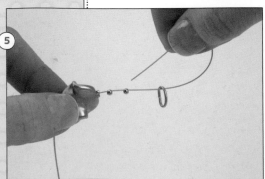

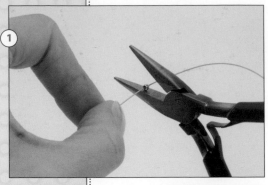

DIRECTIONS

1 :: Cover a clean, flat work surface with a beading cloth to keep the beads in their proper positions. Referring to the beading layout or creating your own random design, lay out the bead groups for strands A, B, C, and D. Use wire cutters to cut four 26-in/66-cm lengths of beading wire. Set three aside. Insert one end of the remaining strand, strand A, into one crimp bead. Slide the bead to the wire's midpoint. Place the crimp bead in the jaws of the chain-nose pliers and crimp it. (See "How to Secure a Crimp Bead or Tube with Chain-Nose Pliers," page 276.)

2 :: From the center of strand A, as shown in the beading layout, thread on one carnelian nugget, one seed bead, one briolette, one seed bead, one bicone in tomato red, and one crimp bead.

3 :: Push the bead group against the crimped bead and use chain-nose pliers to crimp the bead on the opposite side.

4 :: Follow the beading layout to add the remaining bead groups on strand A. You can thread on and secure one group at a time or thread all the bead groups on at once and then secure them to the beading wire. (See Tip, below.) Just be sure to thread a seed bead between each bead and a crimp bead before and after each bead group, and leave 1–2 in/2.5–5 cm of space between the groups. Repeat steps 1–4 to make strands B, C, and D. Set all but strand A aside.

5 :: Insert one end of strand A into two crimp beads and one jump ring. Thread the wire end back through both crimp beads.

6 :: Slide the top crimp bead up the wires toward the jump ring so that a ¼-in/6-mm loop is formed. Use chain-nose pliers to secure the crimp bead.

7 :: Slide the second crimp bead to ½ in/12 mm below the first. Secure the crimp bead using chain-nose pliers. Use wire cutters to trim away excess beading wire below this second crimp bead.

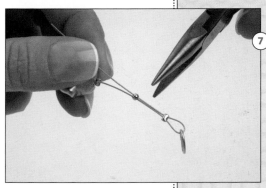

8 :: Repeat steps 5–7 to secure one end of strand C to the same jump ring as strand A. Attach the opposite ends of strands A and C to another jump ring. Attach the ends of strands B and D together using the remaining two jump rings.

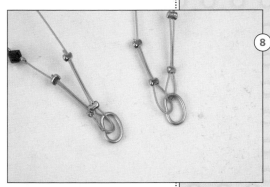

9 :: Use chain-nose pliers to attach one jump ring to one of the two loops on the side of the clasp. (See "How to Open and Close a Jump Ring," page 309.) Attach the jump ring on the opposite end of these strands to the coordinating loop on the opposite side of the clasp. Attach the remaining two jump rings to the other two loops of the clasp.

TIP

The Sun-Kissed necklace is a random design that lets you feature expensive beads without spending a lot of money. But the beading layout shows merely one way to group the beads. There is no wrong way to group them, no specific number of beads to include, and no definitive amount of space to put between them. Just remember that the bead groups should be staggered when the necklace is worn. While you work, periodically lay the strands next to one another and move any groups that clump together.

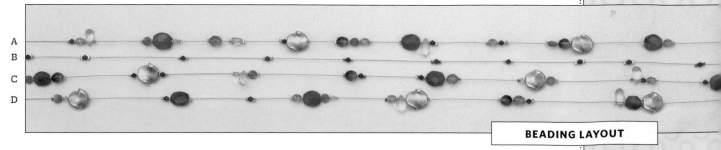

A
B
C
D

BEADING LAYOUT

CRYSTAL SPRINGS

In this pretty necklace, faceted briolette crystals resemble drops of spring water that have been suspended in time and hung from the links of a gold necklace. Light-catching and dainty, each teardrop bead is individually wired, its slender stem accented with a tiny bicone crystal and attached to the chain's links in a symmetrical pattern. A little blue flower from which a pendant-style crystal hangs establishes the focal point of the design.

MATERIALS

1 Austrian crystal briolette, pale yellow, 9 mm dia. × 15 mm long

2 Austrian crystal briolettes, citrine, 6 mm dia. × 12 mm long

4 Austrian crystal briolettes, light pink, 7 mm dia. × 10 mm long

5 opaque faceted dyed quartz briolettes, sky blue, 4 mm wide × 6 mm long × 2 mm thick

10 Austrian crystal bicones, various colors, 4 mm:

> 3 indicolite
>
> 6 powder blue
>
> 1 fuchsia

7 Austrian crystal bicones, various colors, 3 mm:

> 2 blue
>
> 2 pink
>
> 2 green
>
> 1 fuchsia

6 round glass pearls, ivory, 4 mm dia.

6 headpins with 1 mm ball ends, gold, 24 gauge, 2 in/5 cm long

Gold wire, dead-soft, 26 gauge

14 jump rings, gold, 22 gauge, 5 mm dia.

1 lobster clasp, gold, 5 mm wide × 9 mm long

2 ft/61 cm Figaro chain, gold, links 3 mm wide × 7 mm long, separated by three links 2 mm wide × 3 mm long

TOOLS

Ruler

Wire cutters

Chain-nose pliers

Round-nose pliers

FINISHED SIZE

19 in/48 cm

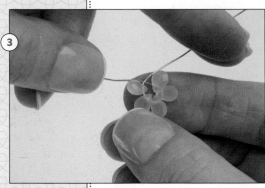

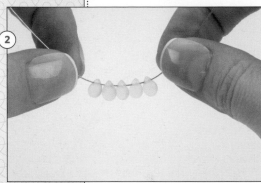

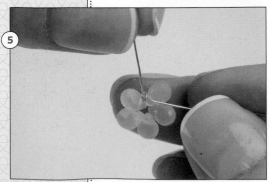

DIRECTIONS

1 :: Use wire cutters to cut one 3-in/7.5-cm length and two 8-in/20-cm lengths of chain. Set these aside. Follow the beading layout and "How to Make a Wire Bail," page 325, to add wire bails to the seven briolettes in pale yellow, citrine, and light pink and their coordinating 3 mm bicones. Then see "How to Make a Wrapped-Wire Loop Using a Headpin," page 316, to add wrapped-wire loops to the six powder-blue bicones and pearl bead combinations using headpins.

2 :: Use wire cutters to cut a 4-in/10-cm length of wire. Thread on the five sky-blue briolettes.

3 :: Bring the wire ends together so the beads curve around to form a flower shape. Cross the wires.

4 :: Use chain-nose pliers to bend one wire end straight up to create a stem, and bend the other wire end at a 90-degree angle to the first wire.

5 :: Wrap the wire placed at the 90-degree angle around the stem. (See "How to Wrap Wire," page 304.) Tighten the wires to secure the beads in place.

6 :: Continue wrapping the wire up and around the stem for ¼ in/6 mm. Use wire cutters to trim away excess wire. Use chain-nose pliers to squeeze the cut end flush against the stem.

7 :: Thread on one indicolite bicone.

8 :: Measure ¼ in/6 mm up from the top of the bicone. Use chain-nose and round-nose pliers to make an eye loop. (See "How to Make an Eye Loop on Both Ends Using Wire," page 311.) Do not cut the wire.

9 :: Insert the wire end through the midpoint of the 3-in/7.5-cm length of chain. Slide the chain down the wire and into the eye loop.

10 :: Thread on the pale yellow briolette bead combination.

(continued page 90)

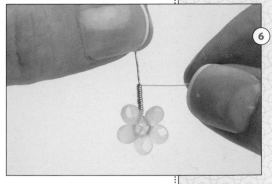

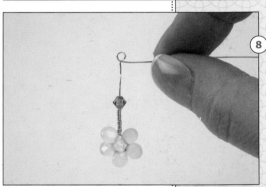

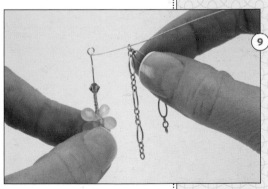

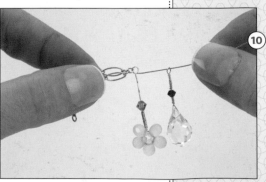

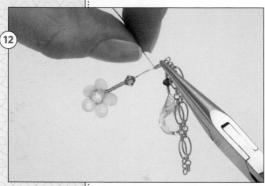

11 :: Slide the pale yellow briolette bead combination down the wire and into the eye loop.

12 :: Grasp the eye loop with chain-nose pliers to stabilize it, and wrap the wire around the stem, moving down toward the blue bicone.

13 :: Use wire cutters to trim away excess wire, and use chain-nose pliers to squeeze the cut end flush against the stem.

14 :: Use wire cutters to cut a 6-in/15-cm length of wire. Position the back side of the blue briolette flower flat against the midpoint of the wire. Wrap one wire end around to the front and bring it diagonally across the front of the flower. Thread it between two beads and bring it around to the back again. Repeat these steps with the other wire end, threading it between two different beads. This will stabilize the flower.

15 :: Insert one wire end from the back through the center of the flower. Thread on the 4 mm fuchsia bicone.

16 :: Thread the wire end with the bicone back through the center of the flower, but on the opposite side of the wire running through the center, so that the bicone is trapped on the front of the flower and the wire end is returned to its starting position on the back side.

17 :: On the back side of the flower, twist the two wire ends together using chain-nose pliers.

18 :: Use round-nose pliers to make a loop with the twisted wire ends. The loop should be flush against the back side of the flower.

19 :: Use wire cutters to cut a 4-in/10-cm length of wire. Make an eye loop at one end, with a 1½-in-/4-cm-long tail. (See "How to Make an Eye Loop on Both Ends Using Wire," page 311.) Insert the longer wire stem through the loop on the back of the flower until the twisted loop sits in the eye loop.

20 :: Wrap the shorter wire tail for ¼ in/6 mm around the stem. Trim away excess wire and squeeze the cut end flush against the stem using chain-nose pliers. Thread on one indicolite bicone.

(continued page 92)

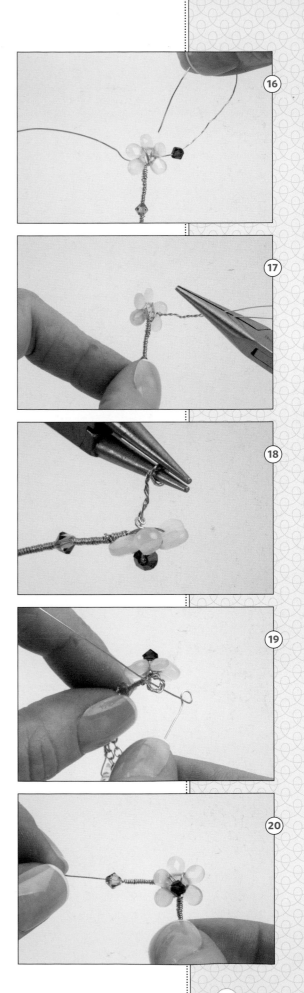

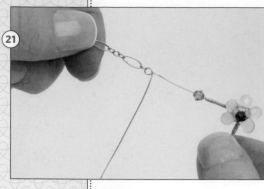

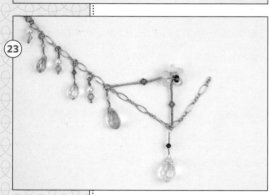

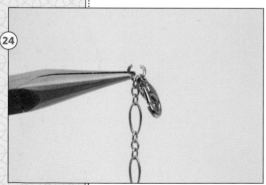

21 :: On the opposite end of the wire, measure ¼ in/6 mm from the bicone and make an eye loop with a long stem. Thread the wire end through the last link of one of the 8-in/20-cm chains.

22 :: Wrap the wire end down the stem toward the bicone. Trim away excess wire and squeeze the cut end flush against the stem using chain-nose pliers. Open one jump ring. (See "How to Open and Close a Jump Ring," page 309.) Insert one end through the last link of the 3-in/7.5-cm chain, the last link of the 8-in/20-cm chain, and the connector loop on one of the citrine briolette bead combinations. Close the jump ring.

23 :: Use five more jump rings to attach two light-pink briolette and bicone bead combinations and three powder-blue bicone and pearl bead combinations to the chain as shown or as desired. Repeat steps 19–23 to complete the opposite side of the necklace.

24 :: Use a jump ring to attach the lobster clasp to the last link of one of the 8-in/20-cm chains. Repeat this step to add a jump ring only to the last link on the other 8-in/20-cm chain.

MOONLIT NIGHT

Sleek and sophisticated, this necklace just grazes the collarbone with the lightest and most elegant rope of beads, woven in a tubular peyote stitch using Delica beads in galvanized silver and hematite. Together these ordinary beads are transformed into a night sky illuminated by a thousand stars, each silver surface sending out tiny points of light. It is finished with a sparkling clasp as round as the moon that can be worn in any position—at the throat in the front, at the back, or anywhere in between.

MATERIALS

Four 5-g bags Delica beads, metallic hematite, size 10/0

One 5-g bag Delica beads, metallic galvanized silver, size 10/0

One bobbin Nymo nylon thread, black, size D

Upholstery cord, white, 6 mm dia.

1 Austrian crystal rhinestone 3-part clasp with silver setting, center ring 16 mm dia., two side parts 13 mm wide × 18 mm long

Masking tape

Cellophane tape

High-tack white glue

TOOLS

Ruler

Scissors

Beading needle, size 10

Tweezers

Mandrel, consistent size throughout, approximately 5 mm dia.

FINISHED SIZE

20 in/51 cm

Before you begin, read the following in the Techniques section:

HOW TO PREPARE BEADS FOR BEAD WEAVING, page 346

HOW TO PREPARE BEADING THREAD, page 347

HOW TO PRESTRETCH BEADING THREAD, page 347

HOW TO CONDITION THREAD, page 348

HOW TO START A SINGLE-THREADED STRAND WITH A BEAD STOPPER, page 348

HOW TO MAKE THE EVEN-COUNT TUBULAR PEYOTE STITCH, page 363

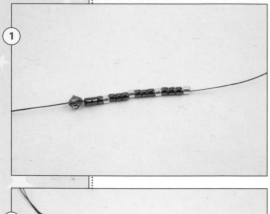

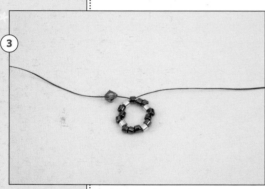

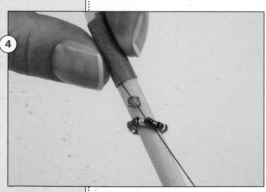

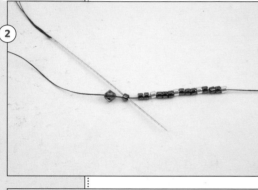

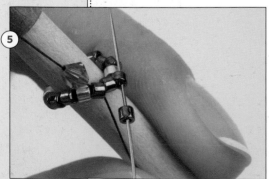

DIRECTIONS

1 :: String a 16-in/40.5-cm single length of pre-stretched and conditioned Nymo thread onto the beading needle. Add a bead stopper at the opposite end. String on three hematite beads and one silver bead. Repeat this stringing pattern three more times.

2 :: Thread the needle through the first bead that was strung. It's the bead closest to the bead stopper.

3 :: Pull the threads to make a beaded loop.

4 :: Slide the beaded loop onto a mandrel and secure the thread end that extends from the bead stopper with masking tape.

5 :: Pick up one new hematite bead with the needle. Working in the same direction as the first row, skip the next bead on the beaded loop and insert the needle into the very next bead; pull the threads taut. (See Tips.)

(continued page 96)

6 :: Repeat step 5 to continue adding hematite beads to the beaded loop, stopping upon reaching the first bead strung in step 1.

7 :: In order to begin the next row, do not thread on an additional new bead, but instead insert the needle into the adjacent raised bead. Pull the thread through. The needle is now in position to add another row of beads.

8 :: Add on the next row of beads. After completing row 4, pass the needle through the adjacent bead to get into position to start row 5, as shown.

9 :: Refer to this photo to add four silver beads to row 5. Four silver beads are added every four rows, with one hematite bead strung between each of them. With each new silver row, their placement shifts two columns to create an alternating staggered pattern.

10 :: Row 5, when completed, should look like the example shown in image 10, below left.

11 :: Continue adding rows while following the beading pattern shown more clearly in step 12. There should be one completely black column of beads between each two columns of staggered silver beads. Each silver bead should have three black beads above and below it within the same column. Silver beads are added in staggered positions every fourth row or with three rows of black beads between them.

12 :: When there is approximately 6 in/15 cm of thread left, stop beading, remove the masking tape, and slide the beaded section off the mandrel. Use tweezers to remove the bead stopper, leaving the thread tail intact.

13 :: Measure and cut a 16-in/40.5-cm length of upholstery cord. To keep the end of the cord from fraying, wrap its perimeter with a piece of cellophane tape and then apply a generous amount of glue to the tip of the cord and to the cord below the tape. Let the glue dry. Trim the end neatly, leaving the glue and tape intact. Repeat this step on the opposite end. Slide the beaded section onto the upholstery cord.

14 :: Repeat steps 1–12 to make another beaded section. Slide the second beaded section onto the upholstery cord below the first section. Before securing the two beaded sections together, first ensure that the beads and the pattern line up. (See "How to Weave Two Peyote Sections Together," page 354.) If they don't, add another row until they match up, but only if there is ample thread. Otherwise, remove rows of beads until they match up by sliding the needle off the thread and using tweezers to pull out the last stitch and slide off the bead. Continue removing stitches and beads with the remaining beads in the same row. Repeat these steps until the beads fit together and the pattern matches.

(continued page 98)

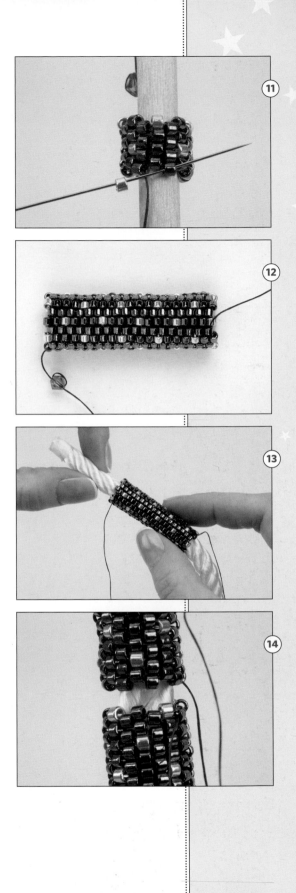

15 :: Thread the needle with one of the 6-in/ 15-cm thread tails from either of the beaded sections. Weave the thread between the two sections all the way around and pull the threads taut. Secure the thread end by weaving it into the beads. (See "How to End a Thread by Weaving In," page 355.)

16 :: Secure the opposite 6-in/15-cm tail length within the beaded sections by weaving it in. Note that you will stitch this thread in the opposite direction from the one in step 15.

17 :: Slide the beaded sections up toward one end of the upholstery cord. Single-thread a needle with a 10-in/25-cm length of thread, adding a double overhand knot at the opposite end. Begin by anchoring the thread lower on the cord, as shown, stitching through the upholstery cord multiple times to prevent the thread from coming loose in the event the cord frays. Make a few stitches farther up the cord with the same thread to secure the upholstery cord to one connector loop on the rhinestone clasp. Do this by threading the needle through the loop and then the upholstery cord. Repeat this step five or six times to sew them together. Use the same thread to secure the second connector loop to the upholstery cord. Tie double overhand knots to finish. (See "How to Make a Single Overhand Knot" and "How to Make a Double Overhand Knot," page 342.) Trim away excess thread.

18 :: Slide the beaded section up over the sewn portion of the upholstery cord so that the first beaded row is flush against the bottom of the clasp.

19 :: Thread the needle with the top 6-in-/ 15-cm-long tail and run the needle through the top row of beads multiple times, tying single overhand knots every few beads to secure them.

20 :: Thread the same needle through the spaces between the beads and the upholstery cord to sew the beaded peyote tube to the cord. Tie a double overhand knot, hiding the knot and the thread within the woven beads, and trim away excess thread. If necessary, cut a second piece of thread to continue stitching the beads to the upholstery cord until it is secure.

21 :: To continue to add rows to the existing beaded section while it is still on the upholstery cord, see "How to Start a New Thread Midproject," page 353. Or make another beaded section on the mandrel and transfer it to the upholstery cord as done in steps 1–12, securing the beaded sections to one another as done in steps 14–16. Upon completing an 18-in-/46-cm-long beaded tube, repeat steps 17–20 to secure the remaining end to the clasp.

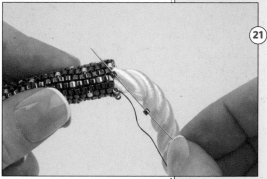

TIPS

Doing this stitch requires that you always work in the same direction. For instance, after you string on the first row, if you bring the needle around counterclockwise to insert it into the first bead, and then transfer it to the mandrel in the same position, you will continue to work counterclockwise as you add all the additional rows.

This necklace is begun by creating beaded sections on a mandrel. The hard surface of the mandrel is easy to work on and will help you to feel comfortable with the peyote stitch and how beads take shape within it. These sections are then transferred to the upholstery cord and stitched together. If you are already comfortable with the even-count tubular peyote stitch and are confident that you will not accidentally stitch the beads to the cord, you can skip using the mandrel and simply start your beading on the upholstery cord.

Remember that in any peyote stitch, each new bead you thread on should always fall on the skipped bead.

When choosing a clasp for this necklace, keep in mind that the cord and the beaded sections must be secured to it, so it has to be substantial and suit the piece. If you can't find a clasp structured like this one, see "How to Attach a Clasp to Peyote Beading Pieces," page 366, for alternatives.

PINK CHAMPAGNE

If champagne bubbles could be threaded onto a necklace, they would look like this near-endless strand of perfectly cut crystal beads in effervescent pink. Measuring 60 in/1.5 m long but strung in one continuous length, the versatile necklace can be worn several ways: wrapped several times so it rides close to the neck; knotted Holly Golightly style; or placed around the neck in a single loop of beads that swings when you walk. Requiring only simple stringing and knotting, Pink Champagne can be created in time to make the first curtain call at the theater.

MATERIALS

131 multifaceted hexagon-cut Chinese crystal round beads, pink AB, 8 mm dia.

131 Chinese crystal round beads, pink, 4 mm dia.

Cyanoacrylate liquid

Masking tape

Transite

TOOLS

Ruler

Wire cutters

Paper clip

FINISHED SIZE

60 in/1.5 m

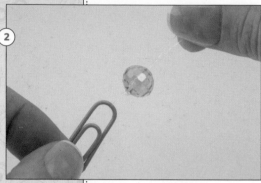

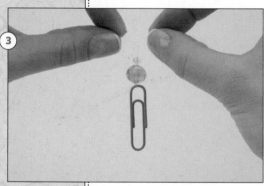

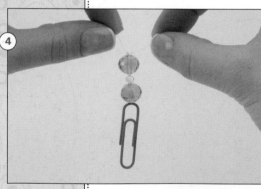

DIRECTIONS

1 :: Cut a 72-in/183-cm length of transite. Tie two single overhand knots 6 in/15 cm from one end. The knot must be bigger than the bead hole to secure it. (See "How to Make a Single Overhand Knot," page 342.) Apply a drop of glue to secure the knot. Thread five beads, alternating between large and small, onto the long end of the transite. Secure this end to a clean, flat work surface using masking tape.

2 :: Thread a paper clip onto the short, 6-in/ 15-cm end of the transite. Thread the short end back through the first bead, trapping the paper clip. Pull the transite to bring the paper clip against the bead. On the opposite side of the bead, tie a single overhand knot close to the bead. (See "How to Anchor Thread Ends Using a Knot," page 352.) Apply a drop of glue to secure it.

3 :: Slide the second bead up the transite to meet the first one. Thread the same short end from step 2 through the second bead. Pull the transite tight so that the knots are flush against the beads. Tie a single overhand knot and secure it with glue.

4 :: Thread the short end through the third bead and repeat step 3.

5 :: Add glued knots between the remaining two beads. Start stringing on the rest of beads, alternating small and large, without knotting between them. Hide the cut end of the transite in the beads and trim away the excess.

6 :: When all the beads are strung, bring both ends of the transite together.

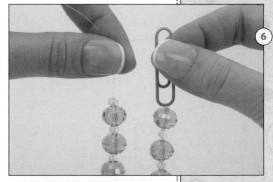

7 :: Remove the paper clip from the loop, and thread the other end of the transite through the loop.

8 :: Thread the end of the transite through the first bead on the side opposite the loop.

9 :: Tie the end into a single overhand knot and secure it with a drop of glue. Repeat this step for the next four beads, threading and knotting the transite as you go. Hide the cut end in the beads and trim away excess.

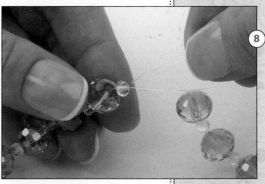

TIP

IMPORTANT :: With the exception of the knots tied in Step 1, every time the directions call for a single-overhand knot, you will need to use the technique "How to Anchor Thread Ends Using a Knot," page 352.

You can use this project's technique to make any kind of continuous-strand necklace. If you are working with a random bead design, using beads of different sizes and shapes (as opposed to the repeating design of this one), you will need to lay out your beads beforehand and pick a starting point, or rather a starting bead, on the necklace. This will be the first bead strung on in step 1 and will be the point where the two strands are joined together. Follow the directions above, working clockwise, to string on the remaining beads until you reach the last bead to the left of the starting point. Then join the strands' ends together.

SNOW QUEEN

As light as frost on a window, a delicate organdy ribbon woven of the finest silvery white thread holds a strand of hollow Venetian-glass beads in a necklace fit for a queen. Made with elements in cool tones, the double rings of ice-blue rhinestones display a winter palette, as do the sterling-silver toggle clasp and the stardust silver beads that are interspersed in the strand pattern.

MATERIALS

12 Venetian-style blown-glass oval beads, clear with white stripes, 13 mm dia. × 25 mm long

14 round beads, laser-finished sterling silver, 6 mm dia.

1 Austrian crystal rhinestone circle pendant, ice blue, 28 mm dia.

1 ring, sterling silver, 8 mm dia. × 2 mm wide

2 round-end end cap connectors, sterling silver, 4 mm wide × 8 mm long

3 jump rings, silver, 24 gauge, 5 mm dia.

1 oval jump ring, silver, 22 gauge, 3 mm wide × 4 mm long

Toggle clasp, sterling silver, 15 mm dia.

¾ yard/69 cm organdy ribbon, white, ¾ in/2 cm wide

Crystal cement

Toothpicks

TOOLS

Ruler

Scissors

Big-eye needle

2 pairs chain-nose pliers

FINISHED SIZE

20 in/50 cm

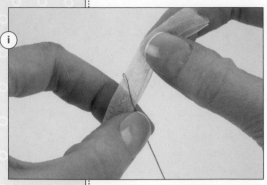

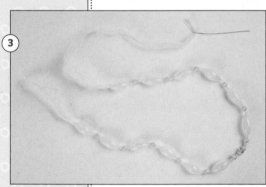

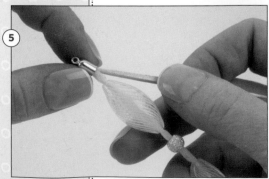

DIRECTIONS

1 :: Fold the ribbon in half lengthwise, and insert one end through the eye of the needle. Pull the ribbon through, creating a 1½-in/4-cm tail. See "How to String Beads on Ribbon," page 287, for help.

2 :: Insert the needle into one blown-glass bead. Slide the bead down the needle and onto the ribbon, stopping 4 in/10 cm before the opposite end.

3 :: Thread on one sterling-silver bead. Continue to thread on blown-glass and sterling-silver beads, alternating between the two, six times in total. Then thread on another sterling-silver bead, the silver ring, and a second sterling-silver bead. Resume the previous pattern by stringing on one sterling-silver bead followed by one blown-glass bead. Repeat five more times. Position the beads on the ribbon as shown, with spaces between the beads, or as desired.

4 :: Tie a single overhand knot at the short, free end of the ribbon. (See "How to Make a Single Overhand Knot," page 342.) Use chain-nose pliers to grasp the end of the ribbon and pull the knot tight. Leave ¼ in/6 mm of ribbon above the knot, then trim away excess using scissors.

5 :: Apply crystal cement to the entire surface area of the knot. Use a toothpick to push the knot into one end cap connector. Let the glue dry. Reposition the beads by sliding them on the ribbon toward the finished end. Repeat steps 4–5 to secure the opposite ribbon end to the remaining end cap connector.

6 :: Open one 5 mm jump ring using both pairs of chain-nose pliers. (See "How to Open and Close a Jump Ring," page 309.) Thread one end through the loop on one half of the clasp and the loop on one end cap connector. Close the jump ring. Attach the second half of the clasp to the opposite connector, using another 5 mm jump ring.

7 :: Open the oval jump ring. Insert one end through the loop on the rhinestone pendant and the last 5 mm jump ring. Close the jump ring. Open the 5 mm jump ring and insert one end through the silver ring on the necklace. Close the jump ring.

• • • TIPS • • •

If you would prefer to showcase more of the ribbon, consider using fewer beads.

Organdy ribbon works well for stringing beads due to its light weight. You will want to test-fit your ribbon and beads before stringing. If the ribbon is too bulky, it could crack your bead as you attempt to thread it on. To prevent this, choose a narrower ribbon or beads with extra-large holes.

CAFÉ AU LAIT

This multistrand necklace has a restrained but sophisticated style that shows off the combination of pearls and crystals, all in a soothing palette: coffee and cream. The beads are arranged randomly on the strands, each one a mix of lustrous pearls in just the faintest blush of cream, champagne, and coffee and the transparent sparkle of crystals in amber, espresso, cola, and smoky brown. Interspersed through the strands are faceted beads in bronze that add a rich glow to the composition. Raising the retro glamour on this necklace is the pretty brooch-style "pin" (really an elaborate connector for the strands) composed of a gold rose with rhinestones that is set on a neat ribbon bow.

MATERIALS

1 faceted smoky-quartz briolette, 3 cm wide × 4 cm long × 4 mm thick

1 rose connector with Austrian crystal rhinestone center, gold, 27 mm dia.

47 round glass pearls in various sizes, cream:

> Four 20 mm dia.
>
> Six 15 mm dia.
>
> Ten 10 mm dia.
>
> Twenty-seven 8 mm dia.

31 round glass pearls in various sizes, champagne pink:

> Six 14 mm dia.
>
> Twenty-five 8 mm dia.

8 round glass pearls, café, 14 mm dia.

1 Austrian crystal round bead, espresso, 9 mm dia.

45 Czech fire-polished round glass beads, bronze, 8 mm dia.

4 Austrian crystal cubes, café, 8 mm

5 Czech fire-polished glass rondelles in various colors and sizes:

> 1 amber, 9 mm dia. × 7 mm wide
>
> 2 cola, 8 mm dia. × 6 mm wide
>
> 2 amber, 8 mm dia. × 5 mm wide

4 round beads, laser-finished gold filled, 2 mm dia.

6 seed beads, gold, size 11/0

1 stamped brass charm with fruit and leaves, 1½ in/4 cm wide × 2¼ in/6 cm long

1 bead cap, gold, 8 mm dia. × 5 mm long

4 clamshells, gold

2 jump rings, gold, 18 gauge, 8 mm dia.

1 spring ring, gold, 18 mm dia.

2 end rings in figure-eight shape, gold

3 packages silk beading cord with needles attached, gold, 2 m per package, size 8

¾ yard/69 cm grosgrain ribbon, coffee, ⅝ in/16 mm wide

Sewing thread, café

1 sewing needle

Masking tape

Cyanoacrylate liquid

Permanent adhesive

High-tack white glue

TOOLS

Ruler

Scissors

2 pairs chain-nose pliers

FINISHED SIZE

25 in/63.5 cm

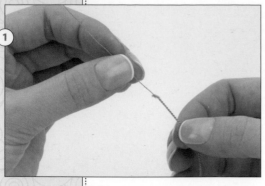

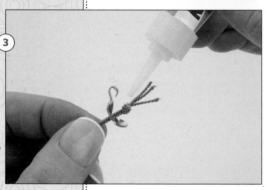

DIRECTIONS

1 :: Remove all three strands of beading cord from their packaging. Ensure that each beading needle is secured to its beading cord. If necessary, tighten them by twisting the needles' eyes with chain-nose pliers.

2 :: Thread all three needles through one clamshell.

3 :: Pull all three cords through the clamshell until the opposite ends of the cords are reached. Tie a single overhand knot to secure them together. (See "How to Make a Single Overhand Knot," page 342.) Ensure that it cannot slip through the clamshell. Apply a drop of cyano-acrylate to the knot. Let dry. Pull the knot into the clamshell. Trim away any excess cord. Close the clamshell using chain-nose pliers.

4 :: Move two of the beading cords aside. On the third beading cord, follow the beading layout for this random design featured in step 6 or create your own design. Then refer to "How to Make a Knotted Necklace," page 284, to see how to add the beads to the silk cord.

5 :: This first finished beaded strand should measure 16½ in/42 cm long. Use masking tape to secure the strand to the work surface.

6 :: Repeat steps 4–5 to make the second and third strands. The middle strand should measure 15½ in/39 cm and the remaining strand 15 in/38 cm.

7 :: Remove the masking tape from the cord ends. Thread all three needles through a clamshell. Tie a single overhand knot. Apply a drop of cyanoacrylate glue. Let dry. Trim away excess beading cord. Set the three strands aside (their needles should still be attached). Close the clamshell using chain-nose pliers.

8 :: Repeat steps 1–7 using the three cords cut away in step 7 to make three short beaded strands, following the beading layout or working as desired. Each strand should measure 5½ in/14 cm.

9 :: See "How to Make a Double Bow," page 367, to make the bow shown here using the grosgrain ribbon. Keep the ends from fraying by adding dabs of high-tack white glue to the cut edges. Attach the leaf charm by hiding the end in the center knot of the bow. Glue the end of the charm in place using permanent adhesive. Secure the bow and the charm further, using a sewing thread and a needle to stitch them together.

10 :: Place a generous amount of permanent adhesive in the center of the bow. Position the rose connector on the glue and press down to adhere. Bend the loops of the bow up slightly so that they hide any glue on the sides of the rose connector. Let dry.

(continued page 112)

11 :: Attach a clamshell on one end of the three longer strands to the bottom loop on the rose connector. (See "How to Attach a Clamshell," page 282.) Secure using chain-nose pliers.

12 :: Attach a clamshell on one end of the three shorter strands to the top loop on the rose connector. Secure using chain-nose pliers.

13 :: Attach the clamshell on the free end of the three longer strands to one jump ring using chain-nose pliers. Attach the jump ring to one figure-eight ring and the figure-eight ring to the spring ring. Use the remaining jump ring and figure-eight ring to attach the free end on the three shorter strands to the spring ring on the opposite side.

14 :: Use one of the remaining beading cords with the needle still attached to string on one seed bead and one laser-finished bead. Repeat this one more time and finish with a seed bead. Then thread on the briolette and repeat the seed bead and laser-finished bead sequence on the opposite side of the briolette.

15 :: Thread both beading cord ends through one bead cap.

16 :: Thread both beading cord ends through the bottom loop on the rose connector. Position one cord to the right of the clamshell hook and the other to the left. Thread both beading cord ends back through the top of the bead cap and trim away the needle.

17 :: Pull both ends of the beading cord to tighten the beads and bring them into the bead cap and to bring the bead cap against the loop on the rose connector. Tie the ends together using a double overhand knot, hiding it within the bead cap. Add a drop of cyanoacrylate to secure the knot. Let the glue dry. Trim away excess beading cord ends.

• • • • TIPS • • • •

If you can find only silk beading cord without a pre-strung needle, you can either buy twisted-wire needles that you attach using chain-nose pliers or make a twisted-wire needle of your own. See "How to Make a Twisted Wire Needle," page 286.

Add a drop pendant to a knotted necklace using the same technique described here. Just move the pendant to the midpoint of a single beaded, knotted strand. Wrap the strands around the knotted beading cord to the right and left of the midpoint bead before threading them back through the bead cap.

BRACELETS

LIME WIRE

Water-clear cubes in juicy lime, lemon, grape, and ice-blue tints are lashed to a gleaming hoop of gold using metallic wire in lime green, adding a quirky industrial note to this bracelet design. The crystal cubes are arranged in a repeating pattern of color that distributes subtle degrees of transparency around the bangle, and when two identical bracelets are paired, their effect is multiplied.

MATERIALS

20 Austrian crystal cubes, violet, 6 mm

20 opalescent Austrian crystal cubes, Pacific blue, 6 mm

18 Austrian crystal cubes, green, 6 mm

18 Austrian crystal cubes, pale yellow, 6 mm

Lime green–colored wire, vinyl-coated copper core, dead-soft, 22 gauge

2 bangle bracelets, silver, 7 cm dia. × 3 mm wide

TOOLS

Ruler

Wire cutters

Chain-nose pliers

FINISHED SIZE

3½ in/8.25 cm dia

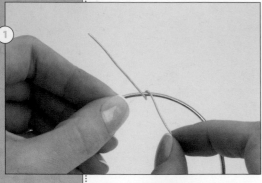

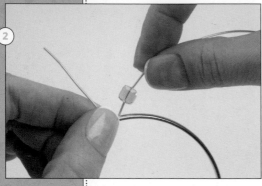

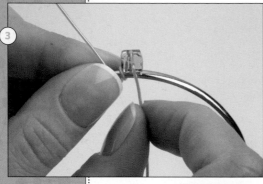

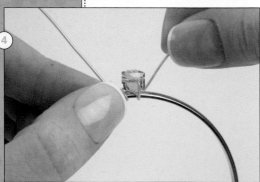

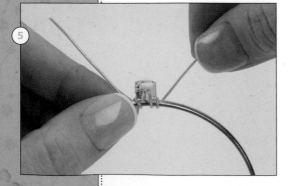

DIRECTIONS

1 :: Use wire cutters to cut two 36-in/91.5-cm lengths of the lime wire. Divide the beads, bangle bracelets, and wire into two equal groups. Set one group aside. Wrap one end of the wire around one bangle bracelet twice to secure it. (See "How to Wrap Thin Wire," page 304.) Finish with the long end of the wire pointing upward, as seen in step 2.

2 :: Slide one violet cube onto the long end of the wire.

3 :: Position the cube on the outside edge of the bangle so that the lime wire is running perpendicular to the bangle bracelet.

4 :: Wrap the wire once around the bangle to secure the cube.

5 :: Wrap the wire around the bangle again, finishing with the wire pointing upward.

MASTERING THE ART *of* BEADING

6 :: Thread on one green cube.

7 :: Repeat steps 3–5 to secure it in place.

8 :: Continue by adding a yellow cube, followed by a blue cube, before starting the four-color pattern again. Repeat the color pattern nine times in total.

9 :: Check the position of the beads as you work, and if necessary twist them slightly to make the cubes and wires lie perpendicular to the bangle.

10 :: After the four-color pattern has been repeated nine times, this bangle will accommodate two more cubes. Fill in these spaces with one violet and one blue cube. (They are accounted for in the materials list.) To finish, wrap the wire around the bangle bracelet two more times. Trim the end and hide it between the first and last cubes. Repeat this step to hide the starting wire end as well. Repeat steps 1–10 to make a second bracelet.

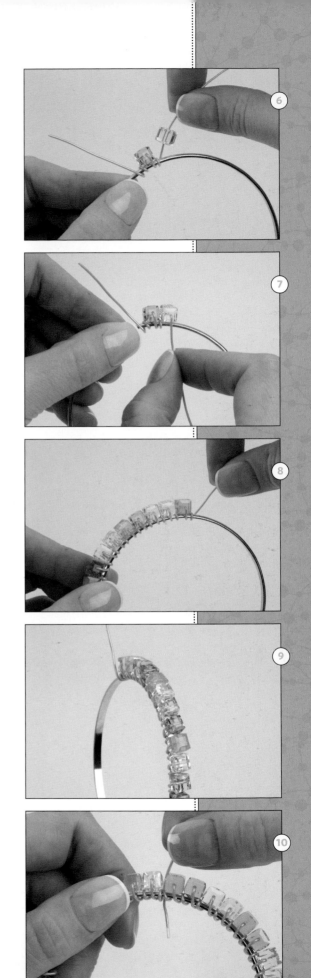

• • • **TIP** • • •

Before you add the last few cubes, make room for them by sliding the other cubes as close together as possible. After the last two cubes are added, you can adjust the spacing.

RENAISSANCE

This multistrand bracelet features an exuberant gathering of chains in gold and antique gold patinas, yet it is relieved of any monochromatic colorway by strand upon strand of sparkling rhinestones, faceted crystals in turquoise and amethyst, and lustrous rainbow pearls that seem picked from a fine needlework tapestry. By design, the careful restraint among the elements shifts attention to the languorous texture of the chains, which seem to flow like streams of liquid metal.

MATERIALS

1 faceted quartz round bead, amethyst, 11 mm dia.

59 freshwater rice rainbow pearls, green, 5 mm dia. × 6 mm long

24 faceted round amethyst beads, purple, 5 mm dia.

3 oval beads, brushed gold, 4 mm dia. × 8 mm long

6 faceted flat amethyst ovals, purple, 4 mm wide × 6 mm long × 2 mm thick

2 Austrian crystal round beads, clear, 4 mm dia.

44 Austrian crystal bicones, turquoise, 4 mm

6 Czech fire-polished round glass beads, gold, 4 mm dia.

7 Czech fire-polished round glass beads, gold, 3 mm dia.

5 ft/152.5 cm curb chain, gold, links 3 mm wide × 4 mm long

2 ft/61 cm rhinestone chain, gold setting, links 2 mm wide × 2 mm long

1 foot/30.5 cm cable-link chain, gold, links 3 mm wide × 4 mm long

1 foot/30.5 cm fine Figaro chain, antique gold, links 2 mm wide × 4 mm long and 1 mm wide × 2 mm long

1 foot/30.5 cm curb chain, gold, links 2 mm wide × 2 mm long

1 foot/30.5 cm curb chain, antique gold, links 1 mm wide × 2 mm long

2 end bars for 13 strands, antique gold, 4 cm long

8 round rhinestone chain end connectors, gold, 3 mm wide × 7 mm long × 2 mm thick

4 crimp beads, gold, size 2

130 (approximately) jump rings, antique gold, 20 gauge, 3 mm dia.

26 jump rings, antique gold, 18 gauge, 5 mm dia.

5 jump rings, antique gold, 22 gauge, 4 mm dia.

1 jump ring, gold, 22 gauge, 4 mm dia.

1 headpin, gold, 20 gauge, 2 in/5 cm long

Beading wire, satin gold, .019 in/0.48 mm dia.

Gold wire, dead-soft, 24 gauge

Toggle clasp with snakeskin pattern, gold, 1.6 cm dia.

Crystal cement

TOOLS

Ruler

Wire cutters

Chain-nose pliers

Crimping pliers

Bent-nose pliers

Round-nose pliers

FINISHED SIZE

8 in/20 cm

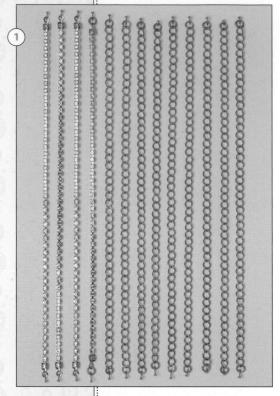

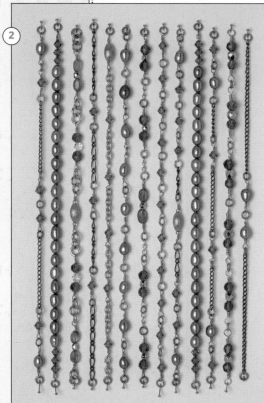

1 :: Use wire cutters to cut the 5 ft/152.5 cm gold curb chain into nine 6-in/15-cm lengths and the 2 ft/61 cm rhinestone chain into four 6-in/15-cm lengths. Set the lengths of gold chain aside. Add rhinestone chain end connectors to both ends of all lengths of rhinestone chain. (See "How to Attach Crimp End Connectors to Rhinestone Chain," page 296.) Set them aside.

2 :: Use wire cutters to cut two 8-in/20-cm lengths of beading wire. Set one aside. Thread on three turquoise bicones, twenty-one pearls, and another three bicones. Use a crimp bead and crimping pliers to secure each end to a 3 mm jump ring. (See "How to Secure a Crimp Tube with Crimping Pliers," page 274.) Repeat with the remaining length of beading wire to make a second pearl strand. Set these aside.

See "How to Make a Wrapped-Wire Loop on Both Ends Using Wire," page 317, to add wrapped-wire loops on both ends to each of the following beads using the gold wire: seventeen pearls, thirty-two turquoise bicones, and three brushed-gold oval beads. Now add wrapped-wire loops on both ends to the following bead combinations: six 3-bead combinations of one 5 mm round amethyst/one 4 mm gold fire-polished/one 5 mm round amethyst; four 3-bead combinations of one 5 mm round amethyst/one 3 mm gold fire-polished/one 5mm round amethyst; two 3-bead combinations of one 5 mm round amethyst/one 4 mm round clear/one 5 mm round amethyst; three 3-bead combinations of one amethyst oval/one 3 mm gold fire-polished/one amethyst oval. Set these aside.

Make eleven 6-in/15-cm lengths of beaded chain, as shown or as desired, by joining the bead and bead combinations with wrapped-wire loops using 3 mm jump rings and short lengths of chain cut from the remaining 1-ft/30.5-cm lengths of uncut chain. Set them aside.

3 :: Pair any one beaded length with one of the nine lengths of curb chain or one rhinestone chain. Use chain-nose and bent-nose pliers to attach one 3 mm jump ring to both ends of each length, using four 3 mm jump rings in total. (See "How to Open and Close a Jump Ring," page 309.) Open one 5 mm jump ring and insert it through both 3 mm jump rings on the same end. Do not close the jump ring.

4 :: Insert one end of the 5 mm jump ring through an outside hole on one end bar. Close the jump ring.

5 :: Use chain-nose pliers to attach one 5 mm jump ring to the opposite ends of the same two strands and to the corresponding outside hole on the second end bar. Close the jump ring. Repeat step 3–5 to continue adding pairs of strands and attaching them to the end bars with 5 mm jump rings, as shown or as desired. Move over one hole on the end bars with each new 5 mm jump ring.

6 :: Attach one of the antique gold 4 mm jump rings to the connector loop on one end bar. Open a second antique gold 4 mm jump ring. Insert one end into the connector loop on the round portion of the toggle clasp and the jump ring connected to the end bar. Close the jump ring.

7 :: Attach an antique gold 4 mm jump ring to the connector loop on the end bar on the opposite side and another to the bar portion of the toggle clasp. Use a third antique gold 4 mm jump ring to join these two jump rings together.

(continued page 124)

8 :: Insert the headpin through the 11 mm faceted amethyst bead. Use chain-nose and round-nose pliers to make a wrapped-wire loop. (See "How to Make a Wrapped-Wire Loop Using a Headpin," page 316.)

9 :: Attach a gold 4 mm jump ring to this wrapped-wire loop and to the jump ring connected to the end bar on the side of the bracelet with the round portion of the toggle clasp.

LOTS OF LUXE

As shimmering as quicksilver, Lots of Luxe is a bracelet woven from rows and rows of tiny silver beads using a needle and thread in traditional even- and odd-count peyote stitches. The silver beads are precisely shaped, fitting together in neat interlocking rows that end in a unique closure: an end loop that is woven into the design, which captures a rhinestone button and adds sparkle and high-end glamour to the bracelet.

MATERIALS

Three 5-g bags Delica beads, metallic galvanized silver, size 10/0

1 rhinestone button with silver setting, crystal, 8 mm dia.

1 bobbin Nymo nylon thread, white, size D

2 small bead stopper beads

TOOLS

Ruler

Scissors

Beading needle, size 10

Tweezers

FINISHED SIZE

7¾ in/18.4 cm

Before you begin, read the following in the Techniques section:

HOW TO PREPARE BEADS FOR BEAD WEAVING, page 346

HOW TO PREPARE BEADING THREAD, page 347

HOW TO PRESTRETCH BEADING THREAD, page 347

HOW TO CONDITION THREAD, page 348

HOW TO START A SINGLE-THREADED STRAND WITH A BEAD STOPPER, page 348

THE PEYOTE STITCH, page 351

HOW TO MAKE THE EVEN-COUNT FLAT PEYOTE STITCH, page 356

HOW TO MAKE THE ODD-COUNT FLAT PEYOTE STITCH USING THREE BEADS, page 360

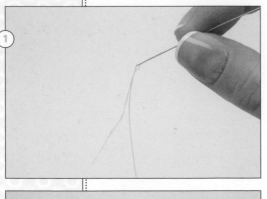

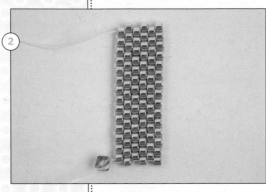

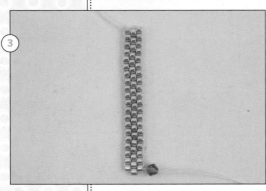

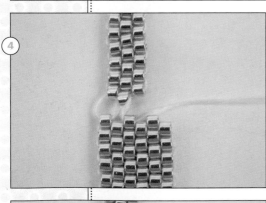

DIRECTIONS

1 :: String a 16-in/40.5-cm single length of pre-stretched and conditioned Nymo thread onto the beading needle. Add a bead stopper at the opposite end. (See "How to Start a Single-Threaded Strand with a Bead Stopper," page 348.)

2 :: String on six silver beads to make row 1. Follow the directions for "How to Make the Even-Count Flat Peyote Stitch," page 356, and continue adding rows of beads until you are left with a 6-in/15-cm tail of excess thread. Remove the needle and set this section aside. Repeat steps 1–2 until you've made enough sections to make a 6½-in-/16.5-cm-long beaded section. See "How to Weave Two Peyote Sections Together," page 354, to join the sections together.

3 :: Repeat step 1 to start a new thread. String on three silver beads to make row 1. Follow the directions for "How to Make the Odd-Count Flat Peyote Stitch Using Three Beads," page 360. Continue adding rows of beads until you've made a 1½-in-/4-cm-long beaded section. Be sure to leave a 6-in/15-cm tail of excess thread. Remove the needle.

4 :: Thread the needle with the thread tail from the even-count (wider) peyote section. Position the odd-count (narrower) peyote section above the wider section and flush to the left. (It should end up looking like the section featured in step 5.) Be sure that the bead patterns line up. If they don't, add or remove a row of beads from either section. Weave the two beaded sections together.

5 :: Pull the threads taut. Do not remove the needle from the thread.

(continued page 128)

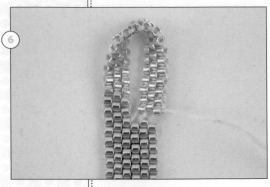

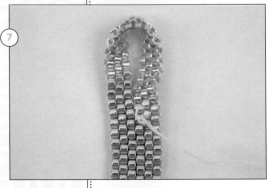

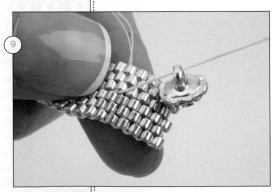

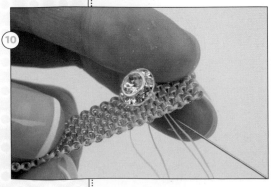

6 :: Bring the narrow strip around as shown, positioning it flush right above the wider beaded section. Be sure that the bead patterns line up. If necessary, add or remove a row of beads. Use the needle and thread from step 5 to weave the narrow section and the wider section together.

7 :: Insert the needle into the bead below the one where you exited the needle in step 6, then continue to weave the thread back to the center of the bracelet and secure it by making a single overhand knot. (See "How to Anchor Thread Ends Using a Knot," page 352.) Hide the thread end by weaving it into the beads. (See "How to End a Thread by Weaving In," page 355.) Cut away the remaining excess. Remove any remaining bead stoppers and secure any remaining threads by weaving them into the bracelet.

8 :: Measure and cut a 12-in/30.5-cm length of thread. Double-thread the needle, but do not add a knot or a bead stopper at the opposite end. See "How to Start a New Thread Midproject," page 353, and start the new thread toward the bottom of the wider section, hiding the thread ends within the beads. Finish weaving the needle through the beads by bringing the needle to the center, three columns in and eleven rows from the bottom. Tie a single overhand knot. Use tweezers to aid in the knot tying if necessary.

9 :: Insert the needle through the shank on the button, and slide the button down the thread.

10 :: Insert the needle down through the bracelet under the button to the underside. Then insert the needle back up to the front side, moving a few beads to the right or left to hide the thread between the rows. Insert the needle through the shank again and back down through the brace-let. Repeat these steps one or two more times to secure the button to the bracelet. Hide the thread ends within the beads. Trim away excess thread.

11 :: To wear, slip the beaded loop over the button. This bracelet can be worn with the button showing or concealed on the back of the wrist.

TIP

This bracelet was made in sections. If you are confident in your peyote stitching, you can continue weaving with the same thread from the even-count wide band directly into the odd-count narrow band simply by reducing the amount of beads by half after reaching 6½ in/16.5 cm.

Row 197 –

Odd-Count Peyote
1½" long
Rows 158–197
3 columns

Row 157 –

Row 157 is the last row of even-count peyote

Row 100–

Even-Count Peyote
6½" long
Rows 1–157
6 columns

Row 11 –

Button Placement
Row 11 between
columns 3 and 4

Row 3 –
Row 1 –

BEADING LAYOUT

BISOU

Oh, the fun you'll have wearing this playful bracelet made up of a collection of small charms that you might find in a Paris flea market. Most in shades of pink, the decorations feature framed letter charms that spell out amour *and its translation, "love," in beaded wire. Other small charms, configured from several glass beads and findings, resemble fine porcelain vases, and dangling between rhinestone silver stars and crystal flowers is a miniature replica of the Eiffel Tower, adding a sentimental* bisou *(or kiss) to this chic piece of jewelry.*

MATERIALS

TO MAKE TWO AUSTRIAN CRYSTAL FLOWER CHARMS AND THE FOUR STAR CHARMS:

2 Austrian crystal flower beads, fuchsia, 13 mm dia. × 7 mm thick

4 star charms with pink pavé Austrian crystal rhinestones, sterling silver, 9 mm wide × 12 mm long × 2 mm thick

12 oval jump rings, sterling silver, 22 gauge, 4 mm wide × 5 mm long

TO MAKE ONE EIFFEL TOWER CHARM:

1 Eiffel Tower charm, silver, 9 mm wide × 25 mm long

1 Austrian crystal cube, pink, 6 mm

1 metal cube, silver, 2 mm

1 headpin with 1 mm ball end, silver, 22 gauge, 2 in/5 cm long

2 oval jump rings, sterling silver, 22 gauge, 4 mm wide × 5 mm long

TO MAKE ONE BRIOLETTE DROP CHARM:

1 glass briolette, clear, 9 mm dia. × 15 mm long

1 metal spacer, gold, 6 mm dia. × 2 mm thick

Gold wire, dead-soft, 26 gauge

1 oval jump ring, sterling silver, 22 gauge, 4 mm wide × 5 mm long

TO MAKE TWO TWISTED GOLD RING CHARMS:

2 twisted wire rings, gold, 16 mm dia.

1 open heart charm, rhodium-plated, 8 mm wide × 10 mm long × 1 mm thick

1 rhinestone circle charm with gold setting, 11 mm dia.

2 jump rings, gold, 22 gauge, 3 mm dia.

2 oval jump rings, sterling silver, 22 gauge, 4 mm wide × 5 mm long

TO MAKE ONE GOLD HEART CHARM:

1 filigree heart charm, gold, 11 mm wide × 14 mm long × 4 mm thick

1 round bead, laser finished, gold-filled, 4 mm dia.

1 jump ring, gold, 22 gauge, 4 mm dia.

1 headpin with 1 mm ball end, silver, 22 gauge, 2 in/5 cm long

1 oval jump ring, sterling silver, 22 gauge, 4 mm wide × 5 mm long

TO MAKE ONE PINK BIRDS CHARM:

1 pendant with 2 pink birds in gold setting, 17 mm dia. × 9 mm thick

1 enamel flower charm with rhinestone center, pink, 12 mm dia. × 3 mm thick

2 Austrian crystal bicones, fuchsia, 3 mm dia.

1 Bali-style daisy spacer, silver, 5 mm dia. × 1 mm thick

1 headpin, silver, 22 gauge, 2 in/5 cm long

2 oval jump rings, sterling silver, 22 gauge, 4 mm wide × 5 mm long

TO MAKE FIVE *AMOUR* CHARMS:

5 circle collage pendants, sterling silver, 15 mm dia. × 2.5 mm thick

5 Austrian crystal bicones, fuchsia, 3 mm

Decorative paper, pink with brown polka dots

Clear adhesive alphabet sticker sheet, with black letters 7 mm high

Clear adhesive sticker sheet, blank

Amazing Glaze

5 oval jump rings, sterling silver, 22 gauge, 4 mm wide × 5 mm long

Permanent adhesive

TO MAKE ONE "LOVE" CHARM:

70 silver-lined seed beads, bubble gum pink, size 10/0

1 star charm with pink pavé Austrian crystal rhinestones, sterling silver, 5 mm wide × 8 mm long × 1½ mm thick

1 puffed-heart charm, sterling silver, 7 mm wide × 8 mm long × 4 mm thick

3 oval jump rings, sterling silver, 22 gauge, 4 mm wide × 5 mm long

Gold wire, dead-soft, 22 gauge

TO MAKE FOUR DOUBLE-SIDED RHINESTONE FLOWER CHARMS:

8 rhinestone flowers with 4 shanks each, antique gold setting, crystal AB rhinestones:

> 2 daisies, 14 mm dia. × 3 mm thick
>
> 2 sunflowers, 12 mm dia. × 3 mm thick
>
> 2 pansies, 10 mm dia. × 3 mm thick
>
> 2 clovers, 10 mm dia. × 3 mm thick

4 oval jump rings, sterling silver, 22 gauge, 4 mm wide × 5 mm long

Gold wire, dead-soft, 24 gauge

Cyanoacrylate gel

TO MAKE NINE CANE BEAD CHARMS:

9 hand-blown glass cane beads, 6 mm–8 mm dia. × 10 mm long:

> 3 pink with black stripes
>
> 3 white with pink stripes
>
> 3 black with pink stripes

12 metal spacers, gold, 6 mm dia. × 2 mm thick

6 Bali-style daisy spacers, gold, 6 mm dia. × 1.5 mm thick

6 Bali-style daisy spacers, silver, 5 mm dia. × 1 mm thick

6 metal cubes, silver, 2 mm

9 headpins with 1 mm ball ends, silver, 22 gauge, 2 in/5 cm long

9 oval jump rings, sterling silver, 22 gauge, 4 mm wide × 5 mm long

TO MAKE SIX POLKA DOT BEAD CHARMS:

3 Czech lampwork round glass beads, fuchsia with black polka dots, 10 mm dia.

3 Czech lampwork round glass beads, amethyst with black polka dots, 8 mm dia.

3 star charms with pink rhinestones, sterling silver, 5 mm wide × 8 mm long × 1.5 mm thick

3 metal cubes, silver, 2 mm

6 Bali-style daisy spacers, gold, 4 mm dia. × 1 mm thick

4 metal spacers, gold, 6 mm dia. × 2 mm thick

1 twisted wire ring, antique gold, 8 mm dia.

1 jump ring, gold, 22 gauge, 3 mm dia.

6 headpins with 1 mm ball ends, silver, 22 gauge, 2 in/5 cm long

9 oval jump rings, sterling silver, 22 gauge, 4 mm wide × 5 mm long

TO MAKE THE JUMP RING CHAIN BRACELET:

76 jump rings, silver, 20 gauge, 6 mm dia.

1 toggle clasp, silver, 12 mm dia.

TOOLS

Chain-nose pliers

Bent-nose pliers

Wire cutters

Round-nose pliers

Ruler

Pencil

Scissors

Tweezers

Small brush

Heat gun

Spatula (for crafting only)

FINISHED SIZE

8 in/20 cm

DIRECTIONS

1 :: To make the bracelet chain that will serve as the base for the charms, use seventy-four of the 6 mm jump rings to create a 7-in/17-cm length of chain. (See "How to Open and Close a Jump Ring," page 309, and "How to Make a Jump Ring Chain," page 329.) Use one of the two remaining 6 mm jump rings to attach the ring portion of the toggle clasp to one end of the chain. Repeat this step, using the last 6 mm jump ring, to attach the bar portion of the clasp to the opposite end.

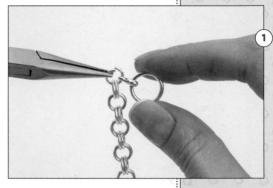

2 :: Follow the beading layout to make the *Bisou* charms as shown or as desired. Add two oval jump rings to each of the following: two Austrian crystal flower charms and the four pink rhinestone star charms. (See "How to Open and Close a Jump Ring," page 309.) Set these aside. To make the Eiffel Tower charm, thread the pink crystal cube and the silver cube onto a headpin and make a wrapped-wire loop. (See "How to Make a Wrapped-Wire Loop Using a Headpin," page 316.) Attach the wrapped loop to the connector loop on the Eiffel Tower charm using an oval jump ring. Attach another oval jump ring to the connector loop. Set this aside. To make the briolette

drop charm, use the gold wire to add a bail to the briolette and one gold spacer bead. (See "How to Make a Wire Bail," page 325.) Add an oval jump ring to the wrapped loop. Set this aside. To make the two twisted gold ring charms, use a gold jump ring to attach one charm to one ring. Attach an oval jump ring to both gold jump rings. Set these aside. To make the gold heart charm, thread a gold laser-finished bead onto a headpin. Make a wrapped-wire loop. Attach the wrapped loop to the connector loop on the heart charm using a gold jump ring. Attach another oval jump ring to the connector loop. Set this aside. To make the pink birds charm, attach two oval jump rings to the pink birds pendant. Thread one bicone, one silver Bali-style spacer, and one bicone onto a headpin. Make a wrapped-wire loop. Thread one oval jump ring onto the wrapped-wire loop, the connector loop on the pink enamel flower, and the first oval jump ring on the bird pendant. Set this aside.

3 :: To make the *amour* charms, place a piece of decorative paper face up on your work surface. Place one circle collage pendant facedown on the paper. (Positioning the pendant on the right side of the paper will allow you to get the most polka dots within the circle.) Use a pencil to trace around its outside edge, and cut out the circle using scissors. Repeat this step to make four more circles. Erase any pencil marks. Use this same technique to cut out five circles from the blank clear adhesive sticker sheet.

4 :: Adhere one clear circle sticker to the polka dot side of each paper circle. Test-fit the newly laminated circles in the collage pendants. Trim away any excess. Place a small dab of permanent adhesive in the recessed portion of the collage pendant to glue the laminated circle to the bottom. Let the glue dry. Repeat this step for the remaining four pendants.

5 :: Cut out the letters that spell *amour* from the alphabet sticker sheet. Remove the paper backing and place one letter on each laminated circle using tweezers.

6 :: Place one collage pendant on a protected, level work surface. Position one fuchsia bicone near the letter using tweezers.

7 :: Fill the pendant with Amazing Glaze. Use a small brush to sweep off any excess granules that fall on the work surface. (These can be collected and placed back in the original container.) Carefully wave the heat gun over the pendant.

8 :: After a minute or so, the powdered glaze will bead up, melt, and pool together. If the pendant is not full enough, add more glaze while it's still hot and continue to run the heat gun over it. Let the pendant cool. If it must be moved, use a metal utensil, such as chain-nose pliers or a spatula, because the metal pendant will be extremely hot! The liquid glaze can spill out of the pendant, so keep it as level as possible. Repeat steps 6–8 to finish the remaining pendants. Add one oval jump ring to each pendant. Set these aside.

9 :: To make the "love" charm, use wire cutters to cut a 4-in/10-cm length of the gold wire. Use round-nose pliers to create a loop at one end to prevent the beads from falling off. This loop will also allow you to attach the charm to the bracelet.

(continued page 136)

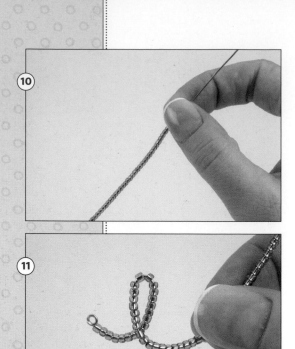

10 :: Thread on 3 in/7.5 cm of pink seed beads. Secure the other wire end by making a loop as in step 9.

11 :: Shape the beaded wire to form an L, pushing the beads toward the nearest wire loop.

12 :: Shape the beaded wire to make an O and a V.

13 :: Continue to shape the beaded wire using your fingers. After completing the E, cut off the wire loop on this end. Remove any excess seed beads and trim the wire ¼ in/6 mm from the last bead on the E.

14 :: Use round-nose pliers to make a loop on the bare wire next to the E.

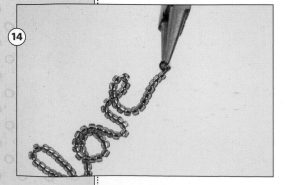

15 :: Attach the puffed-heart charm and the pink pavé star charm to the wire loop after the E, using two oval jump rings. Attach an oval jump ring to the loop next to the L. Set aside.

16 :: To turn the rhinestone flower beads with shanks into double-sided charms, begin with two identical rhinestone flowers.

17 :: Use heavy-duty chain cutters to remove the shanks from both flower beads.

18 :: Use wire cutters to cut a 4-in/10-cm length of wire. Apply cyanoacrylate to the wrong side of one rhinestone flower and position the wire's mid-point in the center of the flower. Be sure that the wire runs straight up and down along the center of the flower.

19 :: Apply cyanoacrylate to the wrong side of the second rhinestone flower. Position it on top of the first, wrong sides together, edges aligned, and press to adhere. Set aside to let the glue dry.

(continued page 138)

20 :: This double-sided rhinestone flower now has a wire extending from each end; using the wire, you can turn the flower into a connector or a charm by adding a wrapped-wire loop or an eye loop at one or both ends.

21 :: To make the charms as shown in step 2, make a wrapped-wire loop on one end. (See "How to Make a Wrapped-Wire Loop Using a Headpin," page 316.) Cut away the wire completely on the opposite end. Repeat steps 16–21 with the rest of the rhinestone flower pairs. Add an oval jump ring to all four flower charms. Set these aside.

22 :: To make the cane bead charms, thread the following onto one headpin: one gold spacer bead, one silver Bali-style spacer bead, one black cane bead, one silver spacer, and one gold spacer bead. Make a wrapped-wire loop. (See "How to Make a Wrapped-Wire Loop Using a Headpin," page 316.) Make eight more cane bead charms with wrapped-wire loops following the beading layout featured in step 2. Attach an oval jump ring to the wrapped-wire loop on each one.

To make the polka dot bead charms, thread one fuchsia polka dot bead and one silver cube onto a headpin. Make a wrapped-wire loop. Attach an oval jump ring to the wrapped loop. Attach an oval jump ring to one pink pavé star charm and the jump ring on the wrapped loop. Repeat these steps to make the two remaining fuchsia polka dot bead charms. Set these aside. Thread one Bali-style gold spacer bead, one gold spacer, one amethyst polka dot bead, one gold spacer, and one Bali-style gold spacer bead onto a head pin. Make a wrapped-wire loop. Attach an oval jump ring to the wrapped loop. Repeat these steps to make a second amethyst bead charm. For the third, thread one Bali-style gold spacer, one amethyst polka dot bead, and one Bali-style gold spacer onto a headpin. Make a wrapped-wire loop. Attach an oval jump ring to the wrapped loop. Attach a second jump ring to one twisted wire ring and the wrapped-wire loop. Set these aside.

23 :: Open the oval jump ring on one cane bead charm, and insert one end through a pair of jump ring links on the bracelet chain. Close the jump ring.

24 :: Repeat step 23 to attach the remaining cane bead charms to the chain. Be sure to space out similar beads with the exception of the *amour* charms, which should be placed closer together. Use the oval jump rings to attach the remaining charms as shown on page 130 or as desired.

● ● ● ● **TIP** ● ● ● ●

If you don't own a heat gun, a tool used typically in paper crafting to melt embossing powder, you can melt Amazing Glaze in the oven. Preheat the oven or toaster oven to 300ºF/150ºC. Place the *amour* collage pendant on a baking tray lined with aluminum foil. When the powdered glaze turns clear, usually after a few minutes, your pendant is done. Remove it from the oven. It will be hot and the glaze will still be liquid at this point, so use pliers or a spatula to move it cautiously onto a protected level surface to cool.

WILDFIRE

Like glowing embers, cut-crystal beads and rhinestones in red, orange, and gold send off sparks of light that ignite the fire of this piece. A rare crystal in violet accents the fiery colorway. The secret structure of this bracelet is its foundation of crocheted gold wire, which forms a flexible and adjustable cuff that fits any wrist size comfortably—just scrunch it for a small size and stretch it for a large size. The bracelet is secured with a pretty gold hook and eye clasp.

MATERIALS

7 round glass pearls, red, 12 mm dia.

3 Austrian crystal rings, red, 12 mm dia. × 3 mm thick

5 faceted glass ovals, orange, 11 mm wide × 15 mm long × 4 mm thick

6 rhinestone buttons, ruby red, with gold casings:

> Two 11 mm dia.

> Four 9 mm dia.

25 clear round glass beads, variegated orange, 8 mm dia.

7 Austrian crystal cubes, 8 mm:

> 2 ruby red

> 3 violet

> 2 olive

103 Austrian crystal bicones:

> 28 red, 6 mm

> 10 orange, 6 mm

> 3 ruby red, 5 mm

> 52 ruby red, 4 mm

> 10 burnt orange, 4 mm

40 Austrian crystal round beads, red, 6 mm dia.

Gold wire, dead-soft, 24 gauge

One 2-part hook and eye clasp for 3 strands, gold, 14 mm dia.

TOOLS

Ruler

Wire cutters

Chain-nose pliers

Round-nose pliers

Tweezers or crochet hook

FINISHED SIZE

7½ in/ 19 cm

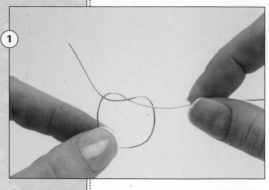

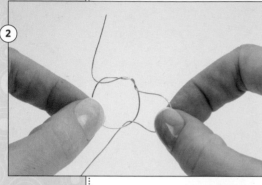

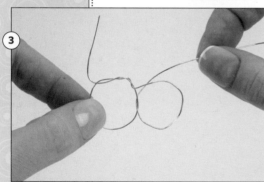

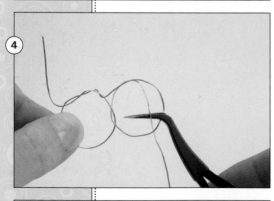

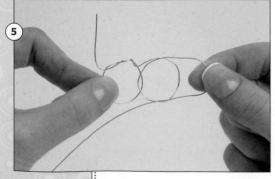

DIRECTIONS

1 :: Use wire cutters to cut an 18-in/46-cm length of wire. Tie a loose single overhand knot 2 in/5 cm from one end, crossing the longer end in front of the tail. (See "How to Make a Single Overhand Knot," page 342.)

2 :: Hold the loop with one hand and grasp the long wire with the other hand approximately 1 in/2.5 cm from the knot. Wrap the long wire behind the loop and pull it through the center to create a second loop. Pull the loop to the right.

3 :: Grasp the long wire and bring it up and behind the loop made in the previous step.

4 :: Pull a third loop through the center using your fingers, tweezers, or a crochet hook.

5 :: Pull the loop to the right.

6 :: Repeat steps 3–5 to make a 6-in/15-cm length of crocheted wire. Secure the wire end by wrapping it a few times around the last loop. Leave a 2-in/5-cm tail and trim away excess wire.

7 :: The finished crocheted wire base should look as it does in image 7, at right.

8 :: Use wire cutters to cut two 36-in/91.5-cm lengths of wire. Set one aside. Leaving a 2-in/5-cm tail, wrap one end of the wire around the bottom of the first loop to secure it to the wire base.

9 :: Thread the opposite end of this wire through a red pearl.

10 :: Run the wire across or along the loops, securing it to the loops by loosely wrapping it a few times. Thread on another red pearl. Repeat this step to add pearls along the length of the bracelet. At the opposite end, set down the excess wire. Do not cut it.

(continued page 144)

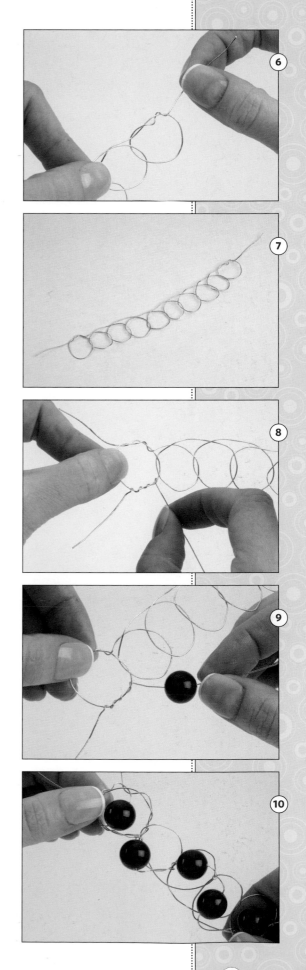

11 :: Secure the second length of wire by wrapping it to the wire base as you did in step 8. Thread the larger beads randomly along the length of the bracelet, loosely wrapping the wire on the crocheted wire base to secure the wire after each bead is added. Use the excess wire from step 10 to fill in the gaps with the smaller beads by working in the opposite direction. If your design is dense like this one, it will be necessary to cut three additional lengths of wire and secure them to the wire base to add more beads.

12 :: To add the clasp, gather the wire tails into three sets of two. If there are fewer wire ends because you used less wire and made fewer passes, cut one 4-in/10-cm length of wire for each tail you are short and secure it to the end of the wire base with the others as shown. Make three wrapped-wire loops using two wire tails for each. (See "How to Join Wrapped-Wire Loops without Using a Connector," page 320.) Use chain-nose pliers to grasp one set of wires ¼ in/6 mm from the base. Bend the wires at a 90-degree angle.

13 :: Use round-nose pliers to grasp the wires ⅛ in/3 mm from the bend. Rotate the pliers toward the bend. Wrap the wires around one jaw of the pliers, crossing them in front of the vertical stem to make a loop.

14 :: Insert one set of wire ends through one outside hole on the clasp. Slide the clasp down the wires until it sits in the wire loop.

15 :: Grasp the loop with chain-nose pliers and wrap the wires around the stem. Trim away excess wire. Use chain-nose pliers to squeeze the cut ends of the wires flush against the stem.

16 :: Use the same technique to attach the remaining sets of wires to the clasp. Repeat steps 12–15 to secure the second half of the clasp to the opposite end of the bracelet. Measure and cut two 10-in/25-cm lengths of wire. Set one aside. Secure the wire to the wire base at one end of the bracelet. Thread on more beads to cover the wrapped-wire loops. Repeat on the opposite end.

16

IMPORTANT :: Do not leave any cut wire ends untreated. Use round-nose pliers to create a small loop at the end before tucking it within the existing wirework.

TIPS

As you add beads to the crocheted wire base, stop every so often to measure the length of the bracelet and test-fit it on your wrist. The loops will often shift and change shape as you work. If you add beads to every wire loop without checking fit, you might inadvertently end up with a narrow bracelet 9-10 in/ 23-25 cm long. If there are wire loops left after you've reached the appropriate length, simply cut away the excess loops and either incorporate the wires back into the bracelet or use them to secure the clasp.

This bracelet is just as beautiful with fewer beads and more wire showing. There are very few times when crimps in the wire will serve a project, but this is one of them. As you weave the wire in and out of the crocheted base to add the beads, it is likely that the wire will crimp up. If you want to remove the crimps, see "How to Unkink Wire," page 304. Otherwise, just flatten the crimped place in the wire between the jaws of your chain-nose pliers and continue weaving on the beads. The crimped wires only add to the design by giving it a modern look, almost as if Jackson Pollock had worked in liquid gold.

HOTHOUSE FLOWERS

Tropical blooms compose this lush lei of incandescent pink, yellow, and green beads made of pressed glass in the shape of delicate flowers, leaves, and buds. The blooms are clustered snugly on a strand of seed beads that forms the base of the bracelet, which fastens with a rhinestone button in the palest lime green.

MATERIALS

BEAD COMBINATIONS TO MAKE FLOWERS, BUDS, AND LEAVES:

4 Czech pressed-glass day lily flower beads, cream, 13 mm dia. × 8 mm thick

4 Czech pressed-glass baby bell flower beads, pink, 5 mm dia. × 3 mm thick

4 transparent seed beads, yellow, size 11/0

.....

6 opaque Czech fire-polished glass rondelles, pale yellow, 9 mm dia. × 6 mm thick

6 Czech fire-polished glass rondelles, frosted pink, 4 mm dia. × 2 mm thick

6 transparent seed beads, yellow, size 11/0

.....

6 opaque Czech pressed-glass buttercup flower beads, pink, 9 mm dia. × 4 mm thick

6 Austrian crystal bicones, green, 4 mm

6 color-lined seed beads, pink, size 11/0

.....

4 opaque Czech pressed-glass day lily flower beads, green and white, 8 mm dia. × 5 mm thick

4 Czech pressed-glass baby bell flower beads, pink, 5 mm dia. × 3 mm thick

4 transparent seed beads, yellow, size 11/0

.....

6 opaque Czech fire-polished glass rondelles, pink and white, 6 mm dia. × 5 mm thick

6 Austrian crystal bicones, pink, 4 mm

6 transparent seed beads, yellow, size 11/0

.....

9 round glass beads, lime, 10 mm dia.

9 pearlized seed beads, yellow, size 11/0

.....

3 Czech foil-lined lampwork round glass beads, yellow, 10 mm dia.

3 opalescent seed beads, cream, size 8/0

.....

8 Czech pressed-glass tulip flower beads, pale yellow AB, 8 mm wide × 11 mm long × 5 mm thick

8 transparent seed beads, yellow, size 11/0

.....

8 opaque Czech pressed-glass discs, pink and white, 8 mm dia. × 2 mm thick

8 Austrian crystal bicones, yellow, 4 mm

.....

9 Czech pressed-glass cherry blossom flower beads, pale yellow AB, 7 mm dia. × 2 mm thick

9 Czech fire-polished round glass beads, pink AB, 3 mm dia.

12 faceted round cat's-eye glass beads, yellow, 6 mm dia.

12 Czech fire-polished round glass beads, pink AB, 3 mm dia.

.....

8 Austrian crystal bicones, pink, 6 mm

8 transparent seed beads, yellow, size 11/0

.....

8 Austrian crystal bicones, yellow, 6 mm

8 color-lined seed beads, pink, size 11/0

.....

5 Austrian crystal bicones, green, 6 mm

5 transparent seed beads, yellow, size 11/0

.....

12 freshwater rice pearls, pale pink, 5 mm dia. × 8 mm long

12 color-lined seed beads, pink, size 11/0

.....

14 dyed-coral round beads, pink, 5 mm dia.

180 color-lined seed beads, pink, size 11/0

.....

24 Czech pressed-glass leaves, 7 mm wide × 12 mm long × 3 mm thick:

    8 opaque pink

    8 opaque green

    8 translucent yellow AB

.....

8 opaque Czech pressed-glass briolettes, pink and white, 8 mm wide × 12 mm long × 5 mm thick

TO MAKE THE BRACELET BASE:

10 g opaque seed beads, cream AB, size 8/0

5 g opaque seed beads, cream AB, size 11/0

1 rhinestone button with gold casing, pale lime green, 11 mm dia. × 10 mm thick

4 crimp tubes, gold, size 2

Beading wire, bright stainless steel, .014 in/0.36 mm dia.

1 bobbin Nymo beading thread, white, size B

Beeswax

TOOLS

Ruler

Scissors

Wire cutters

Crimping pliers

2 beading needles, size 12

FINISHED SIZE

8¼ in/21 cm

(Since this bracelet is bulky, it fits like it is only 7 in/18 cm long. Be sure to test fit before finishing.)

DIRECTIONS

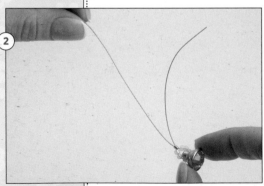

1 :: To make the bracelet base, use wire cutters to cut a 20-in/50-cm length of beading wire. Thread on one crimp tube, three size 8/0 seed beads, the rhinestone button, and another three size 8/0 seed beads.

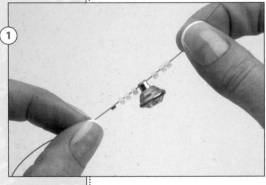

2 :: Insert the wire end into the crimp tube, leaving a 4-in/10-cm tail. Slide the crimp tube and the seed beads up against the button shank. Do not use the crimping pliers to secure the tube.

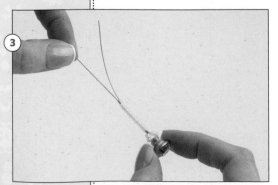

3 :: String ten size 8/0 seed beads and one crimp tube onto both the main beading wire and the tail.

4 :: String on seventy size 8/0 seed beads, followed by a crimp tube.

5 :: String on ten size 8/0 seed beads, followed by a crimp tube.

6 :: String on twenty size 8/0 seed beads. To make the loop clasp, insert the wire end through the last crimp tube you added, the ten seed beads, and the next crimp tube, exiting a few beads after the second crimp tube. Do not use crimping pliers to secure the tube.

7 :: This is the base of the bracelet and will determine its length. The bracelet can be made bigger by loosening the tails on each end and stringing on more beads, but no smaller. If it's too big, undo the loop closure and remove a few beads from the center group of seventy. (Please see note about the finished size before removing any beads.)

8 :: Add one size 8/0 seed bead to the end of one wire tail to create a bead stopper. (See step 3 of "How to Start a Double-Threaded Strand with a Bead Stopper," page 350, and use that technique to add a seed bead to the beading wire tail.) Repeat this step on the second beading wire tail.

(continued page 150)

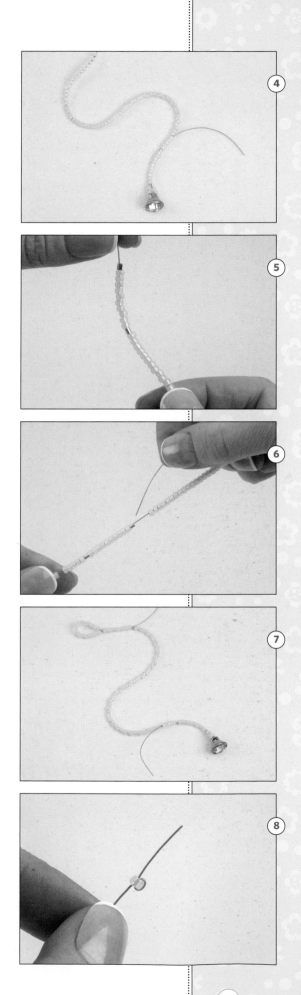

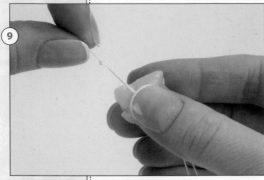

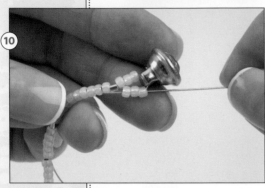

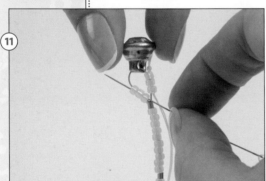

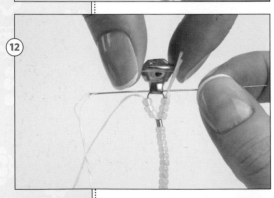

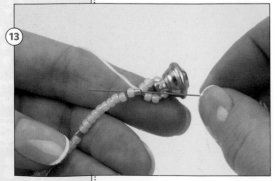

9 :: Measure and cut a 20-in/50-cm length of Nymo thread. Double-thread the prestretched and conditioned thread onto the beading needle and tie a double overhand knot at the opposite end. (See "How to Prestretch Beading Thread," page 347, "How to Condition Thread," page 348, and "How to Make a Double Overhand Knot," page 342.)

10 :: To secure the thread to the base of the bracelet, insert the needle into the three seed beads on one side of the button shank, with the needle moving away from the button. The knot will catch on the seed bead closest to the button shank and will eventually be hidden in the button shank when the beads are tightened up.

11 :: Insert the needle through the three seed beads on the opposite side, this time moving toward the button shank, and pull the thread through.

12 :: Insert the needle through the button shank and pull the thread through.

13 :: Insert the needle back down through the original three seed beads. Go through the crimp tube and one seed bead on the main strand. Pull the threads through.

4 :: Insert the needle into the adjacent seed bead and back through the original seed bead.

5 :: Insert the needle down through the hole in the coral bead and the two cream seed beads and exit it through the next seed bead on the main strand.

IMPORTANT :: To end an old thread and start a new one, stop adding beads when you have about 4 in/10 cm of thread left. Do not cut off the needle. Double-thread the second needle with a prestretched and preconditioned thread, but do not knot the opposite end. (See step 9.) Tie a weaver's knot and then a single overhand knot on top of it to tie the thread ends together. Use the needles to help you negotiate the threads into knots. (See "How to Make a Weaver's Knot," page 343, and "How to Make a Single Overhand Knot," page 342.) Trim the short thread ends to ¼ in/6.5 cm and cut away the needle on the original thread. Continue adding beads with the new threaded needle. The knots should be hidden in the beads when you tighten up the strands before crimping them.

TIPS

Do not add beaded flowers or leaves in the spaces between crimp tubes and seed beads. The sharp edges of the crimp tubes could cut or fray the threads. Instead, skip those spaces and go to the next space between two seed beads.

Not securing the crimp tubes until all the beads have been added allows for some slack in the beading wire, which in this case is a good thing. The seed beads on the base are thus given room to spread out, which creates working space between them and makes navigating the needle and thread easier. When you're done, simply pull on the wire tails to tighten everything up.

GOLD DIGGER

A cluster of golden globes adorns a trio of gold chains whose end links are attached to a toggle clasp. Made to fit snugly against the wrist, the bracelet of oversized gold balls is a study in textural contrast: faceted surfaces that glitter with light; polished surfaces that glow; and a webbing of filigree wire that echoes the delicate chains that extend from each orb.

MATERIALS

1 round metal bead, copper, 19 mm dia.

6 faceted round metal beads, gold, 16 mm dia.

2 filigree round metal beads, gold, 16 mm dia.

3 round metal beads, gold, 15 mm dia.

2 ft/61 cm diamond-cut curb chain, gold, oval links 12 mm wide × 16 mm long

2 ft/61 cm curb chain, gold, oval links 2 mm wide × 4 mm long

2 end bars for 3 strands, gold, 2.5 cm long

14 jump rings, gold, 16 gauge, 7 mm dia.

12 jump rings, gold, 22 gauge, 4 mm dia.

2 jump rings, gold, 18 gauge, 5 mm dia.

1 jump ring, gold, 14 gauge, 14 mm dia.

1 lobster clasp, gold, 22 mm long

Gold wire, dead-soft, 24 gauge

TOOLS

Ruler

Chain cutters

Chain-nose pliers

Bent-nose pliers

Round-nose pliers

Wire cutters

FINISHED SIZE

8½ in/21.5 cm

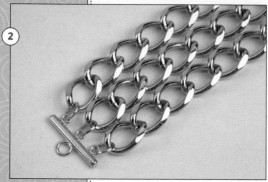

DIRECTIONS

1 :: Use chain cutters to cut three 6-in/15.25-cm lengths of the larger chain.

2 :: Open one 7 mm jump ring. Insert one end into the last link on one length of chain and one connector loop on an end bar. Close the jump ring. (See "How to Open and Close a Jump Ring," page 309.) Attach the remaining two lengths of chain to the same end bar using 7 mm jump rings. Repeat these steps to attach the other end of the three chains to the corresponding loops on the remaining end bar.

3 :: Secure the three chains to one another in the center of the bracelet: Use a 7 mm jump ring to attach a link from the center strand to an adjacent link on an outside strand. Use another jump ring a few links away to join the same two strands. Use two more jump rings to attach the other outside strand to the center strand in the same spots.

4 :: Use wire cutters to cut an 8-in/20-cm length of wire. Thread it through one filigree bead and one 4-mm jump ring. Thread the end of the wire back through the round bead.

5 :: Pull the two wire ends even, trapping the jump ring against the bottom of the bead.

• • • TIP • • •

Sometimes a chain link can be opened using pliers alone. If you have to cut the link instead, see "How to Cut Chain," page 332. Also see "How to Cut Wire," page 301, for important safety tips.

This bracelet should be worn a little snug. If you want it to be smaller than the 8½-in/21.5-cm finished size, shorten the larger lengths of chain or use a smaller lobster clasp and jump ring.

6 :: Make one wrapped-wire loop using both wire ends (see "How to Make a Wrapped-Wire Loop Using a Headpin," page 316).

7 :: Repeat steps 4–6 for the remaining beads. Use wire cutters to cut twelve 2-in/5.2-cm lengths of the smaller chain. On one of the beads, open the jump ring and insert one end through the last link of one of these lengths of chain. Close the jump ring. Repeat this step for the remaining beads.

8 :: Group the beads into four sets of three as shown or as desired. Open one 7 mm jump ring and insert the end through the three wrapped loops in a group. Close the jump ring. Repeat this step with the remaining beads to create three more sets of beads.

9 :: Use chain-nose pliers to open one jump ring on one set of three beads. Insert one end through one side of the center link of the bracelet. Close the jump ring.

10 :: Repeat step 9 to add the remaining three sets of beads, positioning them on the remaining three sides of the same center link. To finish, attach one end bar to the connector loop on the lobster clasp, using a 5 mm jump ring. Attach the 14 mm jump ring to the end bar on the opposite side of the bracelet, using the remaining 5 mm jump ring.

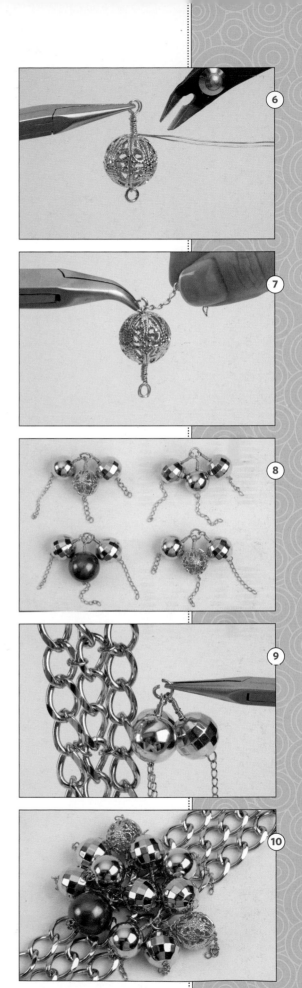

EARRINGS

CARNAVALE

You will want to wear these flirty earrings to your next festival or simply to get yourself into a party mood. They are composed of a handful of small pearls in confetti colors and streams of gold chain set with orange rhinestones. The pearls are secured to lengths of fine chain, and the chains of rhinestones are wrapped with coil ends so that all of the shimmering lengths can be slipped onto the small gold rings that attach to the ear wire. The mechanics of the design allow the dangling beads to move easily, whether you dance or simply tap your foot to the music.

MATERIALS

4 glitter round acrylic beads, light purple, 6 mm dia.

16 freshwater rice pearls, head-drilled, 4 mm to 5 mm dia. × 6 mm long:

> 8 green

> 8 fuchsia

8 opaque Czech fire-polished round beads, teal, 4 mm dia.

8 round glass pearls, purple, 4 mm dia.

8 seed beads, matte gold, size 11/0

4 gold chains with 3 mm dia. round rhinestone detail, orange, 1¾ in/4.5 cm long

16 headpins, gold, 24 gauge, 1 in/2.5 cm long

4 headpins, gold, 22 gauge, 2 in/5 cm long

2 jump rings, gold, 22 gauge, 8 mm dia.

Gold wire, dead-soft, 24 gauge

1 ft/30.5 cm fine Figaro chain, gold, 24-gauge round wire, links 1.5 mm wide × 1.5 mm long and 3 mm long

1 pair of shepherd hook earrings, gold, 1 cm wide × 1.8 cm long

TOOLS

Ruler

Wire cutters

2 pairs chain-nose pliers

Round-nose pliers

FINISHED SIZE

¾ in/1.9 cm wide × 3¼ in/8.3 cm long

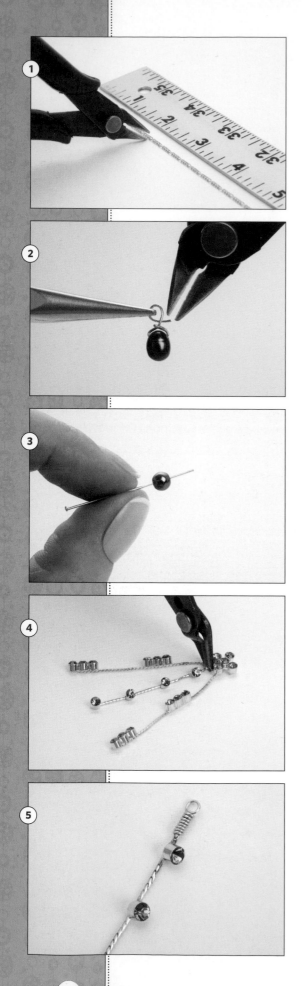

1 :: Use wire cutters to cut two 1-in/2.5-cm lengths, two 1½-in/4-cm lengths, and two 2-in/5-cm lengths of Figaro chain. Be sure the cut chain begins and ends with a larger link. Divide the chains and the beads in half to make two identical groups; set one group aside.

2 :: Use wire cutters to cut sixteen 3-in/7.5-cm lengths of wire. Set one group of wires aside with the chain and beads set aside in step 1. See "How to Make an Eye Loop on a Head-Drilled Bead," page 313, to add an eye loop to one fuchsia freshwater pearl. Repeat these steps to make eye loops on the remaining seven freshwater pearls in this group. Set them aside.

3 :: Insert one 24-gauge headpin into one round purple pearl. Make an eye loop. (See "How to Make an Eye Loop Using a Headpin," page 310.) Repeat this step for the remaining three purple pearls and the four faceted teal beads. Use the 22-gauge headpins to make eye loops on the two glitter round light-purple beads. Set these aside.

4 :: Use wire cutters to cut four 1¾-in/4.5-cm lengths of rhinestone chain. Set one pair aside with the chains, beads, and wires set aside in step 2.

5 :: Use gold wire to make a coil end on one rhinestone chain. (See "How to Make and Use Coil Ends," page 293.) Repeat this step to make a second coil end on the second rhinestone chain.

6 :: Open one jump ring. (See "How to Open and Close a Jump Ring," page 309.) Insert the wire end through the 1-in/2.5-cm length of chain, one seed bead, one rhinestone chain, one seed bead, the 2-in/5-cm length of chain, one seed bead, one rhinestone chain, one seed bead, and the 1½-in/4-cm chain. Do not close the jump ring.

7 :: Insert the end of the jump ring through one ear wire. Close the jump ring.

8 :: Open the eye loop on one fuchsia freshwater pearl. (See "How to Open and Close an Eye Loop," page 315.) Thread the wire end through the bottom link on the 2-in/5-cm chain. Close the eye loop.

9 :: Working upward on the same 2-in/5-cm chain, attach one faceted teal bead to the next large link at the eye loop.

10 :: Follow the beading layout in the photo below to attach the remaining beads to the lengths of chain. To make the second earring, repeat steps 2–3 and 5 to add eye loops to the beads and coil ends to the rhinestone chains and steps 6–10 to assemble it. On step 6, reverse the order of the chains, putting the 1½-in/4-cm chain on first so that the second earring is a mirror image of the first.

> ● ● ● **TIPS** ● ● ●
>
> The gold chain with the orange rhinestone accents used in the Carnavale earrings was repurposed from a piece of costume jewelry. Costume pieces are a great resource, especially for less expensive rhinestones. Search your jewelry box, flea markets, vintage shops, and garage sales for great items (or parts of them) to use in your creations.
>
> When making coil ends on the rhinestone chain, make sure that the eye loop runs from back to front so that, when you thread the coil onto the jump ring, the rhinestones will face forward.

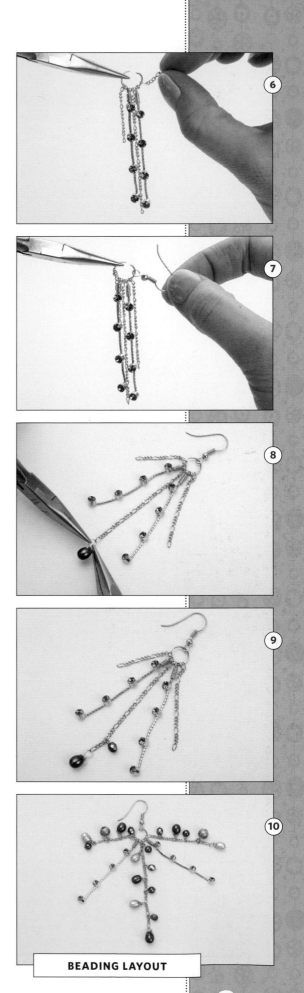

BEADING LAYOUT

HAMPTON CLASSIC

With a subtle nod toward formal tradition, but with a chic choice of color, Hampton Classic turns classy to sassy. Glowing with ripe color, each lustrous, oversized pink pearl is the only ornamentation on a simple ear wire with a small button in brushed gold. Making the earrings takes only minutes, and the design lends itself to single beads with distinctive shapes and textural character. Consider ovals and squares or briolettes and donuts; just make sure the weight of the bead is comfortable to wear.

MATERIALS

2 round glass pearls, pink, 12 mm dia.

2 seed beads, matte gold, size 11/0

2 German metal headpins, 22K gold plated, 22 gauge, 1½ in/4 cm long

1 pair German metal fishhook earrings with round disc detail, 22K gold plated, 1 cm wide × 1.4 cm long

TOOLS

Chain-nose pliers

Round-nose pliers

Wire cutters

FINISHED SIZE

½ in/13mm wide × 1⅛/5.7 cm long

DIRECTIONS

1 :: Insert one headpin through one pearl and one seed bead. Use both pliers and wire cutters to make an eye loop. (See "How to Make an Eye Loop Using a Headpin," page 310.)

2 :: Use chain-nose pliers to open the eye loop. (See "How to Open and Close an Eye Loop," page 315.) Thread it through the base of one earring. Close the eye loop. Repeat steps 1–2 to make the second earring.

ARIA

The Aria earrings have both modern and traditional style and would suit a night at the opera as well as a concert in the park. A broad curve of amber rhinestone flowers is central to these modified hoop-style earrings, but this decorative element also divides the earrings into two sensual spaces. On the lower section, the line of the earring is defined by two loops of fine gold chain that follow the contour of the floral garland. On the top section, two narrow gold tubes form a cathedral arch that mirrors the line of the chains, neatly balancing the design and creating a unified whole.

MATERIALS

2 rhinestone flowers with four shanks each, antique gold setting, amber, 15 mm dia. × 3 mm thick

4 rhinestone flowers with four shanks each, antique gold setting, amber AB, 8 mm dia. × 2 mm thick

4 curved metal tubes, gold, 2 mm dia. × 1¼ in/ 3 cm long

4 Czech fire-polished ovals, copper, 5 mm wide × 6 mm long

8 Czech fire-polished round beads, gold, 3 mm dia.

4 Czech fire-polished round beads, gold, 2 mm dia.

10 metal rondelles, gold, 3 mm dia. × 2 mm long

1 ft/30.5 cm cable-link chain, gold, links 1 mm wide × 2 mm long

2 crimp tubes, gold, size 3

2 crimp covers, gold, size 3

2 jump rings, gold, 22 gauge, 4 mm dia.

Beading wire, gold, .018 in/0.45 mm dia.

1 pair ball post earrings with connector loops, gold-filled, 5 mm dia.

TOOLS

Ruler

Wire cutters

2 pairs chain-nose pliers

Crimping pliers

FINISHED SIZE

1¼ in/3.2 cm wide × 3¼ in/8.25 cm long

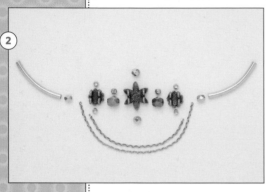

DIRECTIONS

1 :: Use wire cutters to cut two 2½-in/6-cm lengths and two 3½-in/9-cm lengths of chain. Set the chain aside. Use wire cutters to cut two 16-in/40.5-cm lengths of beading wire. Set them aside.

2 :: Divide the beads into two identical groups; set one group aside. Arrange one group of beads facedown by placing one large flower in the center of a flat work surface with one 3 mm faceted gold bead above and below it. To the right and left of the flower, place one 2 mm faceted gold bead, each above one 5 mm faceted copper bead. Working outward to the right and left, place the remaining flowers for this group facedown with one gold rondelle above and below each flower. Position the ends of the 2½-in/6-cm-long chain in line with the bottom row of bead shanks, followed by the 3½-in/9-cm-long chain. Add one 3 mm faceted gold bead at each end of the chain, followed by the curved tubes.

3 :: Thread one end of one length of beading wire through the curved tube, 3 mm gold bead, long chain end, short chain end, and bottom row of bead shanks, picking up the two rondelles and three beads that are positioned below the rhinestone flowers and stringing them between the shanks. (See "How to String Beads between Button or Bead Shanks," page 271.) Continue stringing through the opposite chain ends, 3 mm gold bead, and remaining tube.

4 :: Continuing with the same end of the beading wire, bring it around the top and insert it back into the first gold tube.

(continued page 170)

5 :: Thread the beading wire through the tube and the 3 mm gold bead. Do not thread it through the chain ends.

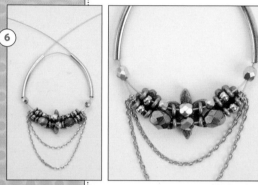

6 :: Continue threading the same end of beading wire through the top row of bead shanks, picking up the two rondelles and three beads that are positioned above the rhinestone flowers and stringing them between the shanks. Bypass the chain ends, but insert the beading wire through the 3 mm gold bead and curved tube again. Both beading wire ends should be at the top of the work surface.

7 :: Simultaneously pull both beading wire ends with one hand while sliding the beads down with the other hand until there is no space between the beads and the tops of the gold tubes are touching. Insert both wire ends through one gold rondelle. Slide the bead down the wires and into the space between the two gold tubes.

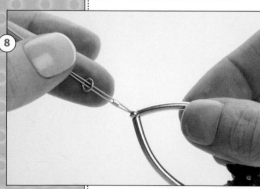

8 :: Use a crimp tube and crimping pliers to attach a jump ring to the ends of the beading wire, passing excess wire back through the crimp tube, rondelle and into the tubes to hide it. (See "How to Secure a Crimp Tube with Crimping Pliers," page 274.) Trim away excess wire if necessary.

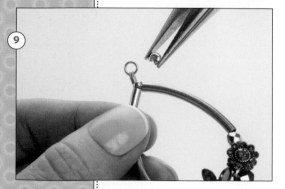

9 :: Conceal the crimp bead with a crimp bead cover. (See "How to Use a Crimp Cover," page 277.)

10 :: Open the jump ring. (See "How to Open and Close a Jump Ring," page 309.) Thread one end through the loop of one post earring. Close the jump ring. Repeat steps 2–10 to make the second earring.

IMPORTANT :: Before starting your design, ensure that the rondelles used at the top of the earrings between the two curved gold tubes have holes large enough to accommodate four strands of beading wire. Also, the 3 mm faceted gold beads must be able to accommodate two strands of beading wire. If your beads' holes are too small, replace them with beads with larger holes or use a thinner beading wire, as long as it can support the weight of the beads.

• • • • **TIPS** • • • •

The design of the Aria earrings could also be accomplished by cutting two strands of beading wire and threading one through the top row of bead shanks and the second through the bottom row. The problem is that you would be left with four wire ends instead of two, which you would then have to thread back through the rondelle and crimp bead, requiring them to accommodate eight strands.

CARIBBEAN SEA

You will feel like you are in a tropical paradise when you wear these earrings. The stunning combination of natural colors in transparent tints of grass and lime green, sky and lemon, conspire with a focal bead in the most breathtaking shade of aqua blue. Made entirely of Austrian crystal, the irregularly cut nuggets of indicolite are balanced by the playful mix of small rondelles that are clustered on the top of each bead.

MATERIALS

2 Austrian crystal nuggets, indicolite, 14 mm wide × 16 mm long × 9 mm thick

16 Austrian crystal rondelles, 6 mm dia. × 4 mm long:

> 4 pale lemon
>
> 4 light lime
>
> 4 lime
>
> 4 grass

16 glass discs, sky blue, 6 mm dia. × 2 mm thick

2 cubes, antique silver, 2 mm

2 headpins, silver, 22 gauge, 2½ in/6 cm long

32 headpins with 1 mm ball ends, silver, 22 gauge, 2 in/5 cm long

8 jump rings, silver, 22 gauge, 4 mm dia.

1 pair post earrings with aquamarine Austrian crystal rhinestones, antique silver, 8 mm wide × 14 mm long × 4 mm thick

TOOLS

2 pairs chain-nose pliers

Round-nose pliers

Wire cutters

FINISHED SIZE

¾ in/19 mm wide × 1½ in/3.8 cm long

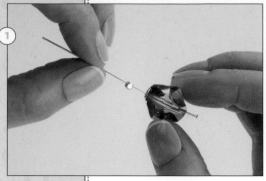

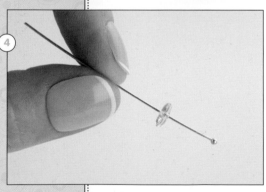

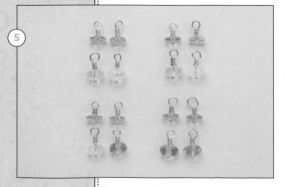

DIRECTIONS

1 :: Insert one 2½-in/6-cm headpin into one indi-colite nugget and one silver cube.

2 :: Use both chain-nose and round-nose pliers to make an eye loop. (See "How to Make an Eye Loop Using a Headpin," page 310.)

3 :: Use chain-nose pliers to open the eye loop. (See "How to Open and Close an Eye Loop," page 315.) Thread one end through the loop on the base of one post earring. Close the eye loop. Set this aside. Repeat steps 1–3 to make the second indicolite–earring post combination.

4 :: Divide the beads into two identical groups; set one group aside. Insert one blue disc onto one headpin with a ball end. Make a wrapped-wire loop. (See "How to Make a Wrapped-Wire Loop Using a Headpin," page 316.)

5 :: Use fifteen more headpins with ball ends to make seven more blue discs, two pale lemon rondelles, two light lime rondelles, two lime ron-delles, and two grass rondelles with wrapped-wire loops. Divide these beads, plus the one in step 4, into groups of four. Each group should have two blue discs and two rondelles of a different color.

6 :: Open one jump ring. (See "How to Open and Close a Jump Ring," page 309.) Thread on one group of four beads, alternating between discs and rondelles.

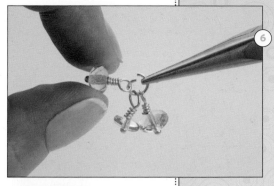

7 :: Thread one end of the open jump ring from step 6 through the loop on the base of the post earring, positioning it to the right of the indicolite nugget eye loop.

8 :: Close the jump ring. The bead cluster should be positioned as shown.

9 :: Open a second jump ring and thread on another group of four beads, alternating between discs and rondelles. Thread one end of the open jump ring through the open wirework on the post earring, positioning it on the right side of and above the first bead cluster. Close the jump ring. Repeat steps 6–9 to add two more bead clusters: one on the left side of the indicolite nugget and one on the left side of the open wirework on the post earring. Repeat steps 4–9 to make the second earring.

•••• TIP ••••

Choosing earring posts with decorative open wirework in addition to the connector loop allows you to create a fuller earring. The bead clusters are attached to these open spaces at different heights, creating a larger, fuller bead cluster. Of course, you can easily use this technique with only one connector, but you may want to reduce the number of bead groups to two or three.

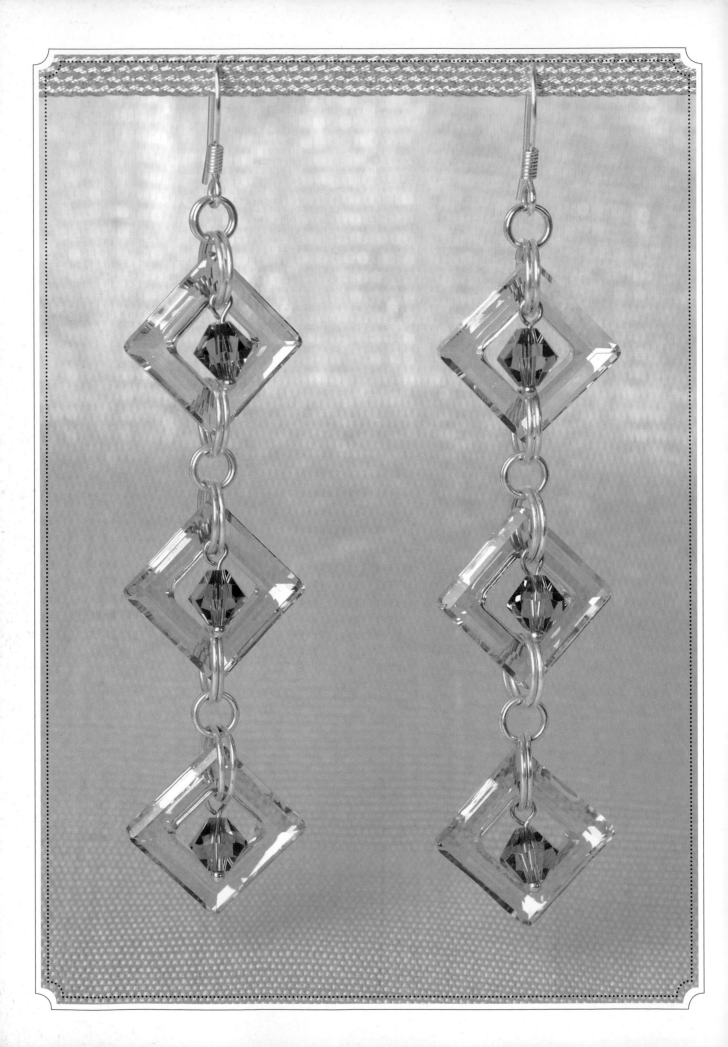

MOONBEAM

A trio of perfect diamond-shaped crystals frames sparkling purple bicones that fall gracefully from silver ear wires in these modern dangle-style earrings. The beads are connected to one another by neat little pairs of jump rings in sterling silver, in keeping with the glacial palette and the elegant simplicity of the design.

MATERIALS

6 Austrian crystal square rings, smoke, 14 mm square

6 Austrian crystal bicones, grape, 6 mm

6 headpins with 1 mm ball ends, antique silver, 22 gauge, 1¼ in/3 cm long

20 jump rings, silver, 22 gauge, 8 mm dia.

12 jump rings, silver, 22 gauge, 5 mm dia.

1 pair shepherd hook earrings, sterling silver, 9 mm wide × 1.6 cm long

TOOLS

2 pairs chain-nose pliers

Round-nose pliers

Wire cutters

FINISHED SIZE

¾ in/19 mm wide × 3½ in/8.9 cm long

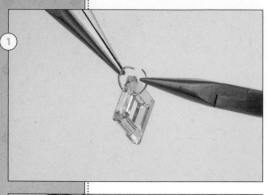

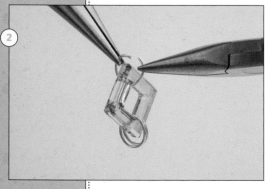

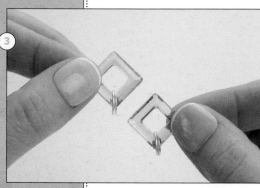

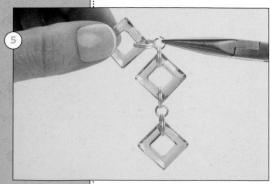

DIRECTIONS

1 :: Divide the beads into two identical groups; set one group aside. Open one 8 mm jump ring. (See "How to Open and Close a Jump Ring," page 309.) Thread one end through a square bead. Close the jump ring. Repeat this step to add a second jump ring next to the first one.

2 :: Rotate the bead so the jump rings are on the bottom. Repeat step 1 to add another two 8 mm jump rings to the opposite corner of the same square bead. This will be the center square bead. Set it aside.

3 :: Use chain-nose pliers to add two 8 mm jump rings to each of the remaining square beads. These will be the top and bottom square beads. Set one aside.

4 :: Use both pairs of chain-nose pliers to open one 5 mm jump ring. Thread one end through the set of 8 mm jump rings on a square bead from step 3 and the opposite end through one set of 8 mm jump rings from the center square bead from step 2. Close the jump ring. Repeat this step to add a second 5 mm jump ring next to the first.

5 :: Repeat step 4, this time attaching the remaining end square bead to the opposite end of the center square bead using two 5 mm jump rings.

6 :: Attach a pair of 8 mm jump rings to the top corner of the top square ring.

7 :: Attach a pair of 5 mm jump rings to the 8 mm jump rings added in step 6. Use chain-nose pliers to open the eye loop on one hook earring, and thread it through both 5 mm jump rings. Close the eye loop. (See "How to Open and Close an Eye Loop," page 315.)

8 :: Insert one headpin into one bicone. Make an eye loop, but do not trim away excess wire. (See "How to Make an Eye Loop Using a Headpin," page 310.)

9 :: Insert the excess wire stem from the bicone through the first set of 8 mm jump rings. If the bicone hangs too low or too high, remove it and adjust the size of the loop. Once the bicone is positioned correctly, trim away excess wire using wire cutters.

10 :: Repeat steps 8–9 to attach the remaining two bicones in the open spaces of the square beads. Repeat steps 1–10 to make the second earring.

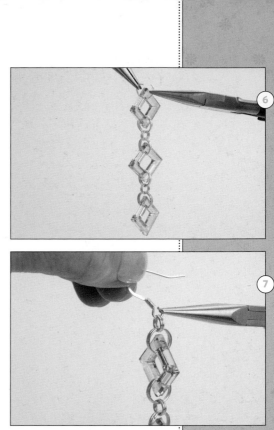

> ● ● ● **TIP** ● ● ●
>
> Using sets of two jump rings together in the corners of the crystal square beads steadies the beads and allows them to hang in the proper diamond position.

FROSTING

You'll love the way the Frosting earrings move when you wear them, so you'll want to pull your hair back to show off these sparklers. The earrings are made in a balanced arrangement of color and bead number. The cut-crystal facets on the water-clear teardrops glow with inner light and counterbalance clusters of dazzling crystals on their tops. The overall palette of the earrings is carefully modulated, with tints of transparent pale smoke, gold, rose, and clear water. Of course, the palette can be changed to suit your own style.

MATERIALS

2 Austrian crystal briolettes, crystal, 12 mm dia. × 22 mm long

32 Austrian crystal bicones, 6 mm:

      8 smoke

      8 crystal

      8 pink

      8 champagne

32 Austrian crystal bicones, 4 mm:

      8 smoke

      8 crystal

      8 pink

      8 champagne

2 headpins with 2 mm ball ends, silver, 22 gauge, 1¼ in/3 cm long

64 headpins, silver, 22 gauge, 1 in/2.5 cm long

2 round Smart Beads, sterling silver, 4 mm dia.

Sterling silver wire, half-hard, 20 gauge

TOOLS

Ruler

Wire cutters

Needle file

Emery cloth, 400 grit

Fine-tip black marker

Round-nose pliers

Chain-nose pliers

Rubbing alcohol

Paper towel

FINISHED SIZE

¾ in/19 mm wide × 2½ in/6.4 cm long

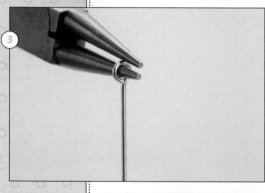

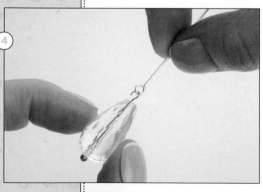

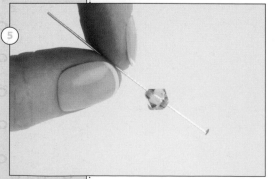

DIRECTIONS

1 :: Divide the beads into two identical groups; set one group aside. Insert one headpin with a ball end through a crystal briolette.

2 :: Use chain-nose and round-nose pliers to make an eye loop. (See "How to Make an Eye Loop Using a Headpin," page 310.) Set aside.

3 :: Use wire cutters to cut a 4-in/10-cm length of 20-gauge wire. (This will become the ear wire.) Use the needle file to deburr one end. Then use emery cloth on the same end until it's smooth. (See "How to Finish Wire Ends," page 302.) Make an eye loop on the opposite end of the wire using round-nose pliers.

4 :: Open the eye loop on the briolette. (See "How to Open and Close an Eye Loop," page 315.) Thread the open eye loop through the loop on the end of the ear wire. Close the eye loop.

5 :: Insert one 1-in/2.5-cm headpin through one 6 mm bicone. Make an eye loop.

6 :: Repeat step 5 to make eye loops on the remaining fifteen 6 mm bicones and the sixteen 4 mm bicones.

7 :: Insert the ear wire through one smoke, one crystal, one pink, and one champagne 6 mm bicone. Continue adding beads in this order until there are no more 6 mm bicones. Then add the 4 mm bicones in the same color order.

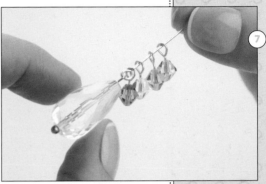

8 :: Thread one Smart Bead onto the wire and slide it down until it butts up against the top bicone, securing the beads in place.

9 :: Using the marker, draw a point on the wire ¾ in/2 cm above the Smart Bead. Hold the wire at this point on the marker (now using it as a mandrel) and bend the wire down. Shape the wire further using your fingers. Remove the mark using alcohol and a paper towel. Test the earring to ensure it hangs properly. Repeat steps 1–9 to make the second earring.

IMPORTANT :: There are several crucial steps in making your own ear wires, including choosing half-hard metals that can maintain their structure while supporting an earring's weight and selecting metals that are hypoallergenic. Be careful to deburr and file wire after cutting it to prevent injury by sharp or pointed ends. See "How to Finish Wire Ends," page 302, and "How to Make Ear Wires," page 339, for more detailed instructions and to learn ways to make other styles of ear wires.

● ● ● ● **TIP** ● ● ● ●

If your completed earrings hang backward, they may be off balance. To check that they're straight, rest the bends of the ear wires over a thin rod, such as a pen or pencil. It may be necessary to increase or decrease the angle of the wires by a few degrees or to manipulate the shape of the end of the ear wire, bending it forward or backward to achieve proper counterbalance.

MINT JULEP

These romantic, pretty earrings are a study in contrasts—attention-grabbing oversized hoops in sterling silver are paired with dainty pressed-glass leaves and faceted quartz beads in whisper-soft shades of mint green and celadon, making the earrings surprisingly sweet and feminine. The construction technique is super-easy—just thread the beads onto the hoops, keeping them in place with Scrimp Beads—and may inspire you to create your own designs using other colors and bead shapes.

MATERIALS

12 German pressed-glass leaves, frosted celadon, 8 mm wide × 11 mm long × 2 mm thick

2 faceted dyed-quartz round beads, mint, 9 mm dia.

4 metal rondelles, silver, 3 mm dia. × 2 mm long

4 Scrimp Beads with screws, silver, 3 mm dia.

1 pair earring hoops, sterling silver, 22 gauge, 3.3 cm dia.

Cyanoacrylate liquid

TOOLS

1 Scrimp Bead screwdriver

Chain-nose pliers

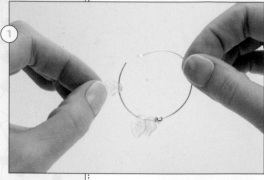

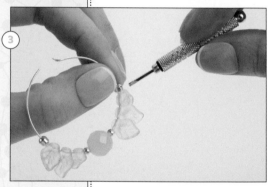

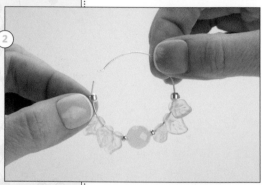

DIRECTIONS

1 :: Insert one end of one earring hoop through a Scrimp Bead, and string on three leaves facing in the same direction.

2 :: Add one silver rondelle, one mint bead, another silver rondelle, three more leaves (facing the same direction as those in step 1), and one more Scrimp Bead.

3 :: Slide the beads along the hoop until they are in the desired position. Use the screwdriver to secure one Scrimp Bead. (See "How to Use a Scrimp Bead," page 280.)

4 :: Read the first tip. Gently press the first leaf up against the first secured Scrimp Bead. Leave a gap between this leaf bead and the rest. Add a small drop of glue to the wire and use gravity to direct it down the wire and into the leaf bead hole. Hold the leaf until it stays in place on its own. Slide the next leaf toward the secured Scrimp Bead, positioning it on the interior of the hoop. Add glue and let dry. Repeat these steps until all the beads are secured in place.

5 :: Use the screwdriver to secure the second Scrimp Bead. Use chain-nose pliers to gently bend the straight wire up.

6 :: Insert the earring wire into the backing end to ensure that it will stay secure when worn. Further adjust the wire angle with chain-nose pliers if necessary. Repeat steps 1–6 to make the second earring.

TIPS

Make sure the beads are next to one another, but don't place them so near that when the earring is closed they will grind against one another. The beads are glass and can chip and break, so check them as you work.

These earring hoops have a backing end into which you insert the opposite wire. This opposite wire must be straight so that beads can be strung on, but you will need to bend it slightly so it will catch in the backing and stay secure when worn.

LORELEI LEE

You will channel Hollywood glamour when you wear the Lorelei Lee earrings, named after a character played by one of the world's most famous blondes, Marilyn Monroe. Although the earrings are eye-catching stunners, the tassel-style design has understated elegance. Made with crystal bicones and bugle beads lined with silver, each tassel is easy to construct; all you do is string the beads on thread, gather several beaded strands together, and secure them to a cap decorated with rhinestones. The length of each of the strands can be adapted to your own style. Make a shorter tassel in jet-black beads or elongate the tassels so they touch your shoulders if you prefer. Either way, you will be ready for your close-up.

MATERIALS

4 Austrian crystal bicones, crystal, 6 mm

114 Austrian crystal bicones, crystal, 4 mm

1 hank silver-lined bugle beads, crystal, 2 mm dia. × 5 mm long

30 round beads, silver, 2.5 mm dia.

60 Austrian crystal flat-back rhinestones, crystal, SS-10, 2.8 mm dia.

2 bead caps, silver, 14 mm dia.

2 jump rings, silver, 16 gauge, 13 mm dia.

4 jump rings, silver, 22 gauge, 3 mm dia.

2 jump rings, silver, 22 gauge, 5 mm dia.

Silver wire, dead-soft, 22 gauge

Silver wire, dead-soft, 20 gauge

1 bobbin Nymo nylon thread, white, size D

1 pair post earrings, sterling silver, 8 mm dia.

Masking tape

Cyanoacrylate gel

Beeswax (optional)

Cardboard (optional)

TOOLS

Toothpick

Tweezers

2 pairs chain-nose pliers

Round-nose pliers

Wire cutters

Scissors

Beading needle, size 10

FINISHED SIZE

½ in/13 mm wide × 5 in/12.7 cm long

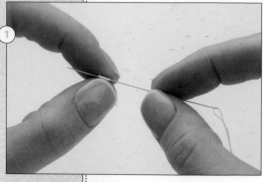

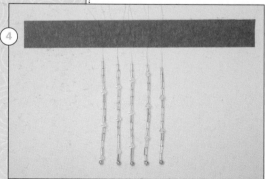

DIRECTIONS

1 :: Thread the beading needle with a pre-stretched single length of nylon thread. (See "How to Prestretch Beading Thread," page 347.) Leave the opposite end attached to the spool. Thread on four bugle beads and then one 4 mm bicone.

2 :: Continue threading on beads by alternating one 4 mm bicone after every four bugle beads, using three such sets in all. Thread on one round silver bead to end the strand. Then bring the needle and thread around the silver bead and insert it into the bottom of the second-to-last bead, in this case a bicone. Continue up through the beads until both thread ends are together.

3 :: Remove the beading needle and cut the thread from the spool using scissors, leaving two 3-in-/7.5-cm-long tails. Use a piece of masking tape to secure the thread ends to your work surface or a sturdy piece of cardboard.

4 :: Follow the beading diagram in this photo to create four more beaded strands. Take note of the staggered placement of the bicones. There will always be two inner sets of four bugle beads with bicones on each end, but the third set of four bugle beads will be split between the top of the strand and the bottom. Repeat steps 1–4 two more times to make a total of fifteen strands. Secure the strands and set them aside. When you remove the tape in step 8, add an additional 4 mm crystal bicone to the top of all fifteen strands.

5 :: Insert a toothpick into the hole of one bead cap. Place one 13 mm dia. jump ring on your work surface. Coat the top and sides of the ring with glue. Press the bead cap onto the jump ring to adhere them together. Let the glue dry.

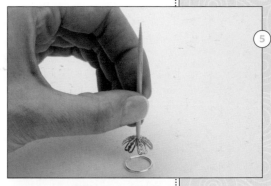

6 :: Grasp one flat-back rhinestone with the tweezers and turn it wrong side up. Apply a small drop of glue. Press the rhinestone against the surface of the bead cap until it adheres.

7 :: Continue gluing rhinestones in concentric circles to the surface of the bead cap until it's covered. Let dry. Remove the toothpick.

8 :: Use wire cutters to cut a 3-in/7.5-cm length of 20-gauge wire. Make an eye loop at one end. (See "How to Make an Eye Loop Using a Headpin," page 310.) Use chain-nose pliers to open the eye loop. (See "How to Open and Close an Eye Loop," page 315.) Remove the tape securing the fifteen beaded strands, add on the additional 4 mm bicones, and gather the thread ends together. Lay them inside the open eye loop. Close the eye loop around them.

9 :: Twist the thread ends together to make them more manageable. Optional: Rub beeswax along the threads. It will help keep them together and make the knot to be created in step 10 more secure. However, because the wax causes the threads to stick together, it will also make sliding the knot down difficult if it is tied too far from the beaded strands.

(continued page 192)

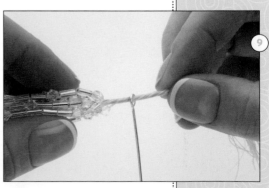

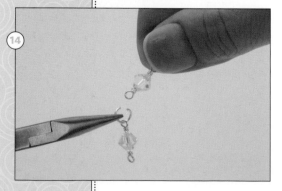

10 :: Make a single overhand knot (see "How to Make a Single Overhand Knot," page 342) on the eye loop, as close to the beads as possible. Use tweezers to help guide the threads into position.

11 :: Apply a drop of cyanoacrylate to the knot. Let dry. Cut away excess threads, leaving a 1/8-in/3-mm tail.

12 :: Insert the end of the wire into the hole in the rhinestone bead cap. Slide the bead cap down the wire until it covers the eye loop and the knot.

13 :: Use chain-nose pliers to make an eye loop above the bead cap. Trim away excess wire. Set this aside.

14 :: Use 22-gauge wire to make wrapped-wire loops on both ends of a 6 mm bicone. (See "How to Make a Wrapped-Wire Loop on Both Ends Using Wire," page 317.) Repeat this step to make a second bicone with wrapped-wire loops. Attach the two bicones to each other using one 5 mm jump ring. (See "How to Open and Close a Jump Ring," page 309.)

15 :: Open one 3 mm jump ring. Insert one end of the jump ring into one end of one of the wrapped-wire loops and the loop on one post earring. Close the jump ring.

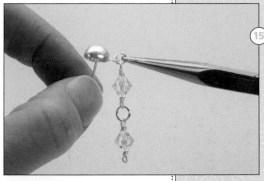

16 :: Open another 3 mm jump ring. Insert one end of the jump ring through the opposite end of the wrapped-wire loop and the eye loop on the bead cap. Close the jump ring. Repeat steps 1–16 to make the second earring.

• • • • TIPS • • • •

Four-millimeter bicones are added to the top of each strand before they are pulled into the bead cap, in order to create the look of a full tassel without adding the weight of extra strands. The bicones bunch together when pulled against the eye loop and cause the strands to bow out a bit, making the bead cap appear full.

You can use these same directions to make a tassel that you attach to a necklace or bracelet. Bead caps and cones come in many sizes, styles, and finishes, so you'll be sure to find one that suits your design.

If you can't find a 13-mm dia. jump ring in 16-gauge silver wire, or one that is the right size for the bead cap you're using, simply make your own. See "How to Make a Jump Ring," page 307.

THE NILE

A serene trio of geometric shapes establishes the pleasing balance of this dangle-style earring design noted for its gemstone colors. Suspended from ornamental disks with swirls of antique gold filigree are bicone crystals in plum to which olivine briolettes wrapped with fine gold wire are attached. Mixing the polished and antique gold patinas and the smooth and textured metals gives these earrings an exotic sensibility.

MATERIALS

2 Austrian crystal flat briolettes, olive green, 14 mm wide × 16 mm long × 6 mm thick

2 Austrian crystal bicones, plum, 6 mm

2 wire filigree metal oval connectors, antique gold, 11 mm wide × 26 mm long × 1 mm thick

Gold wire, dead-soft, 22 gauge

1 pair leverback earrings, gold-filled, 1 cm wide × 1.5 cm long

TOOLS

Ruler

Wire cutters

2 pairs chain-nose pliers

Round-nose pliers

FINISHED SIZE

½ in/13mm wide × 2¾/7 cm long

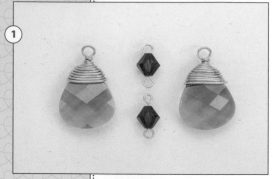

DIRECTIONS

1 :: Use wire cutters to cut two 10-in/25-cm lengths of gold wire. Wrap the green briolettes as shown, using one length of wire for each. (See "How to Make a Wrapped Briolette with a Stem," page 323.) Set them aside. Use wire cutters to cut two 2-in/5-cm lengths of gold wire. Make eye loops on both ends of the plum bicones, using one length of wire for each. (See "How to Make an Eye Loop on Both Ends Using Wire," page 311.) Set them aside.

2 :: Use chain-nose pliers to open one eye loop on one plum bicone, and thread it through the loop on one briolette. (See "How to Open and Close an Eye Loop," page 315.) Close the eye loop.

3 :: Use chain-nose pliers to open the eye loop on the opposite end of the bicone described in step 2, and thread it through the end loop on one filigree connector. Close the eye loop.

4 :: Use chain-nose pliers to open the loop at the base of one leverback earring. Thread it through the loop on the opposite end of the filigree connector used in step 3. Close the loop on the earring. Repeat steps 2–4 to make the second earring.

•••• TIP ••••

Connectors are often looked at as utilitarian and typically recede into the background of a design, along with other metal findings and wirework—but this needn't be the case. In a bracelet or necklace design, a connector could easily play only a supporting role, but this earring design brings it to the forefront. Connectors can be found with not only various motifs and metal finishes but also crystal and bead accents in a variety of colors.

FIREFLY

Whimsical but elegant, these tear-drop hoop earrings in cherry red and gold are as perfect for summer evenings as they are for winter holidays, when a burst of cheerful color is always welcome. Single faceted briolettes accented with wire wraps and suspended within loops of rough-cut beads are wired together and hung from ear wires in matte gold.

MATERIALS

2 cubic zirconia briolettes, red, 9 mm dia. × 16 mm long

40 rough-cut round glass beads, red, 4 mm dia.

Gold wire, dead-soft, 22 gauge

1 pair leverback earrings with scalloped shell detail, brushed gold, 1 cm wide × 1.8 cm long

TOOLS

Ruler

Wire cutters

2 pairs chain-nose pliers

Round-nose pliers

Clip or clamp

FINISHED SIZE

1 in/2.5 cm wide × 2 in/5 cm long

DIRECTIONS

1 :: Divide the beads into two identical groups; set one group aside. Use wire cutters to cut two 8-in/20-cm lengths and two 6-inch/15-cm lengths of wire. Secure one end of an 8-in/20-cm long wire with a clip. (See "How to Keep Beads from Falling Off Your Stringing Material," page 269.) String on 20 rough-cut beads. Slide the beads to the midpoint and remove the clip. Bring both wire ends together, crossing them left over right. Pull the wire ends away from each other until the wires cross directly above the beads.

2 :: Use chain-nose pliers to bend the back wire straight up, centering it where the beads meet to create a stem. While holding the stem stationary, grasp the front wire and wrap it around the stem to the back, then straight down behind the beaded teardrop.

3 :: Reach through the teardrop to pull the wire to the front side. Bend the wire up, wrapping it counterclockwise twice around the stem to secure it. Trim away excess wire. (Caution: Do not pull the wire so tightly that it sits flush against the interior of the teardrop; leave a slight gap between the wire and the beads. The briolette will hang from this interior wire "loop.") Make an eye loop with the remaining wire, the stem. (See "How to Make an Eye Loop Using a Headpin," page 310.) Set this aside.

4 :: Make a wrapped-wire briolette with one briolette and one 6-in/15-cm length of wire. (See "How to Make a Wrapped Briolette with a Stem," page 323.) Make an eye loop with the stem. Attach the eye loop on the briolette to the interior wire "loop" created in step 3. (See "How to Open and Close an Eye Loop," page 315.)

5 :: Attach the loop at the base of one earring wire to the eye loop on the beaded teardrop. (See "How to Open and Close an Eye Loop," page 315.) Repeat steps 1–5 to make the second earring.

RINGS

BEE MINE

The secret to the endless sparkle of these little domes of crystals is that each faceted, warm-as-honey gold rhinestone is set in gold prongs that raise the ring's drama. Deceptively easy to make, these rings are actually constructed from dress buttons and adjustable gold ring bands. The same technique can be applied to any button with open loops or spaces around the outside that allow you to thread the button onto a ring band.

MATERIALS

FOR LARGE "BEEHIVE" RHINESTONE RING:

1 rhinestone button with loops around the base, gold, 23 mm dia. × 15 mm thick

Transite

1 ring form with 13 mm dia. beading disc, gold, 2 cm dia. band

Cyanoacrylate gel

FINISHED SIZE

⅞ in/2.3 cm dia. × ⅝ in/16 mm thick

(Decoration only. Does not include ring band.)

MATERIALS

FOR SMALL FLORET RHINESTONE RING:

1 rhinestone button with flat loops around the base, gold, 15 mm dia. × 8 mm thick

Transite

1 ring form with 13 mm dia. beading disc, gold, 2 cm dia. band

Cyanoacrylate gel

FINISHED SIZE

⅝ in/16 mm dia. × ⅜ in/9.5 cm thick

(Decoration only. Does not include ring band.)

TOOLS

Ruler

Wire cutters

Chain-nose pliers

Bent-nose pliers

DIRECTIONS

1 :: Use wire cutters to cut a 12-in/30.5-cm length of transite, and make a double overhand knot at one end. (See "How to Make a Double Overhand Knot," page 342.) Thread the opposite end through the beading disc from the underside. Pull the transite so that the knot is tight against the bottom of the disc. If necessary, make a second or third knot to keep the knot from slipping through to the other side. Secure the knot with a drop of glue. Let dry. Trim the knot tail to ⅛ in/3 mm long.

2 :: Depending on the type of button, either remove the button shank with wire cutters or bend the shank flush against the bottom of the button using chain-nose and bent-nose pliers. To whipstitch the button to the beading disc, begin by inserting the transite end through one loop on the edge of the button, moving from outside to inside. Then insert the transite into an open hole on the edge of the beading disc, directly below the button loop. Bring the transite around the outside of the disc and back up, inserting it through the adjacent loop on the button. Continue to thread the transite into holes and loops, leaving a ½-in/12-mm space between the button and the ring form. Work around to the starting point.

3 :: Read the Tip section, opposite page, before doing this step. Pull the transite end to tighten the stitches a bit, moving the ring form closer to the button. Apply glue only to the center of the underside of the button by inserting the nozzle between the lengths of transite threads.

4 :: Begin at the original knot and work fairly quickly. Use chain-nose pliers to pull the loops of transite in the direction they were stitched, removing all slack. Work around to the starting point. Secure the end with a knot on the bottom of the beading disc. Apply a drop of glue to the knot. Let the glue dry. Trim away the transite tail.

TIP

Before you apply the glue, be sure you know where the starting thread is and in which direction you need to pull the transite stitches to tighten them. You will need to work fairly quickly so the glue won't dry before the button and ring form can be joined together.

PRIMROSE PATH

A single, smooth bead in celadon green sits in the center of Primrose Path, a ring with vintage style. The large central bead is secured to the ring band with undulating lengths of wire in gunmetal that define a path across the face of the bead and lead the eye to a small bouquet of dainty rosettes. Each flower is crafted in metal and painted in buttercup yellow or pistachio green.

MATERIALS

1 glass olive, celadon, 13 mm wide × 15 mm long × 9 mm thick

6 metal roses, 8 mm dia. × 5 mm thick:

> 3 yellow

> 3 green

Gunmetal-colored wire, enamel-coated copper core, dead-soft, 24 gauge

1 ring form with four holes, antique copper, 2 cm dia. × 8 mm thick

TOOLS

Ruler

Wire cutters

Chain-nose pliers

FINISHED SIZE

½ in/2.5 cm wide × 1⅛/5.7 cm long × ⅜ in/9.5 cm thick

(Decoration only. Does not include ring band.)

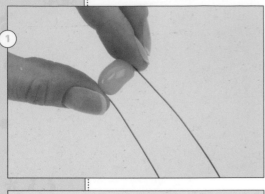

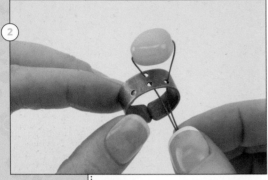

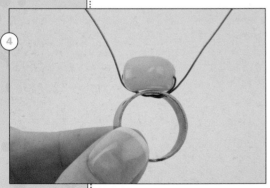

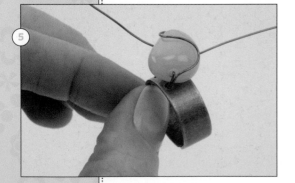

DIRECTIONS

1 :: Use wire cutters to cut a 12-in/30.5-cm length of wire. Insert one end through the celadon bead and slide the bead to the wire's midpoint. Bend both wire ends down.

2 :: Insert the wire ends through one center and one outside hole on the ring form. Pull the wires down until the bead sits on the ring form.

3 :: Insert one wire end back up through the opposite hole with the other wire end.

4 :: Push the second wire end back up through the opposite hole to secure the bead to the ring form.

5 :: From one end of the bead to the other, coil one length of wire across the bead to create an S shape. Both wires should now be at the same end.

6 :: Tuck the coiled wire underneath the wire that runs through the bead to secure it.

7 :: Coil the remaining length of wire along the same S-shaped path in the opposite direction. Tuck the coiled wire underneath the wire that runs through the bead to secure it. The wires should now be at opposite ends.

8 :: At one end, wrap the length of wire around the wire running through the bead approximately five times to hide the bead hole. (Read "How to Make Wrapped Briolettes," page 321, for helpful tips on making successful wraps.)

9 :: Trim away excess wire. Use chain-nose pliers to hide the cut end between the underside of the wire wrap and the ring form. Repeat steps 8–9 with the wire length on the opposite end.

10 :: Use wire cutters to cut a 6-in/15-cm length of wire. Thread on all the rose beads, alternating yellow and green.

(continued page 210)

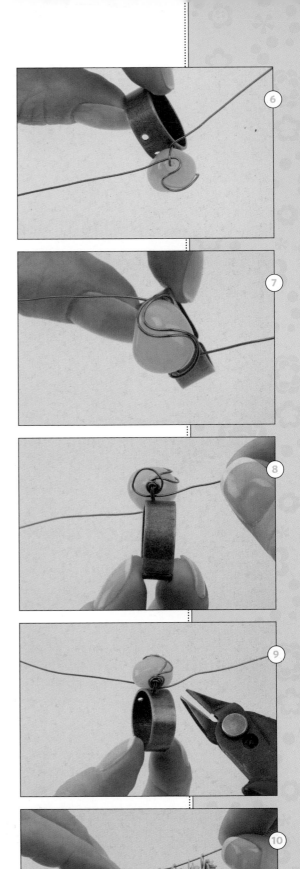

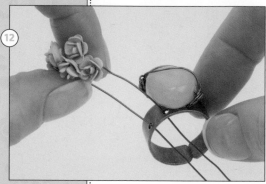

11 :: Slide the flowers to the midpoint of the wire and bend the wire ends up.

12 :: Insert the wire ends through the two remaining holes in the ring form. Cross the wires underneath and insert them back up into the opposite holes. Twist the wire ends together to secure them, concealing them beneath the flowers. Trim away excess wire.

TIP

Premade ring forms are easy to work with and are available with various numbers of holes and loops in different positions. These holes and loops will determine the placement of your beads, so seek out as many examples as you can find. Certain ring forms may inspire you, while others may force you to be clever in executing your designs.

OASIS

A single polished turquoise bead with jagged veins of dark color is the eye-catching focal point of this contemporary ring design with a southwestern sensibility. Made simply by threading the single bead onto sterling-silver wire and then winding and wrapping the wire into a sturdy band, the ring has a straightforward construction technique that allows for a wide variety of interpretations according to your personal tastes. Instead of the opaque turquoise stone, for example, consider threading a crystal bead in sapphire blue onto a length of gold wire for a regal look.

MATERIALS

1 turquoise oval, 16 mm wide × 23 mm long × 11 mm thick

Sterling silver wire, half-hard, 18 gauge

TOOLS

Ruler

Wire cutters

Dowel or ring mandrel

Chain-nose pliers

Needle file

Emery cloth

FINISHED SIZE

1 in/2.5 cm wide × 1¼ in/3.2 cm long

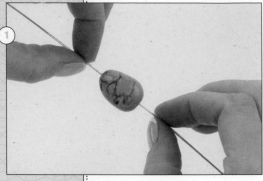

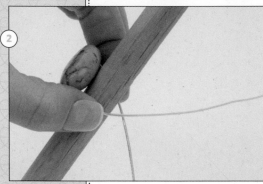

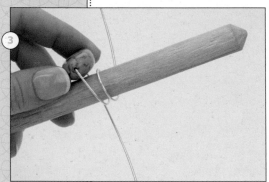

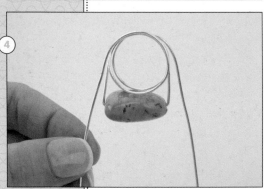

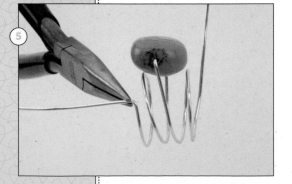

DIRECTIONS

1 :: Use wire cutters to cut a 24-in/61-cm length of wire. Insert one end through the turquoise bead and slide the bead to the wire's midpoint.

2 :: Position the bead on the dowel (or mandrel) and bend the two wires down, crossing them at the base of the dowel.

3 :: Wrap one length of wire one and a half times around the dowel.

4 :: Repeat step 3 in the opposite direction with the opposite length of wire. Slide the ring off the dowel and adjust the loops to the desired size by test-fitting them on your finger or on a ring mandrel with size demarcations.

5 :: Use chain-nose pliers to bend one wire end 90 degrees, pointing away from the ring.

(continued page 214)

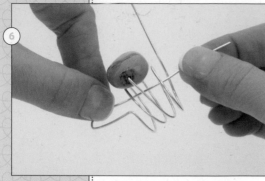

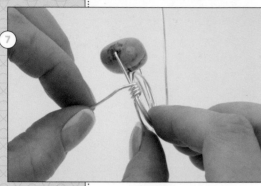

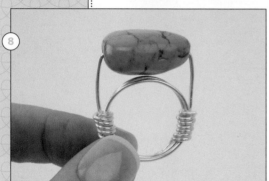

6 :: Insert the end of the same wire used in step 5 back toward the ring and through the center of the wire loops.

7 :: Wrap the wire around the wire loops six times. Repeat steps 5–7 using the other wire end on the opposite side of the ring.

8 :: Trim away excess wire and smooth the cut ends on both sides. (See "How to Finish Wire Ends," page 302.) Use chain-nose pliers to press the cut ends flush against the ring band.

• • • • **TIP** • • • •

You can use any wire to make this ring as long as it is malleable yet strong enough to hold its form. Sterling silver works very well, much better than silver-plated wire, which in lower gauges is very difficult to manipulate and doesn't yield a pretty ring.

PLUM DELICIOUS

Mouth-watering shades of plum and grape sorbet mix with crystals in amethyst and lilac in this sparkling confection of beads that surround a cushion-cut amethyst in deep purple, highlighting the narrow tonal range of the smaller beads. Adding subtle texture to the design are the contrasting shapes of the beads—a combination of crystal bicones and a faceted square.

MATERIALS

1 square pointed back Austrian crystal rhinestone with silver setting, purple, 10 mm wide × 10 mm long × 10 mm thick

12 Austrian crystal bicones in various colors, 6 mm:

> 3 plum
>
> 3 violet
>
> 3 light amethyst
>
> 3 opalescent lilac

12 faceted Austrian crystal bicones in various colors, 4 mm:

> 3 plum
>
> 3 violet
>
> 3 light amethyst
>
> 3 opalescent lilac

Silver wire, dead-soft, 28 gauge

1 ring form with 13 mm dia. beading disc, silver, 2 cm dia. band

TOOLS

Ruler

Wire cutters

Chain-nose pliers

FINISHED SIZE

2 in/5 cm dia. × ½ in/13 mm thick

(Decoration only. Does not include ring band.)

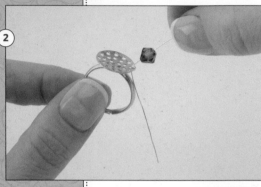

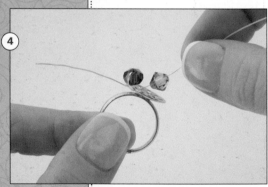

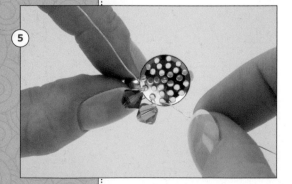

DIRECTIONS

1 :: Use wire cutters to cut a 12-in/30.5-cm length of wire. Insert one wire end into one hole on the outside of the beading disc from the top. Wrap the short end of the wire around the hole three times to secure it, leaving a tail.

2 :: Insert the long end of the wire through one 6 mm plum bicone. Let the bead slide down until it sits on the outside edge of the beading disc.

3 :: Wrap the wire around the outside of the bicone and insert the end into the adjacent hole from underneath the beading disc. Pull the wire until the bead is secure.

4 :: Thread on one 6 mm violet bicone. Let the bead slide down until it sits on the outside edge of the ring form.

5 :: Wrap the wire around the outside of the bicone and insert the end into the adjacent hole from underneath the beading disc. Pull the wire until the bead is secure. Repeat steps 4–5 to add a 6 mm light amethyst bicone followed by a 6 mm opalescent lilac bicone. Continue adding 6 mm bicones, repeating the four-color pattern, until the starting point is reached. Do not cut the wire.

(continued page 218)

MASTERING THE ART *of* BEADING

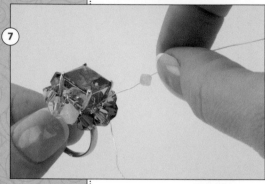

6 :: Cut two 12-in/30.5-cm lengths of wire. Set one aside. Insert one end of the wire through the setting on one side of the square purple rhinestone, sliding the stone to the wire's midpoint. Bend the wires down and insert them through two adjacent holes in the center of the beading disc. Repeat on the opposite side using the remaining length of wire. Pull the wires from underneath to properly position the rhinestone in the center of the beading disc. Securing one side at a time, insert the wire ends back up through the holes, wrap them around the setting, then back down through the disc again. Twist the wires together on the underside; trim away the excess.

7 :: Insert the uncut wire end from step 5 into one opalescent lilac 4 mm bicone. Let the bead slide down until it rests between the rhinestone setting and the top of the 6 mm bicones.

8 :: Wrap the wire around the outside of the 4 mm bicone, between two 6 mm bicones, underneath the beading disc, and up through the adjacent hole. Note: Use the same holes for both sizes of bicones. Thread on one plum 4 mm bicone, followed by one violet and one light amethyst bicone. Continue adding 4 mm bicones around the rhinestone setting, repeating the color pattern, until the starting point is reached. Insert the wire end through the beading disc and secure the wire by wrapping it a few times. Trim away the excess wire including the wire tail and hide the cut ends underneath the beading disc.

●●● **TIP** ●●●

Make sure to check the bead position on the ring after adding each 6 mm bicone. Sometimes the bicones slide down the wire wraps and rest on the underside of the beading disc. To correct this, simply slide the bicone back into the proper position and pull the wire taut before adding the next bead.

MASTERING THE ART *of* BEADING

SEA SPRAY

In Sea Spray, each luminous, irregularly shaped aquamarine chip emits a glow that rivals that of the ocean in moonlight. The chips' edges are tumbled and worn as smooth as sea glass. Each of them is anchored by a headpin topped with a tiny silver ball that secures them in a random pattern to a silver ring band, creating a freeform design.

MATERIALS

26 aquamarine chips, pale blue, approximately 6 mm wide × 6 mm long × 4 mm thick

26 headpins with 1 mm ball ends, silver, 24 gauge, 2 in/5 cm long

Silver wire, dead-soft, 28 gauge (optional)

1 ring form with 2-coiled bands and 9 connector loops, silver, 2 cm dia. × 4 mm thick

TOOLS

Ruler

Wire cutters

Chain-nose pliers

Round-nose pliers

FINISHED SIZE

1 in/2.5 cm wide × 1¼ in/3.2 cm long × ⅝ in/16 mm thick

(Decoration only. Does not include ring band.)

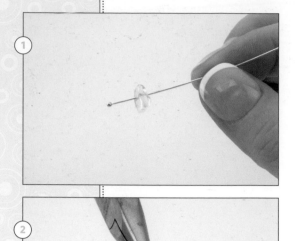

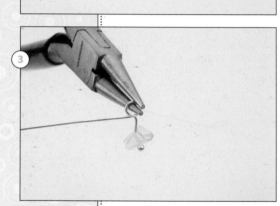

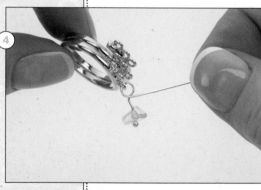

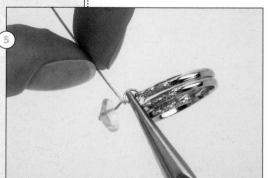

DIRECTIONS

1 :: Thread a chip onto a headpin.

2 :: Use chain-nose pliers to grasp the headpin ⅛ in/3 mm above the bead. Turn the pliers away from yourself to bend the wire at a 90-degree angle.

3 :: Grasp the wire ⅛ in/3 mm from the bend using round-nose pliers. Rotate the pliers toward the bend. Grasp the wire end and wrap it around one jaw of the pliers, crossing the wire in front of the stem to make a loop.

4 :: Insert the end of the headpin into one loop on the ring form. Slide the loop down the wire until the loop on the ring sits in the loop on the headpin, as shown.

5 :: Grasp the loop with chain-nose pliers and wrap the wire end three times around the stem, moving from the loop down toward the first bead.

(continued page 222)

6 :: Use wire cutters to trim away excess. Use chain-nose pliers to squeeze the cut end flush against the stem. Repeat steps 1–6 to add the remaining chips.

7 :: To keep the chips together in a solid bunch, measure and cut two 6-in/15-cm lengths of wire. Insert one wire end through one wrapped-wire loop and twist the wire ends to secure it. Insert the long end of the wire through the other wrapped-wire loops and weave it around the stems of the bead chips, pulling the wire taut to make the chips stand up and cluster together. Secure the wire end to a wrapped loop to finish. Trim away excess wire. Repeat this step with the second wire if necessary.

TIP

After all the chips are added, they will most likely fall in a way that exposes some of the ring form in the center. You may add more chips if you like, but this may make the ring too bulky and uncomfortable to wear. Another option is to add a focal bead in the center. Or use the method described in step 7 to hide small lengths of wire woven below the bead chips to help cluster and secure them.

SONNET

Understated elegance tells the love story of this simple gold band that is suitable for a woman or a man. Surprisingly quick and easy to make, Sonnet is composed of ordinary materials—a few hoops of memory wire and faceted beads in genuine gold, making it perfect for commemorating a wedding or an anniversary. The same band can be made as a friendship or promise ring using any small beads you choose.

MATERIALS

110 (approximately) charlotte (true-cut) seed beads, gold plated, size 13/0

19 Czech fire-polished round beads, gold, 2 mm dia.

Memory wire, gold, ring size

Crystal cement

TOOLS

Memory-wire cutters

Needle file

Emery cloth

Tweezers

FINISHED SIZE

¾ in/19 mm dia. × ¼ in/6.4 cm thick

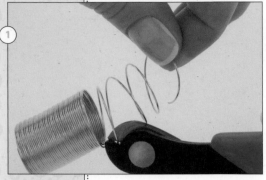

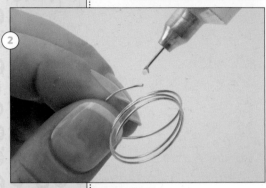

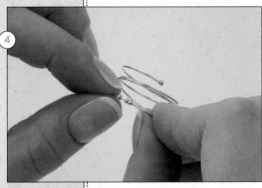

DIRECTIONS

1 :: Count three complete loops of memory wire and use memory-wire cutters to cut the loops from the coil. Use the needle file and emery cloth to smooth the cut ends. (See "How to Finish Wire Ends," page 302.)

2 :: Add a drop of crystal cement to one end of the memory wire.

3 :: Insert the end of the wire into one seed bead, making sure that the bead is flush with the end of the wire. Use tweezers if necessary. Let the glue dry.

4 :: At the opposite end, thread on three more seed beads. Slide the beads down the wire to the end with the glued bead. Before reaching the glued bead, add a drop of glue to the bare wire. Slide the beads in place against the end bead. Let the glue dry. Continue threading on seed beads until you've completed one revolution.

5 :: Thread on one complete revolution of the larger beads, followed by another revolution of seed beads, stopping four beads short of the wire end.

(continued page 226)

MASTERING THE ART *of* BEADING

6 :: Apply glue to the wire end. Thread the remaining seed beads over the glued wire, making sure the end bead is flush with the end of the memory wire. Let the glue dry.

7 :: The underside of the ring should look like this. Notice how the cut ends look and how the transitions between the different types of beads are made.

TIP

Memory wire is typically finished either by looping the wire's ends or by gluing on end beads or caps. End beads are half-drilled and give your pieces a professional, polished finish. For the delicate Sonnet ring, though, the readily available 3 mm end beads are too cumbersome. Instead, four seed beads are glued to the wire on each end to secure it. This technique will work only with very lightweight, small beads and should not be used to finish memory-wire bracelets or necklaces.

VICTORIA

Good taste never goes out of style. Reminiscent of heirloom jewelry from the nineteenth century, this cocktail ring is as perfect with a formal gown as it is with a pair of worn-out jeans. Ornate but demure, the silver setting is a perfect stage for the faceted crystals and tiny blue seed beads that encrust its center. The ring is cleverly constructed from two separate pieces: a vintage-style pendant cast in antique silver and an antique silver ring band.

MATERIALS

2 Austrian crystal rondelles, 7 mm dia. × 5 mm long:

     1 Pacific opal

     1 sea green

1 Austrian crystal rondelle, teal, 6 mm dia. × 4 mm long

1 faceted dyed quartz crystal round bead, teal, 6 mm dia.

1 Austrian crystal bicone, Pacific opal, 6 mm

2 Austrian crystal bicones, pale blue, 4 mm

20 (approximately) opaque seed beads, sky blue pearl, size 11/0

1 filigree oval pendant setting, antique silver, 3.2 cm wide × 3.6 cm long

1 ring form with 19 mm dia. platform disc, antique silver, 19 mm dia. wide band

Five-minute two-part epoxy

Cardboard

Aluminum foil

Toothpicks

Paper towels

TOOLS

Tweezers

FINISHED SIZE

1¼ in/3.2 cm wide × 1½ in/3.8 cm long × ½ in/13mm thick

(Decoration only. Does not include ring band.)

1 :: Cover a small piece of cardboard with aluminum foil. Follow the manufacturer's instructions to squeeze both parts of the epoxy onto the aluminum foil, and use a toothpick to mix it. Use the same toothpick to apply a generous amount to the back side of the pendant. Position the ring form over the pendant and press down to adhere them. Let glue dry thoroughly.

2 :: Plan your bead design. Then apply epoxy within the pendant's frame. Use tweezers to position one bead on the epoxy.

3 :: Continue to add beads, using tweezers, until the frame is filled. To layer the beads and fill gaps between them, use a toothpick to apply a dab of epoxy to the bottom of a bead and then position it in a gap between two beads.

4 :: Apply glue to any remaining open spaces between the beads. Add seed beads to the glued areas using tweezers. Let the glue dry.

TIPS

By the time the first layer of beads is positioned in the glue, the epoxy you've mixed will most likely be dry. Don't rush through the bead placement; just mix small amounts of glue so you don't waste it. And always plan out your next layer of beads before mixing more epoxy.

Pendant settings make great frames for beads or decorative papers and photos fixed with glaze. You can even pour in a layer of colorful nail polish and place charms, rhinestones, or beads directly into the polish while it's still wet. These pendants can be used for rings, bracelets, and necklaces. See "How to Make Collage Pendant Charms," page 372, for tips and ideas.

LA VIE EN ROSE

This beaded rose in sweet pink is composed of a delicate bouquet of petals, made one at a time by threading rows and rows of seed beads onto fine wire. When the petals are gathered together, they form a full-blown flower with a central bud made from a single crystal briolette in the same colorway. The appeal of this beading technique is the variety of flowers you can make by changing the color of your beads and the number of rows you weave to make the petals.

MATERIALS

1 faceted glass briolette, pink, 6 mm dia. × 14 mm long

10 g seed beads, rose pink, size 11/0

Gold wire, dead-soft, 30 gauge

1 German metal ring form with 2 loops, 22K gold plated, 2 cm dia. × 3 mm thick

TOOLS

Ruler

Wire cutters

Chain-nose pliers

FINISHED SIZE

1¾ in/4.4 cm dia. × 1 in/2.5 cm thick

(Decoration only. Does not include ring band.)

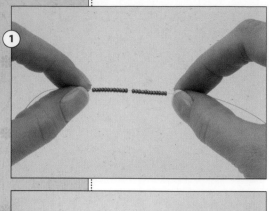

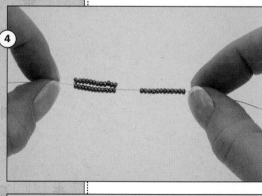

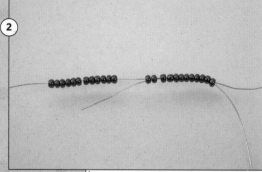

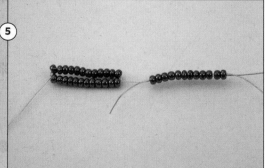

DIRECTIONS

1 :: Use wire cutters to cut a 14-in/35.5-cm length of wire. Follow the beading layout to thread on the first and second rows of seed beads to make a large petal. Slide the beads to the wire's midpoint, leaving a space on the wire between the two rows.

2 :: Insert the left-hand wire end into the last seed bead on the far right. Thread onto this wire the beads that make up the second row only.

3 :: Pull the wire ends to create two rows of beads.

4 :: Position the two rows of beads so that the bare wires that extend from the second row are on the bottom. Insert the wire end on the right into twelve seed beads (row 3). Slide the beads down the wire toward the others.

5 :: Bring the wire end on the left around and insert it into the last seed bead on the far right and the other eleven beads in that row.

BEADING LAYOUT	
LARGE ROSE PETAL:	**SMALL ROSE PETAL:**
Row 1: 12 beads	Row 1: 10 beads
Row 2: 12 beads	Row 2: 9 beads
Row 3: 12 beads	Row 3: 8 beads
Row 4: 11 beads	Row 4: 7 beads
Row 5: 10 beads	Row 5: 6 beads
Row 6: 9 beads	Row 6: 5 beads
Row 7: 8 beads	Row 7: 4 beads
Row 8: 7 beads	Row 8: 3 beads
Row 9: 6 beads	

6 :: Begin to pull the wires.

7 :: Continue to pull the wires until the beads line up under the first two rows, creating row 3. Follow the beading layout to add the remaining six rows. Twist the wires together at the base of the petal. Set aside.

8 :: Repeat steps 1–7 to make eleven more large petals. Follow the beading layout to make an additional four small petals.

9 :: Fit the ring band on your finger or a ring mandrel and adjust it so it will fit snugly. (This will keep the weight of the rose properly positioned when worn.) Use wire cutters to cut one 6-in/15-cm length of wire. Insert one end into the briolette and slide the bead to the wire's midpoint. Bend the wire ends toward each other so that they are parallel, and insert them through one loop on the ring form.

10 :: Secure the briolette by wrapping the wire ends up and around the wire stem and the bottom of the bead. Trim away excess wire.

(continued page 234)

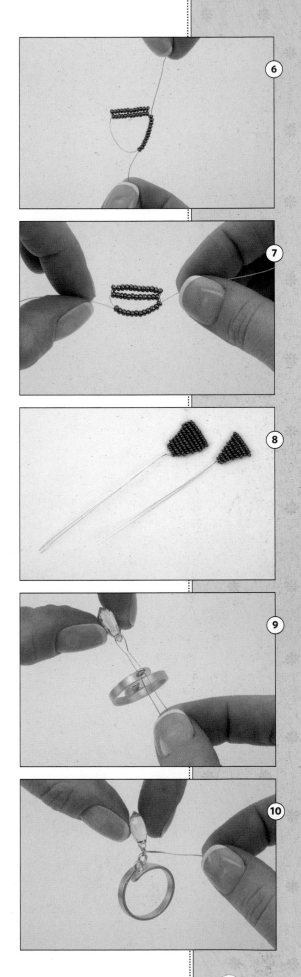

11 :: Insert the wire ends on one small petal through the same loop on the ring form. Wrap the wires around the loop to secure the petal. Do not cut the wire ends.

12 :: Attach a second small petal to the same loop on the opposite side of the briolette and wrap the wires around the loop to secure it.

13 :: Attach the remaining two small petals around the center briolette. Working out from the center, position and secure a large petal to the ring form as before, centering the petal behind the spaces left by the first row of petals. Attach three more large petals around the small petals, securing those closest to the second loop to that loop instead of the first one. Attach the remaining eight petals to either loop to create an outer third row.

14 :: Gather all the wire ends and wrap them around the base of the flower, covering the wire stems and the loops on the ring form. Twist the cut ends together and use chain-nose pliers to hide them within the wrapped wire or tuck them inside an outer petal. Shape the petals as shown or as desired.

TIP

• • • • **TIP** • • •

To make this beaded flower look more like a real rose, it is necessary to shape the petals a bit.

A. Place your index finger along the length of the petal. Support the edges of the petal from underneath with your thumb and middle finger.

B. Apply pressure with your index finger to curve the petal. For the small petals that surround the center briolette, stop here. To shape the large petals, continue with the remaining steps.

C. Use your fingertips to bend back the top edge of the petal.

D. Your finished petal should look like the one shown in image D, at right.

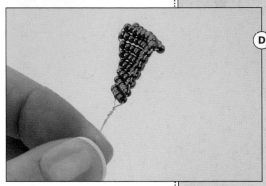

HAIR JEWELRY

DEW DROP BOBBY PINS

You won't need an excuse to add these pretty little pins to your beauty arsenal. Reminiscent of little constellations of delicate dew drops, the bobby pins bring together a dress button with pearlescent blue stones and clear rhinestones and a symmetrical series of wire loops accented with silver beads and faceted briolettes. These are small enough to pin two on one side of your hairstyle, and sparkly enough to highlight any updo.

MATERIALS

2 Austrian crystal rhinestone buttons with silver setting, Pacific blue opal, 23 mm dia. × 13 mm thick

8 Austrian crystal briolettes, crystal, 6 mm dia. × 9 mm long

32 coiled-wire round beads, silver, 4 mm dia.

50 Austrian crystal round beads, sky blue, 3 mm dia.

50 opaque seed beads, Pacific blue pearl, size 11/0

Silver wire, dead-soft, 28 gauge

2 twisted bobby pins, silver, 3 mm wide × 2½ in/6 cm long

TOOLS

Ruler

Wire cutters

Chain-nose pliers

FINISHED SIZE

1¾ in./4.4 cm dia. × 3¼ in/8.25 cm long

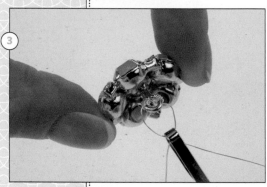

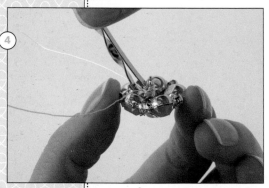

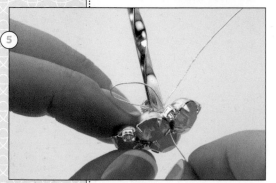

DIRECTIONS

1 :: Divide the bobby pins, buttons, and beads into two identical groups; set one group aside. Use wire cutters to cut a 12-in/30.5-cm length of wire. Insert one end of the wire into the shank of the button, sliding the button to the wire's midpoint. Hold one half of the wire in place at the button shank and wrap the other half around the shank five times to secure it.

2 :: Repeat step 1 with the opposite half of the wire to secure it to the shank.

3 :: Insert the wire ends now secured to the shank into the base of the bobby pin.

4 :: Pull the wires taut, bringing the bobby pin to the shank. Continue to wrap the wire ends around the base of the bobby pin and the shank.

5 :: Thread one wire end up through the bottom of the button, where the bobby pin and button overlap. Let the wire exit out the top. Repeat with the opposite length of wire. Do not cut these wire ends.

6 :: The base of the bobby pin should be securely attached to the button shank, but the top side of the bobby pin, where it overlaps with the button, has not yet been secured. The uncut wires from step 5 will serve this purpose in step 15. Lifting the pin and exposing the underside of the button should still be possible. Set this aside.

7 :: Use wire cutters to cut a 40-in/100-cm length of wire. Make beaded, twisted wire, alternating between the sky-blue crystal beads and the seed beads. (See "How to Make Beaded, Twisted Wire," page 336.)

8 :: Bend the beaded, twisted wire into ten 1½-in/4-cm flat loops, as shown.

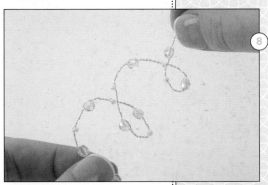

9 :: Use wire cutters to cut an 8-in/20-cm length of wire. Insert one end of the wire through the bead hole of an end bead on the twisted wire. Upon exiting the bead, thread the wire through the bottom loops on the beaded, twisted wire and through the bead hole of the end bead on the opposite side.

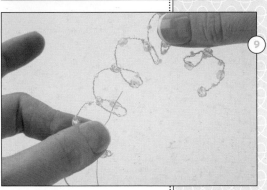

10 :: Bring the two nontwisted wire ends together so that the beaded, twisted wire forms a flower. Hold the wire ends together and shape the petals.

(continued page 242)

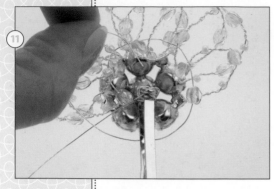

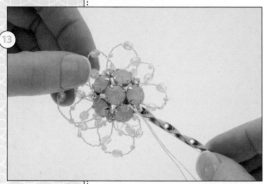

11 :: Center the beaded flower around the button shank. Wrap the beaded flower's wire end on the right clockwise around the shank, and then thread it through the shank. Pull the wire taut. Repeat this step with the other wire end, but wrap it counterclockwise. Twist the two wire ends together a few times at the point where the bobby pin overlaps the button to secure them. Do not trim away the ends.

12 :: Thread one of the wire ends from step 11 up through a hole in the button design. Run the wire across the top of the button between two blue rhinestones so that the silver wire appears to be a part of the matching silver setting, and insert it back down another hole. Move the wire clockwise on the underside of the button so that it traps and secures a portion of the beaded flower. Then insert the wire end up through another hole. Repeat these steps to further secure the beaded flower petals to the button. When you reach the starting point, anchor the wire end by wrapping it to the shank or to another wire on the underside of the button; hide the end within the wirework.

13 :: Repeat step 12 with the remaining wire end from step 11 and weave it in the opposite direction.

14 :: Use wire cutters to cut four 6-in/15-cm lengths of wire. Set three aside. Insert one wire end into a briolette and slide the bead to the wire's midpoint. Fold the wire in half and twist. Using the beaded, twisted wire technique, add four silver coiled-wire beads. Repeat this step using the remaining three wires and beads.

15 :: Attach the beaded wires made in step 14 as shown at four points around the button—northeast, northwest, southeast, and southwest—or as desired. Secure the wire ends by wrapping them to any available space on the shank or around other wires on the back side of the button. Hide the wire ends within the wirework. Now that all the beaded wirework has been completed, you can finish securing the bobby pin to the button at the point where it meets the outer rim of the button. Wrap the two wire ends from step 5 and secure them in the same manner used in step 12. Run your fingers over the underside of the button to feel for any sharp or loose wires. Use chain-nose pliers to bend, tuck, or hide away any cut wire ends that may catch on your hair during use. Repeat steps 1–15 to make the second bobby pin.

TIPS

To make quick and simple beaded bobby pins, stop after step 6 and use the uncut wires to secure the button to the top of the pin. Or you can place a few buttons in a row on a barrette and secure them with wire or transite. Buttons come in a variety of shapes, colors, and styles and are perfect for embellishing hair jewelry. Don't forget to raid flea markets, vintage shops, and your grandmother's button box to find the rarest and most interesting ones.

GREEK GODDESS HEADBAND

Sometimes the simplest things are the most beautiful. Uncomplicated and practical, yet romantic and classic, Greek Goddess joins two narrow gold headbands, accented with lengths of rhinestone chain. The continuous lengths of rhinestones are lashed to the headbands with fine gold wire and finished with demure wraps of ribbon.

MATERIALS

1 yard/91 cm rhinestone chain, gold setting, 2 mm wide

¼ yard/23 cm grosgrain ribbon, ocher, ⅞ in/2.2 cm wide

Gold wire, dead-soft, 30 gauge

Gold wire, dead-soft, 24 gauge

1 place-holding round bead, 24 mm dia.

Scrap wire, 24 or 22 gauge

2 metal headbands, gold, 3 mm wide × 15½ in/
39 cm long

Masking tape

Cyanoacrylate gel

High-tack white glue

Permanent adhesive

TOOLS

Ruler

Wire cutters

Chain-nose pliers

Scissors

FINISHED SIZE

5 in/15.24 cm wide × 6 in/12.7 cm long ×
1¼ in/3.2 cm thick

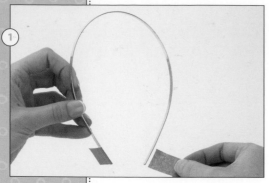

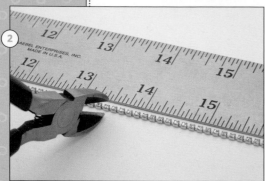

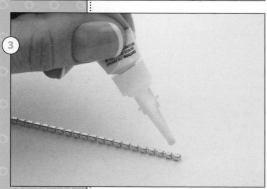

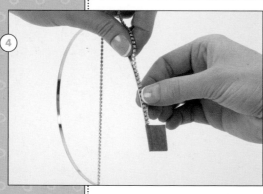

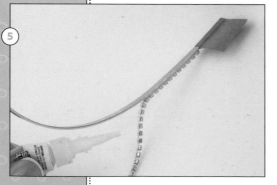

1 :: Using masking tape, cover a 7/8-in/2.2-cm portion of both bottom ends of each headband. The covered area should be equal to the width of the ribbon.

2 :: Measure and cut a 13¾-in/35-cm length of rhinestone chain. This measurement should be equal to the distance along each headband between the two pieces of masking tape.

3 :: Lay the cut length of rhinestone chain wrong side up on a flat work surface. Beginning at one end, apply dabs of cyanoacrylate glue to the backs of the rhinestones for approximately 2 in/5 cm.

4 :: Gently lift the glued end of the rhinestone chain. Turn it so that the right side is facing up and place it on one of the headbands, directly above the masking tape. Press along the chain to adhere it.

5 :: Position the headband on the work surface so that the wrong side of the rhinestone chain is exposed. Continue to apply dabs of glue in 2-in/ 5-cm increments, stopping to adhere the rhine- stone chain one section at a time.

6 :: Continue gluing the rhinestone chain to the headband until you've reached the opposite end. Stop just above the masking tape. Set it aside.

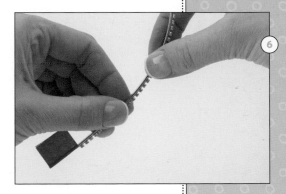

7 :: Repeat steps 2–6 to glue a rhinestone chain to the second headband.

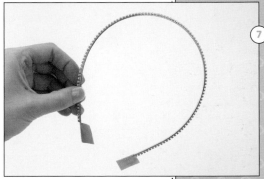

8 :: Remove the masking tape from both ends of one headband. Secure the end of the 30-gauge wire to the headband by wrapping it four times beneath the last rhinestone, leaving a tail. (See "How to Wrap Thin Wire," page 304.) Do not cut the wire from the spool.

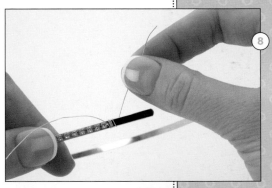

9 :: To further secure the rhinestone chain to the headband, wrap the wire around the headband and bring it to the front, running the wire through the space between the first two rhinestones.

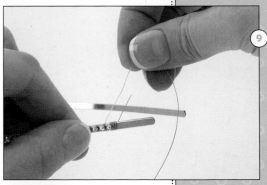

10 :: Continue wrapping the wire around to the back and to the front again, this time running the wire through the space between the second and third rhinestone.

(continued page 248)

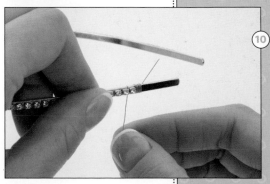

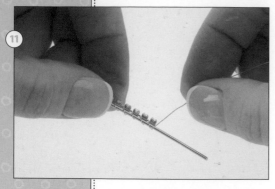

11 :: Continue to wrap the wire between each rhinestone, moving one rhinestone to the left each time, until you've reached the opposite end. Wrap the wire four times beneath the last rhinestone to secure it. Trim away excess wire. Trim away the wire tail on the other end as well.

12 :: Repeat steps 8–11 to secure the rhinestone chain to the second headband with the wire. Secure the place-holding bead to the midpoint of both headbands using scrap wire.

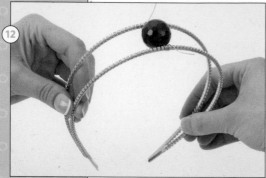

13 :: Hold one end of each headband in the same hand, keeping the bands parallel and ½ in/12 mm apart. In the same hand, hold the tail end of the 24-gauge wire (still attached to the spool) on the back side of the headband farthest away from you. With the opposite hand, wrap the long end of the wire underneath the first headband, bringing it up between the two headband ends.

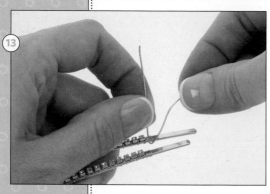

14 :: Bring the wire from between the headbands over the nearest headband.

15 :: Wrap the wire around the headband nearest you, bringing it up between the two headbands.

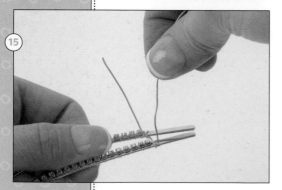

16 :: In this way, continue wrapping the wire around both headbands, creating four figure eights while maintaining a space between them. Do not cut the wire.

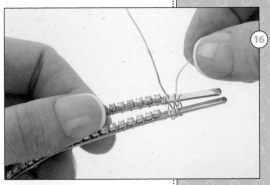

17 :: Position the bottom ends of the headband so that one overlaps the other. Pick up the wire from step 16 and wrap it around the ends, this time around the outside, to secure the ends together.

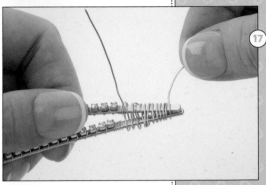

18 :: At the bottommost point, begin to wind the wire back up toward the rhinestones until it is directly below the first rhinestones. Cut away excess wire and use chain-nose pliers to press the cut end flush against the wrapped wire. Do not cut the original wire tail created in step 13.

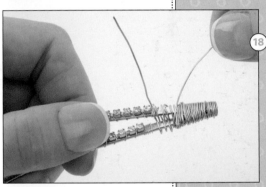

19 :: Measure and cut a 2½-in/6-cm length of ribbon. Apply dabs of white glue to the cut ends to prevent fraying. Let dry. Apply permanent adhesive to the wrapped-wire end. Position the end of the ribbon on the adhesive.

20 :: Wrap the wire tail around the ribbon to further secure it.

(continued page 250)

21 :: Apply permanent adhesive to the wrong side of the ribbon and wrap it around itself, covering the wire. Finish by gluing the ribbon end on the inside of the headband so the ribbon seam will be hidden when it is worn. Repeat steps 13–21 to bind and cover the opposite ends of the headband. Remove the placeholder bead and scrap wire.

• • • TIPS • • •

Rhinestone chain is available in many different sizes and settings, so you're sure to find one that fits a headband of any width.

Try to avoid crimping the 30-gauge wire so it won't crack and break. To make your wrapping easier, as you wrap the wire around the headband rotate it so the space you're working on is closest to you. Also, your wire will crimp less if you can wind the wire with one complete motion. Wind the wire around the headband and then exit the wire through the open space in the headband; then bring it underneath the band and back up again.

RASPBERRY BARRETTE

A chunky collection of cat's-eye, quartz, and seed beads encrusts a barrette in a sweet confection of pink. Sturdy but lightweight, this hair accessory is made in a hue that shows up well on all hair colors. The beading technique is straightforward, one that relies on a die-cut metal disc with predrilled holes through which you can thread transite, making it easy to "sew" on any kinds of beads you wish. This disc is then secured to a barrette backing. The same construction principle used to make the Raspberry Barrette can be used to make both pins and rings, such as the Plum Delicious and Bee Mine rings.

MATERIALS

4 rose quartz round beads, pink, 9 mm dia.

3 cat's-eye round glass beads, pink, 9 mm dia.

4 cat's-eye four-sided ovals, pink, 7 mm wide × 16 mm long × 7 mm thick

9 faceted rose quartz briolettes, pink, 7 mm dia. × 11 mm long

11 flat glass diamonds, rose, 7.5 mm wide × 7.5 mm long × 3 mm thick

5 faceted cat's-eye round glass beads, pink, 7 mm dia.

12 rose quartz rondelles, pink, 6 mm dia. × 4.5 mm wide

5 cat's-eye round glass beads, pink, 5.5 mm dia.

5 g seed beads, silver lined, raspberry, size 11/0

One 2-part barrette (barrette platform and beading oval with holes), gold, 1½ in/4 cm wide × 3 in/7.5 cm long × ½ in/12 mm thick

Transite

Cyanoacrylate liquid

TOOLS

Ruler

Wire cutters

Chain-nose pliers

Tweezers (optional)

FINISHED SIZE

2 in/5 cm wide × 3½ in/8.9 cm long × ½ in/ 13 mm thick

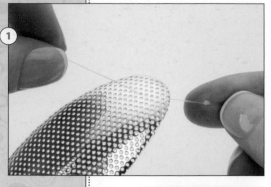

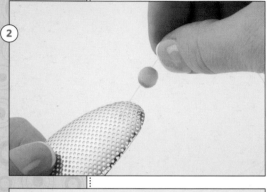

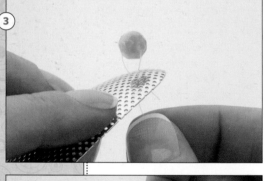

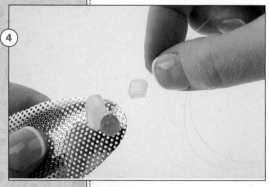

DIRECTIONS

1 :: Use wire cutters to cut a 12-in/30.5-cm length of transite and make a double overhand knot at one end. (See "How to Make a Double Overhand Knot," page 342.) Secure the knot with a drop of glue. Thread the opposite end of the transite through the tip of the beading oval from the back side. Pull it so that the knot is tight against the oval. If necessary, make a second or third knot to make it thicker.

2 :: String one faceted round pink cat's-eye bead onto the nonknotted end of the transite.

3 :: Thread the same end of the transite through an adjacent hole in the beading oval and pull it tight so the bead rests flat. Adjust the bead so its holes are parallel with the oval.

4 :: Insert the transite into an adjacent hole to bring the end back to the front side. Pull tight to eliminate any slack. Thread on the remaining beads in random order, weaving the transite in and out of the beading oval as you go. When the remaining transite is approximately 2 in/5 cm long, make a double overhand knot on the back side of the beading oval to secure it. Add a drop of glue to the knot. Repeat steps 1–4 to start a new strand. Cover the entire surface of the oval with beads.

5 :: Use seed beads on transite to fill in the spaces between the larger beads. Start a new strand as you did in step 1. Thread on five or six seed beads at once. Position the beaded strand between the larger beads, then thread the transite through a nearby hole. Repeat this step to continue filling in the spaces. Use tweezers to maneuver the beads into their proper position.

(continued page 254)

6 :: Position the beading oval on the barrette platform.

7 :: Use chain-nose pliers to close the prongs around the beading oval, securing the barrette platform.

●●● **TIPS** ●●●

If you have trouble securing the prongs on the bar-rette platform to the beading oval because there is a seed bead or two in the way, simply crush the bead between the tips of the pliers. Be sure to wear safety goggles, or cover the area with a cloth to keep the pieces contained.

Read "How to Use a Beading Disc," page 290, for more tips.

ORANGE BLOSSOM HAIR COMB

Go from shrinking violet to tiger lily with Orange Blossom, a hair comb that will add lively color and vintage style to any ensemble. Each flower in its trio is made from beaded-wire loops in citrus colors and accented with a colorful rhinestone raised high in a gold setting. The glamorous hit of sparkle is actually a cut-crystal button with a shank at the back that makes it easy to attach the button to the flower head. The lightweight beaded petals can be articulated in any direction, and, if accidentally crushed, they can be bent back to their original loop shape.

MATERIALS

3 hanks of silver-lined seed beads, size 11/0:

> 1 ruby-red grapefruit

> 1 tangerine

> 1 mandarin orange

3 rhinestone buttons, antique gold setting, 9 mm dia.:

> 1 ruby

> 1 tangerine

> 1 lemon

48 Austrian crystal bicones, 4 mm:

> 16 ruby-red grapefruit

> 16 tangerine

> 16 lemon

Gold wire, dead-soft, 24 gauge

Gold wire, dead-soft, 30 gauge

1 metal hair comb, gold, 3¾ in/9.5 cm long

TOOLS

Ruler

Wire cutters

Chain-nose pliers

Round-nose pliers

FINISHED SIZE

3 in/7.6 cm wide × 5¾ in/14.6 cm long

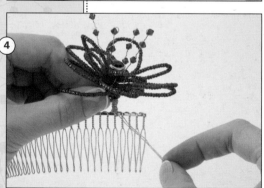

DIRECTIONS

1 :: Make one 3-in/7.5-cm dia. flower using the ruby-red grapefruit seed beads and 24-gauge wire. (See "How to Restring Small Beads" and "How to Make a Beaded Flower," pages 270 and 333.) Set it aside. Use wire cutters to cut four 6-in/15-cm lengths of 30-gauge wire. Using this wire, make four flower "stamens," with four ruby-red grapefruit bicones on each. (See "How to Make Beaded, Twisted Wire," page 336.) Insert one beaded stamen through the flower petals, pressing it against the center of the flower.

2 :: Secure the stamen at the base of the flower by twisting the wire ends around the stem. Add the remaining three beaded stamens, positioning them around the center of the flower and securing them at the base.

3 :: Use wire cutters to cut a 6-in/15-cm length of 30-gauge wire. Insert one end of the wire through the shank of the ruby rhinestone button and slide the button to the midpoint. Secure the wires to the shank by wrapping them a few times. Insert the wire ends through the flower petals until the button sits in the center of the flower. Secure the button by twisting the wire ends around the stem.

4 :: Use the wire flower stem to secure the beaded flower to the hair comb. Wrap the wires around the comb, securing the ends at the base of the flower. Use chain-nose pliers to press the wire ends flush against the base of the flower.

(continued page 258)

5 :: Repeat steps 1–4 to make the additional beaded flowers with their coordinating embellishments and attach them to the comb. Use wire cutters to cut a 6-in/15-cm length of 24-gauge wire. Use round-nose pliers to make a loop at one end of this wire to keep the beads from falling off. Thread on ruby-red grapefruit seed beads, leaving 1 in/2.5 cm of bare wire. Secure the free end of the wire by wrapping it around the base of the visible wire stem. Slide the beads down the wire to the point at which it was just secured. Wrap the beaded wire around the visible wire stem between the hair comb and the base of the flower until it's covered. Cut away the wire loop at the end of the wire and remove any excess beads. Secure the wire end by wrapping it to the base of the flower, hiding the cut wire end within the beadwork. Repeat this step to cover the exposed stems of the remaining two flowers, using the coordinating beads.

● ● ● **TIP** ● ● ●

These beaded flowers can be made in any size you can imagine. Make a field of little flowers and apply them to a barette, bracelet, or necklace. You can even add leaves and vines. If you make larger flowers or use larger beads, be sure to use a lower-gauge wire to support the frame.

TORCH SONG HEADBAND

Feathers and beads combine in a high-style accessory with movie-star glamour. Here, a plain headband is transformed into a modern fashion statement with retro style. A velvet flower with peacock feathers in iridescent greens and blues and light-catching crystal beads, secured to one side, provides a stunning accent. Discreet wraps of velvet ribbon conceal its construction. The headpiece is theatrical, but it may be just the accessory you are looking for when you make your dramatic entrance at your next soirée.

MATERIALS

1 velvet flower pin with 7-in/17-cm eyelash feathers, black, 12 cm wide × 11 cm long

1 Indian peacock eye feather, 6–8 in/15–20 cm long

2 Indian peacock feather pads, turquoise and gold, 3½ in/9 cm wide × 4½ in/11 cm long

9 glass briolettes, kelly green, 8 mm wide × 10½ mm long × 5½ mm thick

3 Austrian crystal bicones, turquoise, 6 mm

3 Austrian crystal bicones, Indian red, 4 mm

12 Austrian crystal flat-back rhinestones, metallic gold, SS-16, 4 mm dia.

¼ yard/23 cm one-sided fusible webbing

⅓ yard/30.5 cm velvet ribbon, black, 9 mm wide

Gold wire, dead-soft, 24 gauge

Gold wire, dead-soft, 26 gauge

1 plastic headband, black, 7 mm wide × 15 in/ 38 cm long

High-tack white glue

Permanent adhesive

Cyanoacrylate gel

TOOLS

Scissors

Household iron

Aluminum foil

Cookie sheet

Pencil or fabric marker

Ruler

Wire cutters

Chain-nose pliers

FINISHED SIZE

3 in/7.6 wide × 9 in/22.9 cm long × 2 in/5 cm thick

(Flower and feather decoration only.)

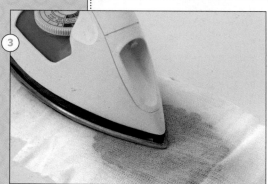

DIRECTIONS

1 :: If necessary, remove the pin, and anything else that doesn't serve the final design, from the premade flower.

2 :: Measure and cut two 4-in/10-cm x 5-in/12-cm rectangles of fusible webbing. Set these aside. Cover a cookie sheet with aluminum foil. Place one feather pad wrong side up on the cookie sheet. Position one rectangle of fusible webbing, glue side down, over the feather pad.

3 :: Run a household iron on a high setting, with all water removed, over the fusible webbing to melt the glue onto the feather pad. Use scissors to trim away any excess webbing. Repeat steps 2–3 with the second feather pad. Then use the velvet flower petals as templates and the pencil to trace them onto the fusible webbing. Cut out the twelve traced petals from the feather pad.

4 :: Use high-tack white glue to adhere the feather petals to the underside of the velvet petals. Trim away any excess. Use the remaining feather scraps to cover the base and stem of the velvet flower. Let dry completely. Use wire cutters to trim the peacock eye feather to 7 in/17 cm. Use wire cutters to cut a 6-in/15-cm length of 26-gauge wire. Wrap a third of the wire around the base of the peacock feather. Position the feather in the center of the flower and use the wire to secure it to the base of the center feathers.

(continued page 262)

5 :: Make a total of nine beaded wires, three of each item shown in the photo at left. Make one beaded branch with three green briolettes. (See "How to Make a Beaded Branch," page 337.) Repeat these steps to make two more branches, each with three green briolettes. Make one twisted wire with one turquoise bicone, and make one twisted wire with one Indian red bicone. (See "How to Make Beaded, Twisted Wire," page 336.) Repeat these steps to make four more twisted wires: two each with one turquoise bicone and two each with one Indian red bicone.

6 :: Separate the twisted wires at the base of one branch. Use chain-nose pliers to bend them at a 90-degree angle. Wrap the wire ends around the base of the center feathers.

7 :: To stabilize and secure the beaded branch, use chain-nose pliers to twist the wire ends on the opposite side. Trim away excess wire.

8 :: Repeat steps 6–7 to add two more green branches, three turquoise bicones, and three red bicones to the center of the flower.

9 :: Cut a 3-in/7.5-cm piece of velvet ribbon. Apply small dabs of permanent adhesive on the wires wrapped around the base of the center feathers in steps 6–8. Wrap the ribbon around the glued area to conceal the twisted wire ends. Trim away excess ribbon.

10 :: Use cyanoacrylate to glue one rhinestone to the tip of every black velvet petal.

11 :: Position the flower on the headband as shown so it sits above the ear or as desired. Wrap an 8-in/20-cm length of 24-gauge wire around the stem and the headband.

12 :: Gently lift the flower to apply permanent adhesive to the headband. Press the flower to the headband and hold it in place. Let dry.

13 :: Apply permanent adhesive to the wire-wrapped flower stem and headband. Use lengths of velvet ribbon to cover the wire. Repeat this step to add velvet ribbon to the opposite headband end. Note: This headband came with grosgrain ribbon on the ends. In this case, simply cover it with the velvet ribbon.

•••• TIPS ••••

If you would prefer to accent a ponytail or a bun, simply wire the finished velvet flower onto a hair comb instead of a headband.

To eliminate any traces of fusible webbing along the edges of the glued petals, run a permanent black marker around the edges.

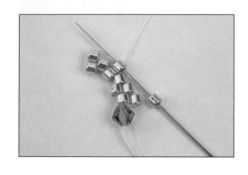

TECHNIQUES

TECHNIQUES TABLE *of* CONTENTS

STRINGING AND FINISHING

You can choose from many kinds of stringing materials, depending on the weight, size, and type of beads you're using and the look you want. Each stringing material can be finished in a variety of ways, as detailed here; see also "Finishing Techniques," page 56. Here are just a few examples of stringing materials and finishing techniques.

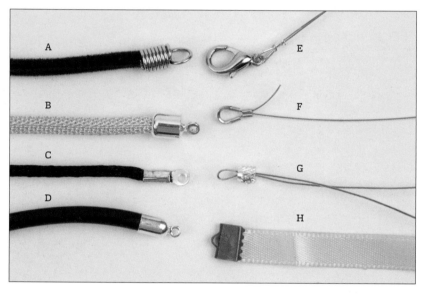

LEFT SIDE, TOP TO BOTTOM

A :: Velvet cord with coil end

B :: Round hollow-mesh chain with end cap

C :: Satin cord with foldover crimp end

D :: Rubber tubing with end cap

RIGHT SIDE, TOP TO BOTTOM:

E :: Beading wire with crimp tube, French bullion wire and lobster clasp

F :: Beading wire with crimp tube and wire guardian

G :: Beading wire with Scrimp Bead

H :: Ribbon with clamp end

how to KEEP BEADS FROM FALLING OFF YOUR STRINGING MATERIAL

Sometimes you'll want to string your beads before you finish the ends of your stringing material. You'll need to temporarily secure one end so the beads stay on until you're ready; there are multiple techniques for keeping them in place.

If you must repeatedly secure and free up stringing material while making a project, a clamp or clip is the best choice (see the Hard Candy Cocktail Rings, www.chroniclebooks.com/beading). They can be used on beading wire, transite, monofilament, and most other stringing materials.

To secure a length of wire, make a small loop at one end using round-nose pliers (see steps 9–11 of the Bisou bracelet, page 131). After you've strung the beads, you can then cut away the end loop.

A tension bead or bead stopper is most commonly used with thread. It is a great way to create tension on a strand when bead weaving; it keeps beads on the thread, and it can easily be removed. (See "How to Start a Single-Threaded Strand with a Bead Stopper," page 348.)

You can also use masking tape to temporarily secure the end of stringing material (see this method used with silk cord in the Café au Lait necklace, page 109).

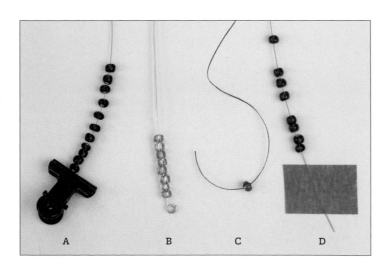

FROM LEFT TO RIGHT:

A :: Clip

B :: Wire loop

C :: Tension bead or bead stopper

D :: Masking tape

Small beads, such as seed beads, are sold both loose (in vials and packages) and pre-strung (in hanks). Prestrung beads are on weak cotton thread, so you must restring them, a laborious process because each must be strung individually. This technique makes the task easier. Use it with any stiff stringing material like wire, nylon-coated beading wire, and transite, or any soft stringing material along with a needle.

DIRECTIONS

1 :: Ready the wire or other stringing material by securing one end. (See "How to Keep Beads from Falling Off Your Stringing Material," page 209.) Lay the hank of beads on a clean, flat work surface. Find the knot or juncture where the strands meet.

2 :: Separate one beaded thread from the hank near the knot. Use scissors to carefully cut the thread from the hank. Knot the end to prevent the beads from falling off. Follow the beaded thread to its opposite end, where it is also attached to the knot. Cut the thread and secure the strand with your fingers.

3 :: Insert the unsecured end of the wire into the unsecured end of the beaded thread while still holding on to the thread end.

4 :: Simultaneously push the wire forward through the bead holes and pull the thread backward. The beads are now on both thread and wire.

5 :: Without letting go of the wire or thread, lift only the tip of the wire. Continue to hold the wire, but let the end of the thread drop, and grasp it again where the thread meets the tip of the wire. Lift the wire and the thread vertically. Gently pull the thread away from the wire; the beads will slide off the thread and down the wire. Repeat steps 3–5 to add more beads to the same wire.

how to STRING BEADS BETWEEN BUTTON OR BEAD SHANKS

Buttons and beads with shanks are generally used only in bracelet and necklace designs because they can lie flat with their back sides concealed. But you don't always need to hide their back sides. I was able to use rhinestone beads with two rows of shanks on their back sides in the Aria earrings (page 167), even though both sides were visible, by threading beads between the shanks. Here is a technique that makes stringing the beads easier.

DIRECTIONS

1 :: Insert one end of the beading wire through only the first shank.

2 :: Push the beading wire up between the shanks and away from the bead. Thread on a bead and let it slide down the wire until it sits against the first shank.

3 :: While keeping the bead tipped at an angle, slowly and gently slide the beading wire back in the direction from which it came until it can be threaded through the second shank.

Wire guardians and French bullion wire are used to hide the utilitarian-looking loops created when stringing material is attached to a jump ring, clasp, end bar, or the like. Stringing material has to withstand friction at these connection points, and French bullion wire and wire guardians help prevent it from wearing out prematurely. Both are typically used with nylon-coated beading wire, but you can use either with other stringing materials. French bullion wire works very well with silk and satin cording. The directions below explain how to use a wire guardian. For details on how to use French bullion wire, see "How to Secure a Crimp Tube with Crimping Pliers," page 274.

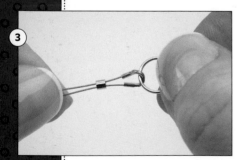

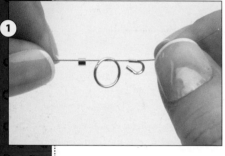

DIRECTIONS

1 :: Thread a crimp tube, a jump ring, or other end piece, and the cylinder on one side of a wire guardian, onto one end of the beading wire.

2 :: Make a loop at the end of the beading wire and insert the end into the cylinder on the opposite side of the wire guardian.

3 :: Pull the end of the beading wire through the wire guardian so it sits in the guardian's horseshoe-shaped channel. Move the jump ring up the beading wire and onto the wire guardian. Now thread the short wire end into the crimp tube. Slide the crimp tube up the wires, stopping $1/32$ in/1 mm before the guardian. Secure the beading wire using crimping pliers. (See "How to Secure a Crimp Tube with Crimping Pliers," page 274.)

Crimp tubes and beads are used to attach nylon-coated beading wire to metal findings such as clasps, jump rings, and end bars, and to secure groups of beads in specific positions on a length of beading wire. (The difference between crimp tubes and crimp beads is explained on page 54 of the glossary.) They are extremely effective in keeping even heavy beads in place, whether you're stringing an entire strand or creating an illusion effect.

Crimp tubes and beads are often paired with beading wire because the wire is strong enough to withstand the friction of the metal crimp. These tubes and beads can be used to secure other stringing materials as well, such as elastic stringing cord and transite, but cord and thread will most likely fray when exposed to their metal edges and are much better secured with knots.

Crimp tubes are secured using chain-nose pliers or crimping pliers. Crimp beads are best secured with chain-nose pliers. It *is* possible to use only the crescent-shaped portion of crimping pliers to secure a crimp bead, but only with crimps made from soft metals. If you use crimping pliers with beads made from base metals, they'll leave jagged shards of metal that do not look very pretty and could cause injury.

When choosing a crimp tube or bead, it is important to select one through which strands can snugly pass (see the chart on page 36 of the glossary for guidelines). There are no hard-and-fast rules stating that you should always use a particular size of crimp with a particular size of beading wire. Some beaders like their crimps slightly bigger (as I do); others, slightly smaller.

Any time you use crimp beads or tubes, remember these important points:

IMPORTANT ::

• When you slide the crimp tube or bead up toward the piece you are attaching it to—the jump ring or clasp—it is important that you not place the tube or bead directly against the piece. The loop you form with the beading wire needs enough room to pivot and swing. If the wire is too snug or unable to move, the beading wire will likely snap.

• After securing the crimp tube or bead, gently tug on the longer beading wire to make sure the wires hold. If the wires slip out of place, you either didn't crimp the tube or bead properly or it is too large. Always be sure to check your wires before you string on any beads.

how to SECURE A CRIMP TUBE WITH CRIMPING PLIERS

The photos here also show you how to use French bullion wire (see "How to Cover and Protect Stringing Material" on page 272 for more details). To use a crimp tube without French bullion wire, disregard the notes in parentheses and move on to the next step.

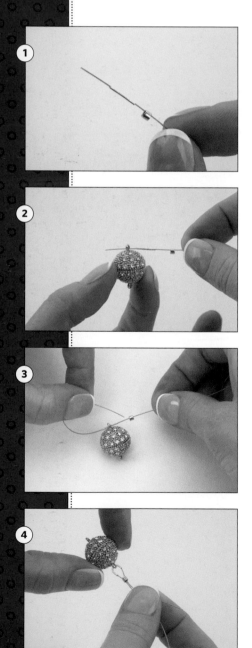

DIRECTIONS

1 :: Thread a crimp tube onto one end of a length of beading wire. (If using French bullion wire, use wire cutters to cut a ¼-in/6-mm length of bullion and thread it onto the beading wire following the crimp tube, as shown.)

2 :: Thread the end of the beading wire onto a clasp.

3 :: Thread the end of the short wire back through the crimp tube to create a loop and a 2-in/5-cm tail.

4 :: Hold both wires and slide the crimp tube up toward the base of the clasp. Stop a few millimeters away from the base of the clasp. (If using French bullion wire, center it on the loop of beading wire so that equal lengths of bullion wire extend from the right and left sides of the clasp, as shown in step 6.)

5 :: Place the crimp tube in the back (crescent) portion of the crimping pliers. Position the beading wires so that one wire is against the far right side and the other wire is against the far left side of the tube's interior. Squeeze the pliers closed.

6 :: One wire now should be in each channel of the crimp tube, as shown in image 6.

7 :: Rotate the crimp tube 90 degrees so it's on its side and place it in the front (round) portion of the crimping pliers. Squeeze the pliers closed to fold the crimp tube in half.

8 :: The completed crimp tube should look as shown in image 8.

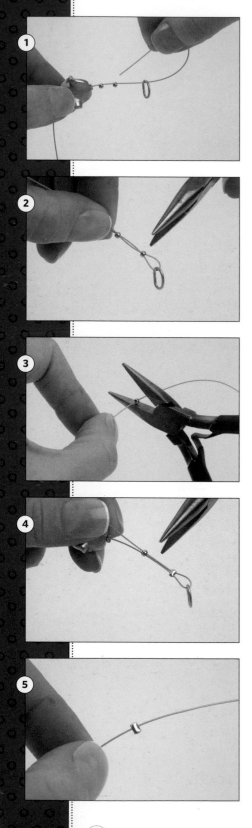

To see this technique used in a project, see the Sun-Kissed necklace (page 83). The photos below show two crimp beads being used, but only one is necessary in this technique.

DIRECTIONS

1 :: Thread a crimp bead and a jump ring onto one end of a length of beading wire. Thread the end of the short wire back through the crimp bead to create a loop and a 2-in/5-cm tail.

2 :: Hold both wires and slide the crimp bead up toward the base of the jump ring. Stop a few millimeters away from the base of the jump ring. Or for a different style, make a larger loop, as shown. Place the crimp bead in the jaws of chain-nose pliers.

3 :: Position the pliers as shown.

4 :: Squeeze the pliers closed to flatten the crimp bead, securing it to the strands. Note the different appearance of the crimped crimp bead (the one closest to the jump ring) and the uncrimped crimp bead.

5 :: The finished, secured crimp bead should look as shown in image 5.

If the appearance of a crimp bead secured with chain-nose pliers or a crimp tube secured with crimping pliers doesn't work with your design, try crimp covers as another decorative option. They are small, hollow, round metal beads that are fitted around crimps to conceal them.

They are easiest to use with a crimp tube that has been secured with crimping pliers, which makes the tube very compact. When choosing a crimp cover (see page 54 in the glossary for more information on crimp covers), select one that is 1 mm wider than the crimp tube. However, since crimp tubes come not only in different widths but in different lengths, choose a crimp cover 1 mm larger than the tube's largest dimension.

You can use crimp covers with crimp beads and tubes secured with chain-nose pliers, but you will need to choose a crimp cover that is 1 mm larger than the flattened width, not the original diameter, of the bead or tube.

I use chain-nose pliers to secure crimp covers around crimp tubes, but you can also use the front (round) portion of crimping pliers. Crimping pliers make closing the crimp cover easy because their round portion exerts leverage on all sides. But standard-size crimping pliers can be used only with 2 mm x 1 mm and 2 mm x 2 mm crimp tubes. Using standard crimping pliers with larger covers dents their metal. Crimping pliers are available in extra-large and micro sizes. But if you don't want to spend money on extra tools, chain-nose pliers work equally well.

DIRECTIONS

1 :: After you're secured a crimp tube to the beading wire, grasp one crimp cover, with the opening facing outward, in the tips of chain-nose pliers.

2 :: Center the crimp cover over the crimp tube.

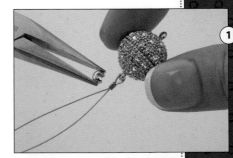

3 :: Squeeze the pliers, using gentle and steady pressure, until the edges of the crimp cover touch. Ensure that there are no gaps or openings. The closed crimp cover should look like a small round bead, as shown.

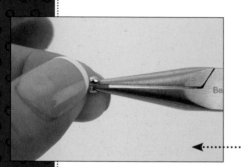

• • • TIP • • •

Sometimes the opening in a crimp cover is not wide enough to accommodate your crimp tube, even though you selected the appropriate size. It's just the way the crimp cover was manufactured. But you can use needle-nose pliers to open the cover a bit more, a trick that works best with sterling-silver or gold-filled (soft metal) crimp covers. With a little practice, you can nudge open crimp covers made from base metals as well. Just remember that opening and closing the cover repeatedly weakens it, so don't overdo it.

Insert the nose of the needle-nose pliers into the crimp cover. Apply gentle pressure on the pliers' handles to open the jaws and widen the cover's opening.

how to USE MAGIC CRIMPING PLIERS

Magic Crimping Pliers are a special tool that turns crimp tubes directly into round beads. This tool not only secures the beading wire with the crimp tube, as regular crimping pliers do, but also shapes the crimp to give you the same look that you would get by using a crimp cover, without the extra step.

Their manufacturer recommends that Magic Crimping Pliers be used only with .018-in/0.46 mm dia. and .019 in/0.48 mm dia. nylon-coated beading wire and 2 mm sterling-silver or gold-filled crimp tubes because these metals are softer and easier to shape without getting overworked and breaking. You can use Magic Crimping Pliers with base-metal crimp tubes, but it takes a lot more practice, and you should definitely be prepared to break some.

DIRECTIONS

1 :: Thread a 2 mm crimp tube and a clasp onto the end of a length of .019-in/0.48-mm dia. beading wire. Thread the short end of the wire back through the crimp tube to create a loop and a 2-in/5-cm tail. Slide the crimp tube up toward the bottom of the clasp. Stop a few millimeters away from the base of the clasp. Position the crimp tube as shown, directly in the center of the Magic Crimping Pliers. Squeeze the pliers closed.

2 :: The four corners of the 2 mm crimp tube should now be pinched flat, and the tube should look like a ravioli.

3 :: Rotate the crimp tube 90 degrees so it's on its side, and position it directly in the center of the pliers. Squeeze the pliers closed.

4 :: The crimp tube should now begin to resemble a round bead.

5 :: Rotate the tube 45 degrees and place it back in the center of the pliers. Squeeze the pliers closed.

6 :: Repeat step 5 every 45 degrees. Work around the entire circumference to shape the tube into a round bead.

IMPORTANT :: When you slide the crimp tube up toward the piece you are attaching it to—the jump ring or clasp—do not place the tube directly against the piece. The loop you form with the beading wire needs enough room to pivot and swing. If the wire is too snug or unable to move, the beading wire will likely snap.

After securing the crimp tube, gently tug on the longer beading wire to make sure the wires hold. If the wires slip out of place, either you didn't crimp it properly or your crimp tube or bead is too large. Always check your wires before you string on any beads.

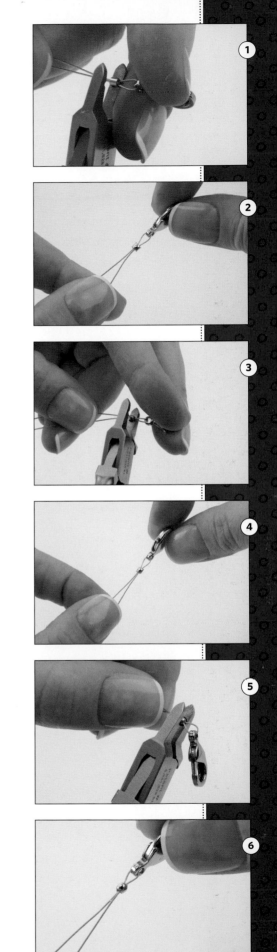

Scrimp Beads can be used instead of crimp beads or crimp tubes. They are strung on nylon-coated beading wire in the same way that crimp beads and tubes are, but they are secured differently: a very small screw on the side of the Scrimp Bead is tightened to hold the wires in place.

You will need to buy a special screwdriver specifically designed for use with Scrimp Beads. I recommend that you buy a kit that includes a screwdriver, Scrimp Beads, and extra screws (see "Sources and Resources"). The screws are tiny and very easy to lose, so you'll really appreciate the extra ones.

Scrimp Beads are adjustable and reusable. If you are unhappy with a bead's original placement, simply unscrew it, reposition it, and secure it again. To permanently fix a Scrimp Bead in place, place a drop of cyanoacrylate into the bead's barrel after securing the screw.

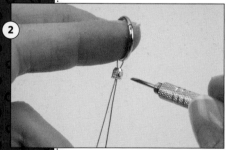

DIRECTIONS

1 :: Place a screw into one Scrimp Bead. Turn the screw only a few times so it catches and holds but doesn't obstruct the bead hole. Thread it and a jump ring (or clasp) onto the end of a length of beading wire.

2 :: Thread the short end of the wire back through the Scrimp Bead to create a loop and a 2-in/5-cm tail. Slide the Scrimp Bead up toward the bottom of the jump ring. Stop a few millimeters away from the base of the jump ring. Use the screwdriver to tighten the screw.

3 :: Optional: Put a drop of glue into the barrel of the Scrimp Bead. Let dry.

IMPORTANT :: After securing the Scrimp Bead, gently tug on the longer beading wire to make sure the wires hold. If the wires slip out of place, make sure the screw has been properly tightened. Always check your wires before you string on any beads.

> ● ● ● **TIP** ● ● ●
>
> Scrimp Beads can also be used to secure beads on wire. For this alternative way to use them, see the Mint Julep earrings, page 185.

how to USE SMART BEADS

Smart Beads look like ordinary gold and silver round beads but have a silicone lining that allows them to grip stringing materials, which make them easy to use. They are ideal replacements for crimp beads to keep groups of lightweight beads clustered together and secure, as in a floating illusion necklace like Sun-Kissed (page 82) and the Frosting earrings (page 181).

DIRECTIONS

1 :: Thread a Smart Bead onto the wire or other stringing material.

2 :: Slide the Smart Bead against a group of beads to hold them in place.

> ● ● ● **TIP** ● ● ●
>
> To secure beads on an illusion necklace, thread one Smart Bead on each side of the group of beads to hold them in place.

how to ATTACH A CLAMSHELL

Clamshells are part of a finding category called bead tips. They are used mainly with stringing materials that you finish by knotting, such as cord and thread, but they can be used with other stringing materials, too.

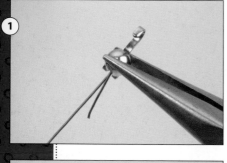

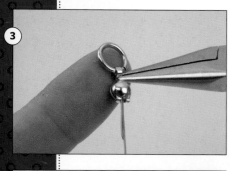

DIRECTIONS

1 :: Use chain-nose pliers to grasp the open halves of the clamshell. Slowly squeeze the halves together, trapping the knot inside.

2 :: Place a jump ring or other connector in the clamshell's hook as shown. Grasp the front of the hook using chain-nose pliers.

3 :: Rotate the pliers toward yourself, bending the hook around the jump ring to secure it.

4 :: Detail: This is a side view of a properly closed clamshell.

IMPORTANT :: Clamshells should be added or removed only by rolling or unrolling them by their hooks, as described in steps 2–3. Do not squeeze the entire clamshell (hook and clam) in the jaws of the pliers. You will weaken the metal and break off the hook.

how to USE A CLAMSHELL TO COVER A CRIMP TUBE OR BEAD

When I'm making a necklace, such as Bali Ha'i (page 79), that uses heavy beads, I use a clamshell in addition to a crimp tube and beading wire for extra security. This is a nontraditional choice: clamshells are typically used with thread and cord, and crimps are used with beading wire. In this case, though, the clamshell serves two purposes. It conceals the crimp (as a crimp cover would) and helps the crimp support the beads' weight.

DIRECTIONS

1 :: Use wire cutters to cut a length of beading wire. Thread one end of the strand through a clamshell, a crimp tube, and the connector loop on a clasp.

2 :: Thread the short end of the strand back through the crimp tube. Use the crimp tube and crimping pliers to secure the strands. (See "How to Secure a Crimp Tube with Crimping Pliers," page 274.)

3 :: Slide the clamshell up along the strands until the crimp bead is inside the clamshell and the hook on the clamshell is threaded onto the clasp.

4 :: Use chain-nose pliers to close the clamshell, trapping the crimp bead inside.

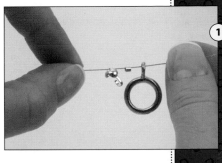

5 :: Use chain-nose pliers to grasp the hook and roll it forward to secure the clamshell to the clasp and to hide the beading-wire loop.

Creating a knotted necklace has not only a practical purpose but an aesthetic one. Knots keep beads from rubbing against one another (particularly important for delicate pearls and semiprecious stones) and protect you from losing any beads should the necklace break. Knotting also elevates the look of your pieces by allowing beads to drape elegantly, even if they're not expensive ones.

Knotted necklaces are traditionally made with soft stringing materials such as silk cord. Choose a cord size that fills the bead hole. When you combine different-size beads with accordingly different-size holes, as I did in the Café au Lait necklace (page 109), things get tricky. The cord has to be narrow enough to fit through the smallest bead hole, but not so narrow that when it's knotted the largest bead hole can slide over the knot; the knots must keep the beads in position. Test your beads on a few sizes of cord to see which works.

A useful tip: Some beads, including pearls and crystal rondelles, are available with extra-large holes. You can combine small pearls with extra-large holes and larger pearls with regular-size holes, making finding the right size of cord easier.

Knotting silk cord requires a needle. You can buy silk cord with a twisted wire needle already attached to it. It is usually sold wrapped on a card. Open the package and remove all the cord from the card. Do not cut it! Straighten out both the needle (it's usually folded in half) and the cord; you might iron the cord if its folds are especially stubborn.

Always try to make your knots as uniform as possible. And knot the cord in the same direction every time. Doing so will prevent the line of beads from becoming too stiff, bunching up, or lying incorrectly when the necklace is worn.

IMPORTANT :: A knotted strand requires more cord than an unknotted piece. For example, 20 in/51 cm of strung beads is the equivalent of a 22-in/56-cm strand of beads with knots tied between them. To calculate the amount of cord you need, multiply the finished strand length you want by three. You will need a 66-in/128-cm-length of cord to achieve a 22-in/56-cm knotted strand.

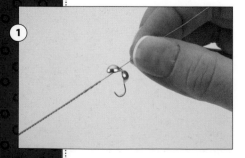

DIRECTIONS

1 :: Make an overhand knot on the end of the silk beading cord. (See "How to Make a Single Overhand Knot," page 342.) On the opposite needle end, thread on one clamshell, inserting the needle into the hole from the inside. Slide the clamshell down toward the knot.

2 :: When the knot is about 1 in/2.5 cm away from the clamshell, apply a drop of crystal cement or cyanoacrylate to secure it; let the glue dry. Pull the knot into the clamshell. Trim off the excess cord end and use chain-nose pliers to close the clamshell.

3 :: Thread on one bead and slide it to the end with the clamshell.

4 :: Tie a single overhand knot, but do not pull it tight.

5 :: While holding the cord with one hand, use the other hand to place the tips of tweezers through the knot and against the bead.

6 :: While holding the tweezers, pull the cord to tighten the knot flush against the bead.

7 :: Repeat steps 3–6 as many times as necessary to achieve the desired strand length. To finish the strand, thread the needle through the remaining clamshell. Tie a single overhand knot that sits in the clamshell; add glue. Trim away excess cord and close the clamshell. The strand is now complete. See "How to Attach a Clamshell," page 282, to learn how the strand can be attached to end bars, jump rings, and other findings.

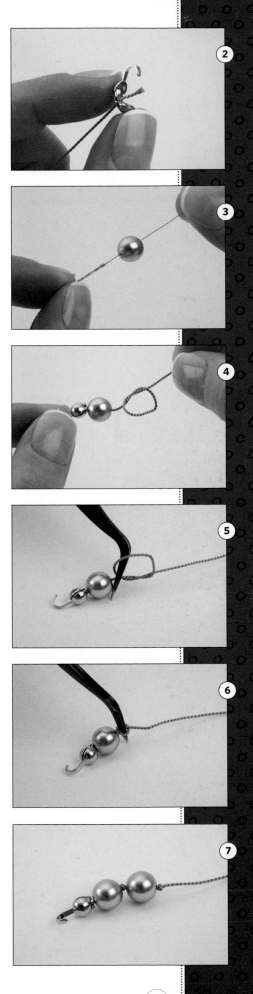

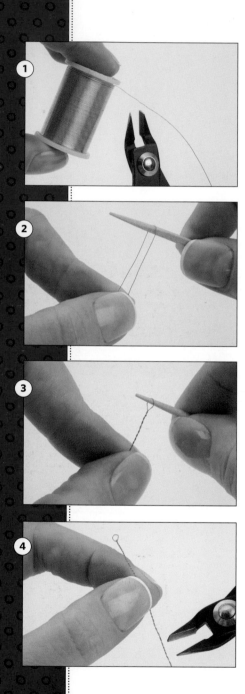

You can buy ready-made twisted wire needles, but there are always those occasions when you break your last one midproject. Never fear: they are super-simple to make, allowing you to get right back to your beading.

DIRECTIONS

1 :: Measure and cut a 6-in/15-cm length of 28-gauge half-hard wire. Note: You can also use nylon pliers to harden the dead-soft wire that you're more likely to have on hand. See "How to Work-Harden Wire," page 303.

2 :: Fold the wire around a toothpick as shown.

3 :: Twist the pair of wires between your fingers to form a straight spiral with a loop. Do not overtwist the wire.

4 :: Slide the loop off the toothpick. Using wire cutters, snip the wires evenly across to make the needle.

Ribbon has more body than other stringing materials and can hold beads in place without the use of crimps or knots, allowing you to create a floating design. You will be most successful using narrow widths of ribbon made from light fabrics, such as organdy and organza. To see this technique used, see the Snow Queen necklace, page 105.

Beads can be strung directly onto lengths of ribbon with the help of a twisted wire needle with a large collapsible eye that can accommodate the width and bulk of the ribbon.

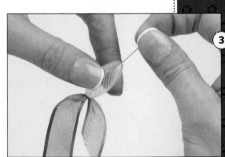

DIRECTIONS

1 :: Use scissors to cut a sharp angle at one end of the ribbon. (This will aid in threading the needle.) Thread the ribbon through the eye. Pull the ribbon through, leaving a 1-in/2.5-cm to 1½-in/4-cm tail.

2 :: Thread one bead onto the needle.

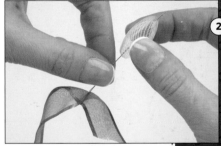

3 :: Slide the bead down the needle and onto the ribbon.

• • • TIP • • •

You need only gentle pressure to slide the bead onto the ribbon. Do not force it or you may crack or break your bead. If your bead won't move past the needle's eye, use a narrower ribbon.

how to USE A CLAMP END WITH RIBBON

There are a number of ways to finish ribbon used as stringing material. If you prefer not to gather the ends inside an end cap (see below), you can maintain the flat look of a ribbon from end to end by choosing a clamp end. They are available in various metal finishes and widths, so you can always find one that coordinates with your piece. Select one that is as wide as the ribbon. If one size seems a little too wide and another a little too narrow, choose the one that is slightly wider than the ribbon.

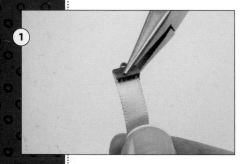

DIRECTIONS

1 :: Apply a small amount of permanent adhesive or crystal cement to the interior of one clamp end. Position the ribbon end on the glue. Use chain-nose pliers to squeeze the clamp end together, securing the ribbon inside. Let the glue dry. Repeat this step on the opposite ribbon end.

how to USE AN END CAP WITH RIBBON

End caps are another way to finish ribbon. The ribbon end is gathered, fitted, and glued into an end cap with a connector loop so you can attach a clasp. To see this technique used in a project, see the Snow Queen necklace, page 105.

DIRECTIONS

1 :: Tie a knot at one end of the ribbon. Use chain-nose pliers to grasp the end of the ribbon, and pull to tighten the knot. Trim away excess ribbon.

2 :: Apply crystal cement to the knot. Use a toothpick to push the knot into one end cap connector. Let the glue dry. Repeat steps 1–2 to secure another end cap connector to the opposite ribbon end.

how to MAKE A RIBBON CLASP

Ribbon clasps can add a bold, dramatic statement or an understated, elegant element to your designs. See the Watercolors necklace, www.chroniclebooks.com/beading, for inspiration.

DIRECTIONS

1 :: The easiest way to make a ribbon clasp is to attach all the beaded strands in a multistrand piece to large jump rings at both ends. Then thread the ribbon through the rings and tie it in a bow at the back of your neck or wrist.

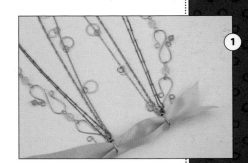

• • • TIP • • •

An alternative is to cut the desired length of ribbon into two equal parts. Tie one half to one jump ring using a double overhand knot. (See "How to Make a Double Overhand Knot," page 342.) Trim away the excess ribbon and use high-tack white glue to secure the short trimmed end to the long end. Repeat these steps with the remaining length of ribbon. Tie a bow at the back of your neck or wrist.

how to MAKE A CONTINUOUS-STRAND NECKLACE

A continuous-strand necklace has no clasp, so it has to be long enough to fit over your head. The recommended minimum length is at least 24 in/61 cm. The longer the necklace is, the more ways you can wear it—doubling and tripling the strands around your neck or tying it in a knot.

This technique requires securing the strand's two ends together with knots that can be hidden within the beads, so you must choose a stringing material that can be knotted easily, such as silk cord, transite, or beading thread. See the Pink Champagne necklace, page 101, for step-by-step instructions.

how to USE A BEADING DISC

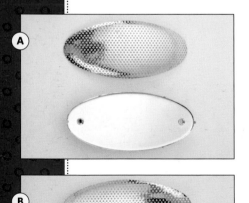

Perforated beading discs are thin, convex metal discs with small holes on which you "sew" beads. Then you secure the beaded discs to various kinds of backings, such as pin backs, clip earrings, post earrings, ring forms, and barrettes, to name just a few. Beading discs can also be purchased alone and turned into finished beaded elements that you can add to necklaces or bracelets any way you want. You can find them in gold and silver and all sorts of shapes. For examples of how to use a beading disc, see the following projects:

BEE MINE RING, page 203

PLUM DELICIOUS RING, page 215

RASPBERRY BARRETTE, page 251

A ∷ **TOP VIEW OF BEADING DISC AND BARRETTE BACKING**

B ∷ **BOTTOM VIEW OF BEADING DISC AND BARRETTE BACKING**

The simplest project to make with elastic stringing cord is a bracelet. Since no clasp is required, you need to know only how to make a simple square knot to secure its ends together. This is a wonderful project if you're just learning how to bead: it's easy and gives you near-instant results. Despite this technique's simplicity, you will still be able to make elegant and beautiful jewelry with it if you choose attractive beads.

DIRECTIONS

1 :: Cut a length of cord 4 in/10 cm longer than the desired finished length. Temporarily secure one end of the elastic cord. (See "How to Keep Beads from Falling Off Your Stringing Material," page 269.)

2 :: String on the beads.

3 :: Free up both ends, bring them together, and tie a square knot. (See "How to Make a Square Knot," page 344.) Add a drop of crystal cement; let the glue dry.

4 :: Trim the elastic tails and use a toothpick to push the knot inside the nearest bead hole to hide it.

YOU CAN ALSO SECURE ELASTIC STRINGING CORD WITH A CRIMP TUBE INSTEAD OF A KNOT.

1 :: Choose a crimp tube large enough that the cord can pass through twice. Repeat steps 1–2. Bring the ends together, but do not tie a knot.

2 :: Thread a crimp tube onto one cord end. Thread the other cord end through the crimp tube from its opposite side. The cord ends should form an X, intersecting in the crimp tube.

3 :: Pull both ends to eliminate slack in the cord, and use chain-nose pliers to flatten the crimp tube. Trim away excess cord.

NOTE :: SOME BEADERS WARN AGAINST USING CRIMP TUBES WITH ELASTIC BECAUSE THEIR SHARP METAL EDGES CAN CUT INTO THE CORD.

IMPORTANT :: ELASTIC STRINGING CORD WEARS OUT MORE QUICKLY THAN OTHER STRINGING MATERIALS, SO KEEP THESE THINGS IN MIND:

• Elastic stringing cord is not a good choice for heavy beads or ones with rough or sharp holes.

• The elastic cord should be as wide as the bead holes. Elastic cord with a smaller diameter will rub against the inside of the bead holes, causing it to fray and break.

• When you tie the knot, try to stretch only the tails making the knot. The rest of the elastic running through the beads should be in the relaxed, unstretched position as much as possible.

• If the beads are strung too tightly, the bracelet is more likely to weaken and break under the repeated strain it endures as you put it on and take it off.

Needles are usually necessary to string beads on soft stringing materials. Sometimes, though, there isn't enough room in a bead hole to accommodate the width of both the stringing material and its tail (the stringing material that is threaded through the needle and folded over). In such cases, turn your stringing material itself into a needle. This technique works on elastic stringing cord, silk cord, and satin rattail, to name a few.

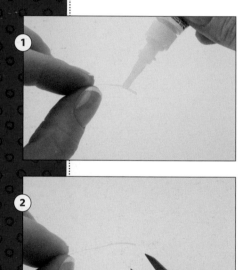

DIRECTIONS

1 :: Apply a few small drops of cyanoacrylate to a ½-in/12-mm length at the end of the stringing material. Let the glue dry. Apply more glue if necessary until the end is stiff and will maintain its shape as it passes through a bead.

2 :: Cut the very tip at an angle to create the point of the "needle." Repeat steps 1–2 to refresh the "needle" when necessary.

> ••• **TIP** •••
>
> If you don't have cyanoacrylate on hand, you can use other types of glues, even clear nail polish, as long as it makes the stringing material rigid.

Coil ends (see page 51 in the glossary) are most commonly used to secure the ends of soft stringing materials such as velvet or satin cord. They can be purchased, but it's just as easy to make your own.

To use ready-made coil ends, add a drop of crystal cement or permanent adhesive to the end of the cord. Slide the coil end onto the cord until the top wire coil is flush with the cut end of the cord. Then use chain-nose pliers to squeeze the bottom few coils around the cord to secure it. After the glue has dried, tug on the cord to make sure it will hold.

Here I used coil ends in a nontraditional way, applying them to a length of rhinestone-studded chain I harvested from costume jewelry. If you use parts of costume jewelry, you should salvage any loops or links that are attached to the pieces you want. In this case, there were none, so I needed to find a way to add a connector to the ends of the chain. A coil end was the best solution. See the directions below to add a coil end to chain and the Carnavale earrings (page 161) for inspiration.

DIRECTIONS

1 :: Use wire cutters to cut a 6-in/15-cm length of 24-gauge wire. Position the wire across the top of the rhinestone chain, leaving a 1-in/2.5-cm tail. Hold the 1-in/2.5-cm tail against the rhinestone chain stem. With the other hand, grasp the 24-gauge wire and begin to wrap it tightly around the rhinestone chain.

2 :: Continue wrapping the wire until it reaches the top of the rhinestone chain, completing the last wind when you reach the back (the side opposite the rhinestones). Use wire cutters to trim away the 1-in/2.5-cm tail only.

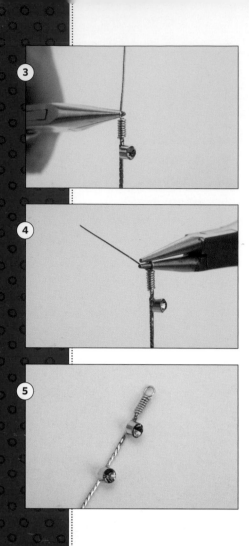

3 :: Use chain-nose pliers to gently squeeze the coil at its base to force the cut wire end flush against the chain and to secure the coil to the rhinestone chain. Use chain-nose pliers to bend the wire so that it is straight up and centered in the back.

4 :: Use round-nose pliers to make an eye loop. (See "How to Make an Eye Loop Using a Headpin," page 310.)

5 :: Trim away excess wire.

how to USE FOLDOVER CRIMP ENDS

Foldover crimp ends are generally used to secure soft stringing materials such as satin cord, suede, and leather. Some have a small prong at their base that will pierce the stringing material to help hold it in place. I also put a drop of glue in the crimp end's interior before adding the stringing material.

I used foldover crimp ends to finish the fine chain I used in the Watercolors necklace, www.chroniclebooks.com/beading. Usually chain is finished by threading a jump ring through the last link, but this chain was too fine for that. Instead, I used a foldover crimp end with a prong and a drop of glue to secure the chain so I could incorporate it into my design.

DIRECTIONS

1 :: Position a foldover crimp end face up on a flat work surface. Apply a small amount of crystal cement to the inside of the end. Place the end of a fine chain, cord, or other stringing material in the crimp end.

2 :: Use chain-nose pliers to fold over one half of the crimp end toward the center until it covers the end of the stringing material.

3 :: Use chain-nose pliers to fold over the opposite half of the crimp end. Let the glue dry. Use wire cutters to remove any excess chain or stringing material that obstructs the connector loop.

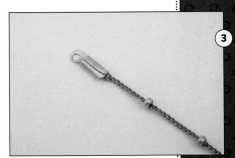

Rhinestone chain is a great way to add sparkle to your designs. It's usually sold by the foot/30.5 cm and is available in many sizes and metal settings. If you use the chain alone or secure it to another element, as I did in the Greek Goddess headband (page 245) and the Stardust hair combs (www.chroniclebooks.com/beading), you don't need to finish its ends. But if you use it as you would a strand of beads in a necklace, bracelet, or earring design, you must add crimp end connectors, which allow you to attach the chain to other elements, such as jump rings, clasps, and end bars. See the Renaissance bracelet (page 121) for inspiration.

DIRECTIONS

1 :: Use chain cutters to cut the desired length of rhinestone chain. Position one end of the chain near one rhinestone chain crimp end connector.

2 :: Add a drop of crystal cement or cyanoacrylate gel to the basin of the end connector. Use chain-nose pliers or tweezers to lift the last rhinestone on the chain and place it within the basin of the end connector. Let the glue dry.

3 :: Use chain-nose pliers to bend the connector's prongs flush against the rhinestone. Repeat steps 1–3 to attach another end connector to the opposite end of the chain.

how to MAKE A BUTTON OR BEAD CLASP

Instead of using a metal clasp, you can thread beads on the end of your stringing material and make a loop, which you can then secure around a button or bead to hold your piece in place. This clasp is similar to a toggle clasp: here the button or bead functions like the bar portion of the toggle. See the Lots of Luxe bracelet (page 125) and the Hothouse Flowers bracelet (page 147) for two versions of this technique.

A :: THE WOVEN LOOP AND BUTTON CLASP ON THE LOTS OF LUXE BRACELET

B :: THE BUTTON END ON THE HOTHOUSE FLOWERS BRACELET

C :: THE LOOP END ON THE HOTHOUSE FLOWERS BRACELET

how to MAKE A TASSEL *and how to* USE BEAD CAPS, CONE ENDS, AND BULLET ENDS TO MAKE MULTISTRAND PIECES

Tassels are a pretty addition to necklaces and bracelets and are made by gathering multiple strands on one end, leaving the opposite ends to dangle freely. I used them in the Lorelei Lee earrings (page 189). This technique can be applied in many other ways in your jewelry designs.

DIRECTIONS

1 :: In a multistrand piece, gather the multiple beaded strands together and secure them with an overhand knot to the eye loop end of a wire. Secure the knot with a drop of glue. Trim away the excess stringing material.

2 :: Thread the free end of the wire into a bead cap, cone end, or bullet end to hide the gathering point and knot.

3 :: Use round-nose pliers to make an eye loop (a connector) on the wire. The tassel can now be attached and incorporated into any design.

• • • **TIPS** • • •

If you use the above technique on both ends of your strands, all you need to do is add a clasp to make a multistrand bracelet.

Lengthen the beaded strands and gather the ends in bead caps, cone ends or bullet ends to make a multistrand necklace.

To use this technique with a stringing material you can't knot, attach multiple strands of beading wire to an eye loop using crimp beads. Or gather crimped loops together with another piece of beading wire you string through all of them. Then feed the beading wire ends through a bead cap, bullet end, or cone end, and attach it to a clasp.

ALTERNATIVE WAYS TO MAKE MULTISTRAND PIECES

Multistrand pieces don't have to use bead caps, bullet ends, or cone ends; there are many other ways to finish them. Take a look at the following multi-strand projects to see the stringing materials that are used and the ways in which they are finished to inspire your own designs.

MULTISTRAND NECKLACES

A :: **SUN-KISSED NECKLACE, PAGE 83:** *Beading wires are attached to a multi-strand clasp using crimp beads.*

B :: **CAFÉ AU LAIT NECKLACE, PAGE 109:** *Silk cords are knotted together and secured in clamshells.*

C :: **L'HEURE BLEUE NECKLACE, WWW.CHRONICLEBOOKS.COM/BEADING:** *Beading wires are attached to lobster clasps using crimp beads. The clasps are attached to a silver ring with jump rings.*

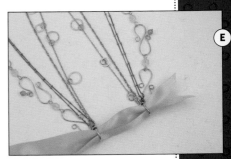

D-E :: **WATERCOLORS NECKLACE, WWW.CHRONICLEBOOKS.COM/BEADING:** *Multiple chains are attached to large jump rings. A ribbon is threaded through the rings and tied in a bow to make a clasp.*

MULTISTRAND BRACELETS

....

F :: **RENAISSANCE BRACELET, PAGE 121:** *Chains and beaded strands are attached to end bars with jump rings.*

G :: **GOLD DIGGER BRACELET, PAGE 155:** *Large link chains are attached to end bars with jump rings.*

WIREWORK

Working with wire is an integral part of making beautiful beaded jewelry. Wire is extremely versatile and can be used to make links, connectors, jump rings, and loops and to wrap beads. The more you practice, the better your wirework will get. Here are a few basic things to keep in mind when working with wire.

how to **PROTECT WIRE**

Wire can easily be marred and scratched by metal tools such as pliers. As your wirework improves, this will become less of a problem, but there are a few things you can do to prevent it in the meantime.

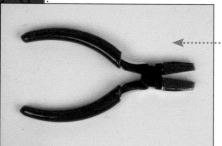

Masking tape: Simply cover the jaws of your pliers with masking tape.

Nylon pliers: The jaws of nylon pliers are covered with permanent or replaceable pads of thick nylon that cushion the wire. These pliers are available with square jaws, pointed jaws, round jaws, and half-round/half-flat jaws for all kinds of wirework. You can use them to shape and manipulate wire without scratching or denting it. They work particularly well on colored wire, which can scratch easily. (See the Primrose Path ring, page 207.)

Rubber coating: You can dip the jaws of pliers into a liquid rubber coating such as Tool Magic. After a few hours, the rubber cures and the pliers can be used as usual, only now they will have a soft cushion between the metal and the wire; this will keep the wire from being dented or scratched. The rubber coating can be simply peeled away at any time.

how to CUT WIRE

Choosing the right wire cutters is very important. The harder the wire temper and the thicker its gauge, the stronger the wire cutters will need to be. If you try to cut 20-gauge wire with nippers, the wire will leave divots in the blades and render them useless. When you buy cutters, read the manufacturer's recommendations on what gauge and temper the cutters are best suited for. Cutting the right wire with the right cutters will keep them sharp, extend their longevity, and permit you to make to make clean cuts. Here is a general guide to choosing the right wire cutters for dead-soft wire. A good rule of thumb: when in doubt, choose the stronger cutter.

30 gauge–26 gauge: Nippers

24 gauge–18 gauge: Cutters

16 gauge–12 gauge: Heavy-duty chain cutters

Nylon-coated beading wire: Cutters

Memory wire: Memory wire cutters

A :: NIPPERS CUTTING WIRE

B :: HEAVY-DUTY CHAIN CUTTERS CUTTING CHAIN

C :: MEMORY WIRE CUTTERS CUTTING MEMORY WIRE

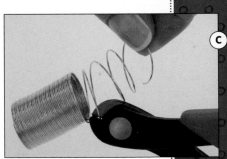

IMPORTANT :: The smaller the piece of wire you're cutting away, the higher and faster it will fly across the room. You should always wear eye protection when cutting wire. There are a few precautions you can take to prevent flying wire shards, too. Simply cup your hand over your planned cut once your cutters are positioned. Or place a dish towel or swatch of fabric over the piece to keep the wire from flying away.

Never cut memory wire with anything other than memory wire cutters, or you will hurt your hand and ruin your cutters.

how to **MAKE CLEAN CUTS**

Your goal should be to make a clean, close flush cut that will leave no jagged edges that could cut or scratch you. Flush cutters are specifically designed for this work. Try this exercise: Use flush cutters to cut a piece of scrap wire in half. Now examine the two cut ends. Most flush cutters yield one end with a clean, straight flush cut and another with an angled cut. As you work, make sure you use the side with the straight cut in your jewelry pieces and leave the angled cut on the spool end or on the excess wire you are trimming away.

how to **FINISH WIRE ENDS**

It's important to smooth sharp or jagged wire edges and remove any metal shards from cut wire. This is especially important when you are making your own ear wires. (See "How To Make Ear Wires," page 339.) This process is called deburring. Begin by using an abrasive needle file, then move on to medium-grit emery cloth, and then finish by using fine-grit emery cloth.

DIRECTIONS

1 :: Run the end of the wire across the needle file to remove large shards and sharp edges. Rotate the wire to smooth all sides and edges.

2 :: Run the wire end across a piece of medium-grit emery cloth to further smooth rough edges. Rotate the wire to smooth all sides and edges.

3 :: Run the wire across a piece of fine-grit emery cloth. Rotate the wire to smooth all sides and edges until it is completely smooth to the touch and safe to wear.

Unless you make your components, such as jump rings, chain links, clasps, and ear wires, from full-hard wire, which is difficult to work with, you must work-harden your wire. This can be done by hammering it or by using nylon pliers on it. Both methods realign the molecules in the wire, stiffening it. Hardening is essential; it enables the components you make to keep their shape and tolerate the weight of beads while they're worn.

Work-harden wire with a hammer with a nylon or rawhide head. Such hammers keep the wire from being marred or scratched and should not change the shape of your wirework. Some beaders prefer to shape a component before placing it on a bench block and striking it with the hammer. This is simple to do if the wire piece is flat, such as a jump ring or an S-link. If you've made a more complex component in which wires cross, you can use the hammer to strike the portions that do not overlap or hammer the wire prior to shaping it. As the wire hardens, it also becomes trickier to work with. Overhammering wire may cause it to break, as will hammering two wires that cross or overlap.

Another option is to work-harden the wire by pulling it through the closed jaws of a pair of nylon pliers a number of times. Hold one end of the wire with chain-nose pliers. Grasp the wire next to the chain-nose pliers with nylon pliers. Keep the jaws of the nylon pliers clamped down on the wire while you use the chain-nose pliers to pull the wire through them. Repeat this a few times until the wire is stiff but springy. Be careful not to overwork the wire; if you do, it will become brittle and break when you try to shape it. I have read that it is also possible to simply squeeze sterling-silver or gold-filled wires between the jaws of nylon pliers a few times to harden them, but I have yet to try this myself.

The more you work with the same piece of wire, bending it, wrapping it, or unwrapping it to fix a mistake, the less malleable it will get. If you overwork wire, it will weaken, snap, and break. When you work with higher-gauge wires, such as 26, 28, or 30, this will happen quickly. It should also be noted that wire and findings made from base metals will crack and break much more quickly than wires made from softer metals, such as sterling silver and gold-filled.

how to UNKINK WIRE

A kink is an unwanted loop in the wire you're working with. Kinks occur when you're using long pieces of wire, as in the Wildfire bracelet (page 141) and the Calypso earrings (www. chroniclebooks.com/beading). If a loop starts to form, stop your work immediately. Do not pull on the wire; that will tighten the loop and only make it worse. Use your fingers or another tool to loosen the loop until it's wide enough to flatten out. If a dent remains in the wire, use nylon pliers to flatten it. Then run the nylon pliers along the length of the wire to straighten it out further. This will harden the wire, so don't do it too many times. If the loop cannot be fixed, start over with a fresh piece of wire, or your piece may break midproject.

how to WRAP WIRE

Knowing how to wrap wire successfully is a basic skill every beader should possess. You will need it to create a wrapped-wire loop, a wrapped briolette, a wire bail, jump rings, and ring forms, to name just a few items.

Sloppy wirework—wrapped wires with gaps or bunches—detracts from your jewelry pieces, but the following techniques will get you professional-looking results.

how to WRAP THIN WIRE

Wire with a gauge between 24 and 30 is simple to wrap around other, thicker wires. But always secure its short end with one hand while winding with the other. Wind the wire only a few times before stopping to check your work, and always keep the wire taut.

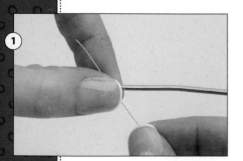

1

DIRECTIONS

1 :: Use your thumb and forefinger to position the thin wire against the foundation wire. Leave a 1-in/2.5-cm wire tail on the thin wire. Hold the tail securely in place.

2 :: Wrap the thin wire around the foundation wire. Keep the wire wraps close together, but don't worry about gaps between them.

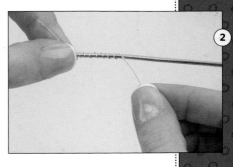

3 :: Use chain-nose pliers to slide the wraps back toward your fingers until they are pressed up against one another.

4 :: Repeat steps 2–3 as necessary.

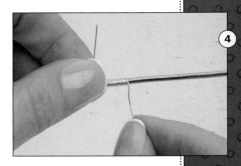

IMPORTANT :: Do not use this technique to wrap thick wire or you'll create large gaps that you can't correct with chain-nose pliers.

how to **WRAP THICK WIRE**

Wrapping thick wire, with a gauge between 16 and 22, requires more precision than wrapping thin wire. Always secure its short end with one hand while winding with the other. Wind the wire only a few times before stopping to check your work, and always keep the wire taut.

DIRECTIONS

1 :: Use your thumb and forefinger to position the thick wire against the foundation wire. Leave a 1-in/2.5-cm wire tail on the thick wire. Hold the tail securely in place.

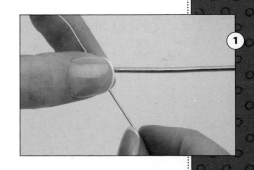

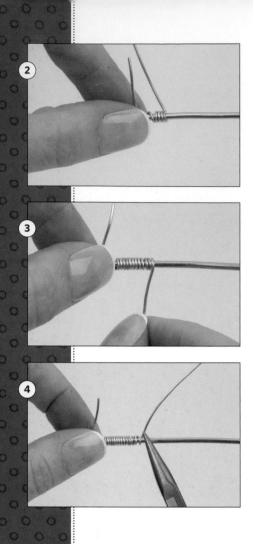

2 :: Wrap the thick wire around the foundation wire. With each wrap, pull the thick wire back toward the hand holding the tail so that no gaps are left between the wire wraps.

3 :: Continue wrapping the wire, stopping every few wraps to check for gaps or spaces.

4 :: If a gap is present, reduce or eliminate it by using chain-nose pliers to slide the wraps back toward the hand holding the tail.

IMPORTANT :: Do not use this technique to wrap thin wire or the wire wraps will pile atop themselves. Thin wire is much more malleable than thick wire and doesn't require so much precision.

• • • TIP • • •

Gaps between wraps of thick wire can be corrected only when there are just two or three wraps. If there are more, chain-nose pliers cannot exert enough leverage to slide them together, and the pliers could slip and mar the wire.

how to **COVER A COMPONENT WITH WRAPPED WIRE**

This technique will give you near-instant results. You can quickly and easily secure beads to a component such as a bangle bracelet or hoop earring simply by threading beads on a wire and wrapping it. Higher gauges of wire and dead-soft wire yield the best results because they are malleable and narrow enough to be incorporated into a design without detracting from it. This technique can also be used to secure rhinestone chain to components.

See the following projects for inspiration:

LIME WIRE BRACELET, page 117

CALYPSO EARRINGS, www.chroniclebooks.com/beading

STARDUST HAIR COMBS, www.chroniclebooks.com/beading

GREEK GODDESS HEADBAND, page 245

Jump rings are readily available, so you will most likely buy them ready-made, particularly when you need them in large amounts. On occasion, though, you may not be able to find jump rings in the gauge, finish, or size you need for a specific project. But you will be able to find wire that fits the exact specifications you want, which is all you need to make your own jump rings. Either use half-hard wire or work-harden dead-soft or soft wire to make sure your jump rings will be stiff enough to support weight while maintaining their shape and staying closed. Making your own jump rings is simple, but please read the directions for wrapping wire on pages 304-305 for more information first.

DIRECTIONS

1 :: Use wire cutters to cut an 8-in/20-cm length of wire. Position one end of the wire against a mandrel. Use your thumb and forefinger to secure the wire end against the mandrel. Leave a 1-in/2.5-cm tail.

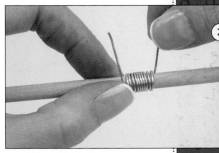

2 :: Wrap the wire around the mandrel as many times as necessary. One revolution equals one jump ring.

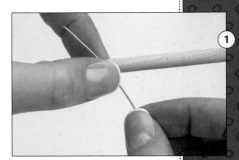

3 :: Slide the wire coil off the mandrel. Use flush cutters to cut away the long unwrapped ends (the tails) so that the flush ends remain on the coil and the angled ends are cut away. At one end, count one complete revolution of wire (one ring). Cut away one ring with the flush side of the cutters. The ring will fall off the coil and should have two flush-cut ends.

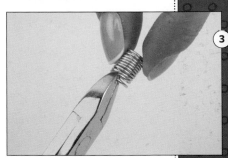

4 :: To make the next ring, use the flush end of the cutters to trim away the angled wire end left on the coil from the last cut on the first ring. Count one complete revolution of wire and cut away the ring with the flush side of the cutters. Repeat step 3 to cut away the remaining rings. If necessary, smooth the cut ends with emery cloth. Note: To ensure that each wire end is flush cut, you will have to rotate the pliers 180 degrees each time you make a cut.

TIPS

Determine the diameter of the jump ring you need. Next, select a mandrel. Please note that the diameter of the mandrel will determine only the inner diameter of the jump ring. Try to choose a mandrel whose diameter is the same all along its length, or at least along a portion long enough to create multiple wire wraps. It should have a smooth exterior. Pens, dowels, and other household tools work perfectly. I prefer not to use pencils because of their ridges.

If you need only a few jump rings, use a permanent marker to mark a position on one jaw on round-nose pliers to make consistently sized rings. (The line can be removed with rubbing alcohol.) Cut a 6-in/15-cm length of wire. Place one end of the wire on the marked line and rotate the pliers, always feeding the wire into the pliers along the line. The finished rings will move up the pliers as you add more. Then follow steps 3–4, above.

how to OPEN AND CLOSE A JUMP RING

Jump rings need to be opened and closed in a specific way so you do not stress their wire, which could cause them to crack or break. This technique also keeps the ring from becoming misshapen.

DIRECTIONS

1 :: Use two pairs of pliers (chain-nose, bent-nose, or one of each) to grasp the closed jump ring on opposite sides, as shown. The split in the ring should be between the pliers.

2 :: Rotate your wrists, moving one toward yourself and the other away to open the ring. Reverse the action to close the jump ring.

TIP

If a small gap remains when you close a jump ring, first reopen the ring. As you begin to close it again, moving one pair of pliers toward yourself and the other pair away, also gently move the pliers in toward each other. This should eliminate the gap.

how to MAKE EYE LOOPS

An eye loop is a simple wire loop that allows you to attach beads or bead units to other components in your jewelry designs, such as a pendant on a necklace or a drop on an ear wire. They can be easily opened and closed with chain-nose pliers, and they work just as a jump ring does.

When beads are strung on a headpin, ball pin, or eye pin, it is the pin that keeps them from sliding off the wire. There are a few things to keep in mind when selecting the right size of pin.

The metal disk at the base of a headpin or the metal ball at the base of a ball pin needs to be large enough to cover the bead hole and keep the beads in place. If the bead at the base has a particularly large hole and the large pin thus required doesn't work with your design, first place a smaller bead at the base before adding the bead with the large hole. Now you can select a smaller-gauge pin. The loop at the base of an eye pin should be large enough to support the beads, and using an eye pin allows you to attach another element to it.

To make an eye loop (connector) at the opposite end of a headpin, ball pin, or eye pin, choose one that will leave ½ in/12 mm of bare wire *after* the beads have been strung onto it.

DIRECTIONS

1 :: Insert a headpin through a bead or beads.

2 :: Use chain-nose pliers to grasp the headpin directly above the top bead. Turn the pliers away from yourself to bend the stem at a 90-degree angle.

3 :: Use round-nose pliers to grasp the stem ⅛ in/3 mm from the bend, rotating the pliers toward the bend. Use your fingers to wrap the wire around one jaw of the pliers, crossing the wire in front to make a loop. (See steps 2–3 in "How to Make an Eye Loop on Both Ends Using Wire," page 311, for more detailed illustrations.)

4 :: Use wire cutters to cut away the wire where the end of the loop meets the stem. Use emery cloth to smooth the cut wire end.

5 :: A finished eye loop should look like the one shown in image 5, with the eye loop centered directly above the bead hole.

••• TIP •••

Use a permanent marker to mark a position on one jaw of the round-nose pliers to make consistently sized loops. The line can be removed later with rubbing alcohol.

---

how to **MAKE AN EYE LOOP ON BOTH ENDS USING WIRE**

You can make eye loops on both ends of a bead or beads with wire. The loops on each end allow you to attach the bead to other components on both sides. For instance, it can become part of a chain or a middle component of an earring.

DIRECTIONS

1 :: Use wire cutters to cut a 3-in/7.5-cm length of wire. Use chain-nose pliers to grasp the wire 1 in/2.5 cm from its end. Turn the pliers away from yourself to bend the wire at a 90-degree angle.

2 :: Use round-nose pliers to grasp the wire ⅛ in/3 mm from the bend. Rotate the pliers toward the bend.

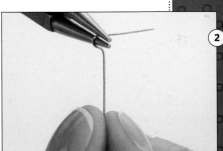

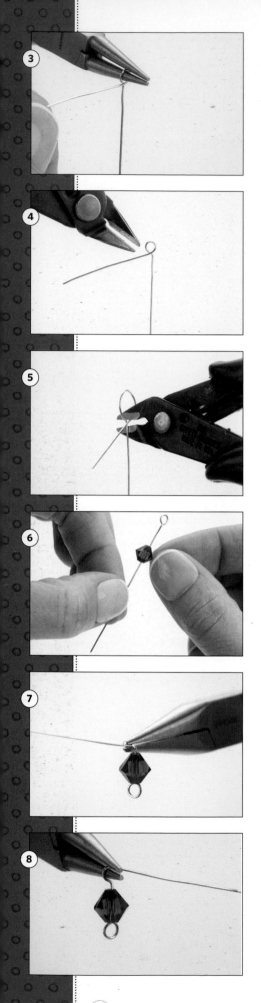

3 :: Use your fingers to bend the wire around one jaw of the pliers, crossing the wire in front to make a loop.

4 :: Use wire cutters to cut away the wire where the end of the loop meets the stem. Use emery cloth to smooth the cut wire end.

5 :: Detail: To ensure perfect cuts, place the wire cutters inside the eye loop. Press the blades against the loop and the stem, as shown. Cut away excess wire.

6 :: Thread a bead onto the wire.

7 :: Rotate the wire so that the bead sits on the eye loop. Use chain-nose pliers to grasp the wire directly above the bead. Turn the pliers away from yourself to bend the headpin at a 90-degree angle.

8 :: Use round-nose pliers to grasp the wire ⅛ in/3 mm from the bend. Rotate the pliers toward the bend.

9 :: Bend the wire around one jaw of the pliers and cross it in front to make a loop.

10 :: Use wire cutters to cut away the wire where the end of the loop meets the stem. Use emery cloth to smooth the cut wire end.

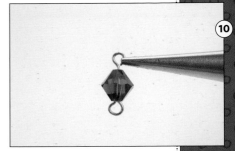

> • • • **TIP** • • •
>
> Using a 3-in/7.5-cm length of wire will allow you to make eye loops on even large beads. After practicing a few times, adjust the amount of wire you need accordingly.

how to **MAKE AN EYE LOOP ON A HEAD-DRILLED BEAD**

A head-drilled bead, also called top-drilled (depending on the shape of the bead), has a hole that is drilled horizontally close to its top, rather than through its center. Freshwater pearls are usually top-drilled so that when they're strung, they will hang below the stringing material. Eye loops made from wire can be added to lightweight, head-drilled, or top-drilled beads such as the freshwater pearls in the Carnavale earrings (page 161). When you choose heavier beads, use techniques with more intricate and secure wirework, such as the ones detailed for wrapped-wire loops (page 315), wrapped briolettes (page 321), and wire bails (page 325).

DIRECTIONS

1 :: Insert one end of a length of wire into a freshwater pearl.

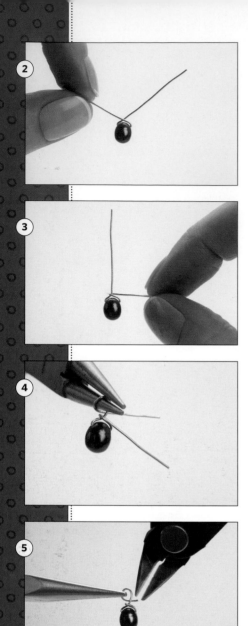

2 :: Slide the pearl to the wire's midpoint. Bring both ends of the wire to the top of the pearl and cross them right over left.

3 :: Use chain-nose pliers to bend the back wire so that it is straight up and centered on the top of the pearl, creating a stem. Wrap the front wire around the stem.

4 :: Use round-nose pliers to make an eye loop with the wire stem. (See steps 7 through 10 in "How to Make an Eye Loop on Both Ends Using Wire," page 311, for more details.)

5 :: Trim away excess wire.

how to OPEN AND CLOSE AN EYE LOOP

This is the correct way to open and close an eye loop while putting the least stress on the wire. Never open an eye loop by pulling the wire directly from the side: the loop will weaken and break.

DIRECTIONS

1 :: To open the loop, grasp the cut end of the wire loop and rotate it toward yourself using chain-nose pliers, making a gap.

2 :: To close the loop, use chain-nose pliers to grasp the cut end of the wire and rotate it away from yourself until the cut end touches the stem.

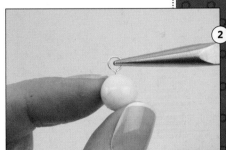

how to MAKE WRAPPED-WIRE LOOPS

Adding wrapped-wire loops to your beads or bead units allows you to attach them to other components in your designs. They are similar to eye loops but are more decorative because they use more complicated wire-work. An eye loop is made directly above the top bead. A wrapped-wire loop is made ⅛ in/3 mm above the top bead, and then the wire tail is wrapped around the wire stem. Wrapped-wire loops are more secure than eye loops because they cannot be accidentally opened or closed, so beads with such loops make great chain links and drops and can support heavy beads. See page 304, on wrapping wire, for more information.

The decision to use a wrapped-wire loop rather than an eye loop can be about aesthetics as well as security. A wrapped-wire loop allows the bead to hang down farther, as it is farther from its connecting loop. (See the Sea Spray ring on page 219.) This can lend the beads movement and swing. It also makes room to add more beads. (See the Bisou bracelet on page 131.)

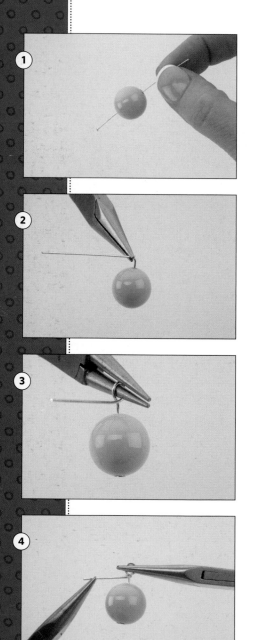

DIRECTIONS

1 :: Insert a headpin through a bead.

2 :: Use chain-nose pliers to grasp the headpin ⅛ in/3 mm above the bead. Turn the pliers away from yourself to bend the stem at a 90-degree angle.

3 :: Use round-nose pliers to grasp the stem ⅛ in/3 mm from the bend, rotating the pliers toward the bend. Use your fingers to wrap the wire around one jaw of the pliers, crossing the wire in front to make a loop. (See steps 2–3 and 9–10 in "How to Make a Wrapped-Wire Loop on Both Ends Using Wire," facing page, for more detailed illustrations of this step.)

4 :: Grasp the loop with chain-nose pliers. Use a second pair of chain-nose pliers to wrap the wire around the stem two to three times, moving from the loop downward.

5 :: Use wire cutters to trim away excess wire. Use emery cloth to smooth the rough wire end.

6 :: Use chain-nose pliers to squeeze the cut end of the wire flush against the stem.

TIPS

FOR SUCCESSFUL WIRE WRAPS:

1 :: Center the loop above the bead hole.

2 :: Hold the wire taut and wind it tightly around the stem.

3 :: Position each wire wrap up against the wrap before.

4 :: Don't leave any gaps between wraps.

---

how to **MAKE A WRAPPED-WIRE LOOP ON BOTH ENDS USING WIRE**

The key to making these successful is to make sure that the loops on both ends of the bead are the same size and have the same number of wraps.

Making the first wrapped-wire loop on one end is always much easier than making the second one on the opposite end after you've threaded on a bead. When you begin the second loop, make the first bend the same distance away from the bead that you did on the opposite end. Then make sure your loops are the same size. Otherwise, you will end up with too much or too little wire to wrap around the stem, resulting in either too many wraps that don't match the other side or a partially bare stem (see above).

DIRECTIONS

1 :: Cut a 6-in/15-cm length of wire. Use chain-nose pliers to grasp the wire 2 in/5 cm from one end. Turn the pliers away from yourself to bend the wire at a 90-degree angle.

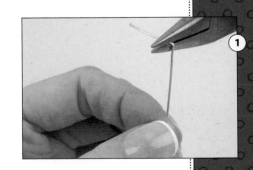

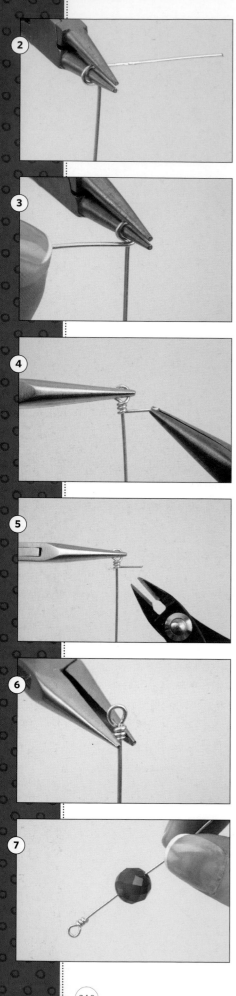

2 :: Grasp the wire ⅛ in/3 mm from the bend using round-nose pliers. Rotate the pliers toward the bend.

3 :: Use your fingers to wrap the wire around one jaw of the pliers, crossing the wire in front of the stem to make a loop.

4 :: Grasp the loop with chain-nose pliers. Use a second pair of chain-nose pliers to wrap the wire around the stem two to three times, moving from the loop downward.

5 :: Use wire cutters to trim away excess wire. Use emery cloth to smooth the rough wire end.

6 :: Use chain-nose pliers to squeeze the cut end of the wire flush against the stem.

7 :: Thread on one bead.

8 :: Grasp the straight wire ⅛ in/3 mm above the bead using chain-nose pliers. Turn the pliers away from yourself to bend the wire at a 90-degree angle.

9 :: Grasp the wire ⅛ in/3 mm from the bend using round-nose pliers. Rotate the pliers toward the bend.

10 :: Use your fingers to wrap the wire around one jaw of the pliers, crossing the wire in front of the stem to make a loop.

11 :: Grasp the loop with chain-nose pliers. Use a second pair of chain-nose pliers to wrap the wire around the stem two to three times, moving from the loop downward. Use wire cutters to trim away excess wire.

12 :: Use emery cloth to smooth the rough wire end. Use chain-nose pliers to squeeze the cut end of the wire flush against the stem.

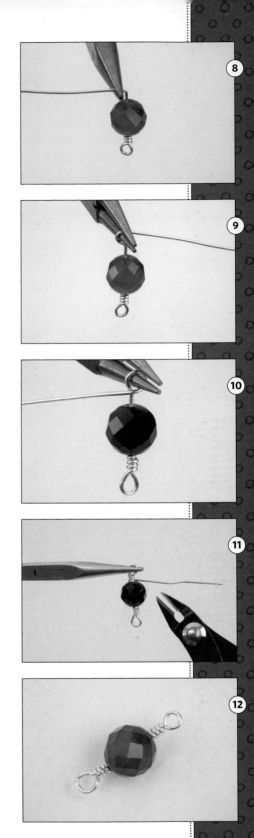

Because wrapped-wire loops cannot be opened or closed, you attach them to other components with a connector, for instance a jump ring. However, when making a wrapped-wire loop, you can stop midway to join it directly to another element without the use of a connector. Use this technique to join wrapped-wire loops together to make secure beaded chains or to attach bead components directly to chain links on a bracelet.

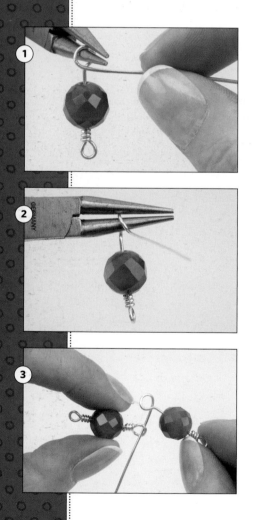

DIRECTIONS

1 :: Follow steps 1–12 from "How to Make a Wrapped-Wire Loop on Both Ends Using Wire," page 317, to prepare a bead with a wrapped-wire loop at each end; set the bead unit aside. Make a wrapped-wire loop on one end of a 6-in/15-cm length of wire, and thread on one bead. Rotate the bead so that it rests on the wrapped-wire loop. Grasp the straight wire 1/8 in/3 mm above the bead using chain-nose pliers. Turn the pliers away from yourself to bend the wire at a 90-degree angle. Grasp the wire 1/8 in/3 mm from the bend using round-nose pliers. Rotate the pliers toward the bend and use your fingers to bend the wire around the jaw of the pliers. Cross the wire in front of the stem to make a loop, leaving a narrow gap.

2 :: Side view: The loop should have a gap large enough that a wrapped-wire loop from another bead unit can pass through it.

3 :: Insert the wire that extends from the bead (worked in steps 1–2) through one wrapped-wire loop on the bead unit set aside in step 1, sliding the bead unit along the wire until the two beads are connected at their loops.

4 :: Grasp the loop on the unfinished bead with chain-nose pliers. Use the wire that extends from the bead to complete the wrapped-wire loop, moving the finished bead unit aside to do so.

5 :: Use wire cutters to trim away excess wire. Use emery cloth to smooth the rough wire end. Use chain-nose pliers to squeeze the cut end of the wire flush against the stem.

6 :: To add another bead unit, follow steps 1–5. Continue to add as many bead units as needed to make a beaded chain of the length you desire. See the Sea Spray ring (page 219) and the Crystal Springs necklace (page 87) for more ways to apply this technique.

how to **MAKE WRAPPED BRIOLETTES**

Using wire to make a wrapped collar on a briolette not only adds a beautiful decorative accent but also hides the bead holes. Use the same technique as you would to make a wrapped-wire loop, but, instead of wrapping just the stem, continue wrapping until you reach the bead holes. (See "How to Make a Wrapped-Wire Loop Using a Headpin," page 316.)

First practice this technique with inexpensive wire and briolettes. Briolette tips are fragile and can be broken or chipped by wire that is wrapped too tightly and by

pliers that are squeezed too firmly when you're readjusting messy wraps. When you begin wrapping, make sure the loop is directly over the tip of the bead and that it stays there. Stop every few wraps to gently shift the wires back into place, because they have a tendency to slide off the tip. If you don't stop to fix these, you'll end up with wires that grind off the tip of the briolette and a wire collar that is lopsided.

Wrapping wire around the tip of a briolette requires a lighter hand than making the tight wraps of a wrapped-wire loop.

Wrapping wire is trickiest for the ⅛-in/3-mm section where you move from the base of the wire loop to the top of the bead. If you wrap too tightly, the wires will bunch up and overlap, never transitioning onto the top of the bead. Position each new wrap against the earlier one, but keep a little slack in the wire as you wrap until the wire can be supported by a wider part of the bead.

how to MAKE A WRAPPED BRIOLETTE WITHOUT A STEM

If you'll use a connector to attach a wrapped briolette, this is the technique to employ. Much like a wrapped-wire loop, the loop on this wrapped briolette cannot be opened or closed. This technique also works very well with heavy beads because the loop cannot be pulled open.

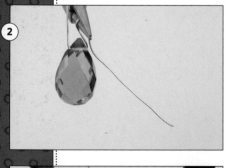

DIRECTIONS

1 :: Use wire cutters to cut a 6-in/15-cm length of wire. Insert the wire through a briolette and slide the bead to the wire's mid-point, bending the two wire ends up.

2 :: Push one wire up against the side of the briolette so it sits at the same angle as the bead. Using round-nose pliers, grip the angled wire ¼ in/6 mm from the top of the bead. Rotate the pliers away from the briolette to make a loop directly over the tip of the bead. Use your fingers to wrap the wire around one jaw of the pliers. When the wire reaches the tip of the bead (completing the loop), use your fingers to bend the wire end out to the side.

3 :: Use wire cutters to trim away excess wire, trimming it slightly above the bead hole.

4 :: Grasp the loop with chain-nose pliers. With the other hand, grasp the long wire and bring it behind the loop and around to the front, trapping both wires at the base of the loop.

5 :: Continue to wrap the long wire around the wires at the base of the loop and down the briolette until the wire wraps conceal the bead holes.

6 :: Cut off excess wire.

7 :: Use the tips of chain-nose pliers to gently squeeze the cut wire end flush against the briolette.

how to **MAKE A WRAPPED BRIOLETTE WITH A STEM**

This technique allows you to make a wrapped briolette without committing the stem to a wrapped-wire loop that cannot be opened. By leaving the stem untouched, it can be turned into an eye loop or a wrapped-wire loop. Then the briolette can be attached to any other component. If you add an eye loop, the stem can be opened and closed. It can also be repositioned if you change your mind mid-design. (If you want to add a wrapped-wire loop and attach it without a jump ring, see "How to Join Wrapped-Wire Loops without Using a Connector," page 320.)

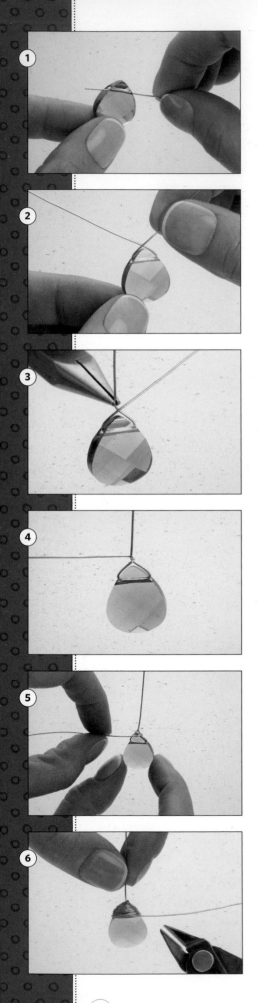

DIRECTIONS

1 :: Use wire cutters to cut a 6-in/15-cm length of wire. Insert the wire through a briolette and slide the briolette to the wire's midpoint.

2 :: Bring both wires up and cross them above the tip of the briolette.

3 :: Use chain-nose pliers to bend the back wire straight up at the point where the wires cross, directly above the tip of the briolette. This is now the wire stem.

4 :: Hold the wire stem with one hand. Grasp the front wire with the other hand and wrap the wire around the stem.

5 :: Continue wrapping the wire down the stem and around the top of the briolette until it conceals the bead holes.

6 :: Trim away excess wire. Use chain-nose pliers to gently press the cut wire end flush against the briolette. Turn the stem into the desired style of connector.

how to MAKE A WIRE BAIL

A bail is used to join a pendant to a neck-lace. Although you can buy ready-made bails, you can make your own decorative ones with or without bead accents. In this example, crystal briolettes are paired with crystal bicones, but you can use briolettes of any material and pair them with coordi-nating or contrasting beads. This type of wire bail allows a pendant movement, so it is important that you leave space between the top of the briolette pendant and the crossed wires so it can move freely.

DIRECTIONS

1 :: Use wire cutters to cut one 4-in/10-cm length of wire. Insert one wire end into one briolette and slide the briolette to the wire's midpoint.

2 :: Bend the wires up and cross them.

3 :: Use chain-nose pliers to bend the back wire straight up at the point where the wires cross, directly above the tip of the briolette. This is now the wire stem. Bend the front wire at a 90-degree angle at the point where the wires cross, above the tip of the briolette.

4 :: Rotate the wires 90 degrees so that they are away from the top of the briolette. Grasp the wires with chain-nose pliers at the point where they originally crossed and wrap the front wire around the stem, moving up ¼ in/6 mm.

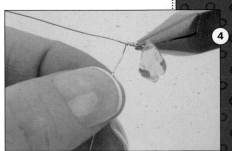

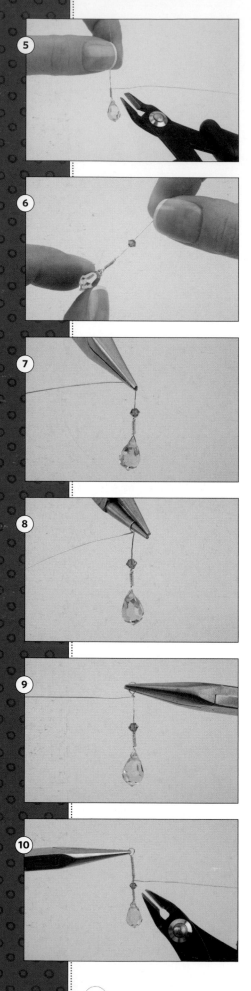

5 :: Use wire cutters to trim away excess wire. Use chain-nose pliers to squeeze the cut end flush against the stem.

6 :: Thread on one bicone.

7 :: Use chain-nose pliers to bend the wire stem at a 90-degree angle ¼ in/6 mm above the bicone.

8 :: Grasp the wire ⅛ in/3 mm from the bend, using round-nose pliers. Rotate the pliers toward the bend. Use your fingers to wrap the wire around one jaw of the pliers, crossing the wire in front of the stem to make a loop.

9 :: Grasp the loop with chain-nose pliers to stabilize it. Wrap the wire around the stem, working downward until the wire reaches the top of the bicone.

10 :: Use wire cutters to trim away excess wire. Use chain-nose pliers to squeeze the cut end flush against the stem.

● ● ● **TIP** ● ● ●

You move the wires off the top of the briolette in step 4 to prevent yourself from accidentally chipping or cracking the top of the briolette. It is always better to do the wirework off the bead (if you can) so you won't damage it. This technique also makes creating neat wire wraps easy.

MASTERING THE ART *of* BEADING

how to ATTACH A BAIL

DIRECTIONS

1 :: To attach a ready-made bail to a briolette, bead, or pendant, first test-fit the bail to ensure that it's wide enough to safely slip its pegs into the bead holes. If not, use chain-nose pliers to gently widen the bail's opening. Add a drop of crystal cement to the pegs inside the bail.

2 :: Position the bail over the bead. Place one peg into one side of the bead hole, sliding it in as far as it can go. Now there will be enough room to place the opposite peg into the opposite side of the hole.

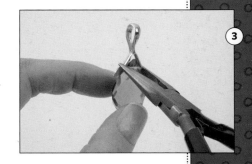

3 :: Use chain-nose pliers to gently squeeze the sides of the bail together. Let the cement dry.

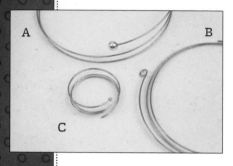

Memory wire can be finished in a number of ways. The simplest is to use round-nose pliers to make a loop at the end of the wire, bending the wire against its natural curve. Or use GS Hypo Cement or cyanoacrylate to glue a half-drilled bead or bead cap onto the wire end. Or, particularly when you are using small beads (as you do when making a ring), apply glue to the last three or four beads on each wire end to secure them. See the Romantic Notions bracelet (www.chroniclebooks.com/beading) and the Sonnet ring (page 223) for examples of how to use memory wire.

CLOCKWISE STARTING AT THE TOP:

A :: Half-drilled bead
B :: Wire loop
C :: End bead

---

how to CROCHET WIRE

Higher-gauge wires can easily be crocheted to form a sturdy base for a cuff bracelet, as seen in the Wildfire bracelet (page 141). First, you manipulate wire into a length of connected loops to give the bracelet structure. Then you use more wire to "sew" beads onto this base, weaving the wire in and out of the loops to secure them. You can use only a few beads for a light and airy look that shows off the wirework, or you can cover the wire base completely for a stunning bejeweled bracelet.

A :: **ADDING THE FIRST BEAD TO THE CROCHETED WIRE BASE**
B :: **SHOWING OFF THE BEADS AND THE WIREWORK**
C :: **COVERING THE WIRE BASE COMPLETELY WITH BEADS**

MASTERING THE ART *of* BEADING

Jump rings are available in a variety of sizes and metals and you can link them together to design your own chains. If you can't purchase jump rings in the exact style, gauge, or metal you're looking for, you can custom-make your own (see "How to Make a Jump Ring," page 307.) Linking single jump rings together is one approach, but linking pairs of jump rings makes a substantial chain and produces a great base for a charm bracelet.

The open links provide ample space to attach charms and beads. If you continue adding links, your jump ring chain will make a great industrial-style necklace as well. You can simply link rings, as in the Bisou bracelet (page 131), or add beads between rings, as in the Moonbeam earrings (page 177).

The jump rings used to make this chain are all the same size, 6 mm dia.

DIRECTIONS

1 :: Open one jump ring. Insert the wire end through two closed jump rings. Close the first jump ring. (See "How to Open and Close a Jump Ring," page 309.)

2 :: Open another jump ring and insert the wire end through the original pair of jump rings. Close the jump ring to create two pairs of two jump rings each.

3 :: Repeat steps 1–2 until you've reached the desired length of chain.

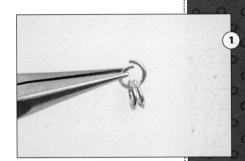

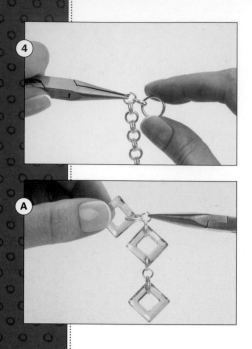

4 :: To attach a toggle clasp, open one jump ring and insert it through the last two links on the chain. Thread on the round portion of the toggle clasp and close the jump ring. Repeat this step on the opposite side to attach the bar portion of the toggle clasp, using another jump ring.

A :: **HERE IS AN EXAMPLE OF BEADS ADDED BETWEEN THE JUMP RING LINKS.**

how to **MAKE AN S-LINK**

An S-link is a simple wire link shaped like an S. It can be combined with an eye link or jump ring and used as a clasp. Or S-links can be joined together to form a chain, as in the Watercolors necklace (www.chroniclebooks.com/ beading).

DIRECTIONS

1 :: Use wire cutters to flush-cut a 4½-in/11-cm length of wire. Make a small loop at one end using round-nose pliers. Use a permanent marker to mark the wire's position on the pliers to make consistently sized loops.

2 :: Bend the wire over a mandrel 1 in/2.5 cm from the loop.

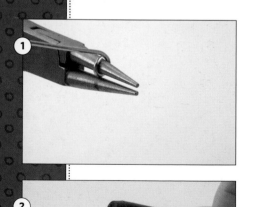

3 :: Identify the midpoint on the wire, which is 1 in/2.5 cm from the bend made in step 2. Shape the wire with your fingers so that the midpoint bends inward toward the eye loop.

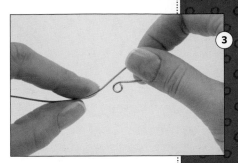

4 :: Bend the wire over the mandrel 1 in/2.5 cm from the midpoint (2 in/5 cm from the bend created in step 2) in the opposite direction.

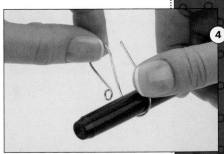

5 :: The wire should now look as shown in image 5.

6 :: Grasp the wire end in round-nose pliers at the marked point.

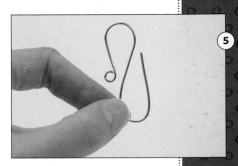

7 :: Rotate the pliers away from the center wire to create a small loop.

8 :: If your wire loops are uneven, place your fingers in the wires and adjust the shape.

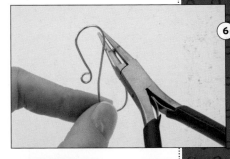

IMPORTANT :: These directions yield S-links that are approximately 1½ in/ 4 cm long. Adjust the wire measurement to make larger or smaller S-links.

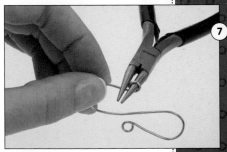

••• **TIP** •••

If you want to make small S-links, cut a piece of wire 2½ in/6 cm long. Then use round-nose pliers only, and forgo using a mandrel. Use the tips of the pliers for the small end loops and the base of the pliers to make the larger bends.

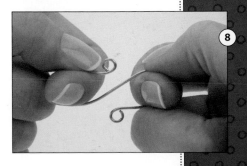

To cut chain into useful lengths, first identify how you want to use it and about how long you'd like it. Certain chains, like the Figaro chain, combine long and short links which may affect your design. In the Carnavale earrings, page 161, I attached freshwater pearls to lengths of fine Figaro chain. It was much easier to attach the pearls to the larger links because there was more room to work, so I made sure that the long links began and ended each length of chain. This in turn, determined their measurements. There were only so many pre-determined lengths that allowed for the long links to be on both ends.

WHERE TO CUT CHAIN:

Once you've established the length, identify the last link on the chain length you want. Then, move one link over into the excess chain that will be trimmed away. This is the link you will cut so the exact length of chain you want stays intact.

Now examine the link you intend to cut. If it has a split link you'll see a place where both ends of the link meet but are not joined together. This looks like the split in a jump ring. These types of links are easy to separate. You can open them just as you would a jump ring (see page 309) using two pairs of chain- or bent-nose pliers. If you don't see two distinct ends, but a place where the ends were soldered together, use wire cutters to cut the link on this spot. It is the weakest point and the easiest to cut. Then, open it like a jump ring to separate the two lengths. If you cannot find any connection point on the link, cut the link on its sharpest curve. This is usually where it meets an adjacent link. Then use two pairs of pliers to open the link and separate the lengths.

WHAT TO USE:

Cut chain using the same tools for wire cutting. Here is a general guide about what cutter to use for what gauge of chain. When in doubt, though, use a heavier cutter.

Fine chain: Nippers

Medium chain: Cutters

Large chain: Heavy-duty chain cutters

HOW TO USE CHAIN:

To see examples of how to incorporate different types of chain into your jewelry designs, see the following:

COCO NECKLACE page 69

CRYSTAL SPRINGS NECKLACE page 87

WATERCOLORS NECKLACE www.chroniclebooks.com/beading

COUNTRY GARDEN NECKLACE page 73

RENAISSANCE BRACELET page 121

GOLD DIGGER BRACELET page 155

STORYBOOK BRACELET www.chroniclebooks.com/beading

BISOU BRACELET page 131

ARIA EARRINGS page 167

CARNAVALE EARRINGS page 161

CALYPSO EARRINGS www.chroniclebooks.com/beading

how to MAKE A BEADED FLOWER

These directions explain how to make one beaded flower, with twelve petals, that measures 3 in/7.5 cm in diameter. You can adjust these measurements to increase or decrease the number of petals or the size of the flower.

DIRECTIONS

1 :: Thread seed beads onto a 36-in/91.5-cm length of 24-gauge wire, leaving the wire attached to the spool. (See "How to Restring Small Beads," page 270.) Unspool extra wire to enable the beads to slide up and down the wire.

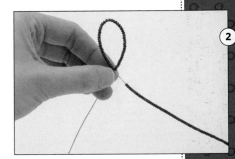

2 :: Create a 4-in/10-cm bare wire stem by sliding the seed beads toward the spool. Measure off a 3-in/7.5-cm length of seed beads and bend only the beaded section of the wire into a loop, crossing the wires at the base.

3 :: Wrap the stem wire around the long wire at the base of the loop to secure it.

4 :: Measure off a 3-in/7.5-cm length of seed beads and slide them up the wire toward the loop.

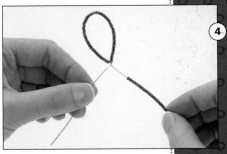

5 :: Bend only the beaded section of wire into a loop.

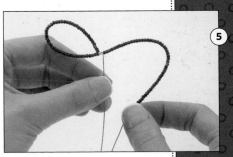

6 :: Cross the beaded wire over the wire stem just below the last seed bead.

7 :: Wrap the beaded wire behind the stem wire and out to the right.

8 :: Measure off a 3-in/7.5-cm length of seed beads and slide them up the wire toward the loops.

9 :: Bend the beaded wire into a loop. Cross the beaded wire over the wire stem just below the last seed bead.

10 :: Wrap the beaded wire behind the stem wire at the center point where the "petals" meet.

11 :: Press the wires at the base of the newly added petal together. While holding the center of the flower, rotate the stem wire clockwise and away from the beaded wire. This helps the wires to interlock and will keep them in place.

12 :: Move the petals closer together. Repeat steps 8–11 to add another petal.

13 :: Continue to add petals, working in a circular direction around the center point, rotating the stem wire clockwise each time.

14 :: As the number of petals increases, you must use chain-nose pliers to secure the beaded wire by flattening it around the stem wire.

15 :: Make a total of twelve petals. Measure an additional 4-in/10-cm length of bare wire to make a second stem. Cut the wire from the spool. Use chain-nose pliers to twist the stem wires together at the center of the flower.

ALTERNATIVE WAYS TO MAKE AND USE BEADED FLOWERS

See the following projects for inspiration, as well as the technique used in the Orange Blossom Hair Comb (page 255):

Use wires with higher gauges in this technique. You can simply use your hands to twist 26-, 28-, and 30-gauge wires. Twist thicker, heavier wire with chain-nose pliers by holding the bead with one hand while using the other hand to grasp the wires with the tips of pliers just below the bead. Rotate the pliers to twist the wires together, moving down the wires with every rotation.

DIRECTIONS

1 :: Use wire cutters to cut a 6-in/15-cm length of wire. Thread on one bead and slide it to the wire's midpoint. Bring the wire ends together, bending the wire in half.

2 :: Use one hand to hold the bead while twisting the wire ¼ in/6 mm with the opposite hand. Use chain-nose pliers if necessary.

3 :: Insert one of the wire ends into another bead. Slide the bead down the wire to a point just below the twisted wires.

4 :: Wrap the remaining wire end (not the one used in step 3) around the outside of the bead until both wires come together at the base of the bead. Twist the wires ¼ in/6 mm. Repeat steps 3–4 to add as many beads as desired.

You'll have the most ease making beaded branches when you use wires in higher gauges. The simplest wires to twist using only your hands are 26, 28, and 30 gauge. To twist thicker, heavier wires, use chain-nose pliers. Hold the bead with one hand while using the other hand to grasp the wires with the tips of chain-nose pliers just below the bead. Rotate the pliers to twist the wires together, moving down the wires with every rotation.

DIRECTIONS

1 :: Use wire cutters to cut a 12-in/30.5-cm length of wire. Insert one wire end into a briolette and slide it to the midpoint. Bend the wires down and cross them directly below the base of the briolette.

2 :: Hold the briolette with one hand while twisting the wire ends ½ in/12 mm with the opposite hand. Use chain-nose pliers if necessary.

3 :: Bend up the left wire stem. Insert its end into another briolette and slide it to the midpoint.

4 :: Bend down the wires on the right and left sides of the briolette, crossing them at the base of the briolette.

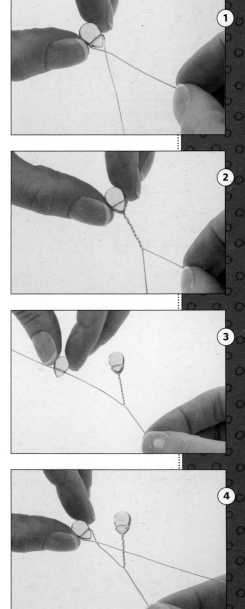

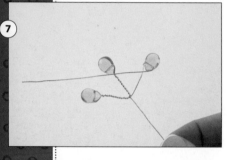

5 :: Hold the briolette in one hand while twisting the wire ½ in/12 mm with the opposite hand.

6 :: Bend the long wire up to the right. Insert the wire end into a third briolette and slide it to the midpoint.

7 :: Bend the wires down, crossing them at the base of the briolette.

8 :: Hold the briolette in one hand while twisting the wire ½ in/12 mm with the opposite hand.

9 :: Twist the remaining two wires together to form a stem.

IMPORTANT :: These directions yield one branch 4 in/10 cm long, with three sub-branches. Adjust these measurements to increase or decrease the size of the branch.

Although ready-made ear wires can be purchased from practically every bead supplier, it is simple to make your own. Since ear wires need to be relatively stiff to support the weight of beads, use half-hard wire or dead-soft wire that is work-hardened in 22 or 20 gauge.

Always finish wire ends by deburring them to prevent injury by metal shards and sharp edges (see "How to Finish Wire Ends," page 302).

For another example of how to make your own ear wires, see the Frosting earrings (page 181).

The French hooks below are made from 1½-in-/4-cm-long sterling-silver headpins with ball ends.

DIRECTIONS

1 :: Use the tips of round-nose pliers to make a small loop on the ball end of a headpin.

2 :: Bend the wire over a wide mandrel.

3 :: Use round-nose pliers on the opposite end to bend the back wire out slightly.

4 :: To make the second ear wire, repeat steps 1–3, making sure to match it to the first ear wire as you work. Deburr both wire ends.

IMPORTANT :: To avoid allergic reactions, make ear wires only out of sterling-silver, gold-filled, or niobium wire.

Many styles of ready-made ring forms can be purchased, but you can make your own as well. The simplest ones are made by wrapping wire. One example, the Oasis ring, is on page 211. When making ring forms of your own it's helpful to use a ring mandrel to size them correctly. But if you're making a ring that involves wrapping wire around the band, like the Oasis ring, make the ring one-half size larger than the size you want. Wrapping wire around the band, as well as using beads that sit low in the setting, like the ones in the Hard Candy Cocktail Rings (www.chroniclebooks.com/beading), will infringe upon the inner diameter of the band, making it necessary to increase the size to compensate for the lost space.

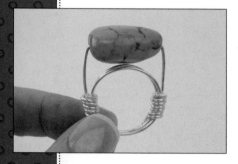

KNOTTING, STITCHING,
AND WEAVING

KNOTTING

You'll need to know how to make different types of knots to properly secure soft stringing materials such as thread and silk cord. Some knots are used on single strands, while others are used to secure two strands together.

The most helpful advice I can give about knots is that you always need more thread than you think to tie them properly. When your thread end is getting shorter and you're tempted to string on just a few more beads, resist the impulse. Even though it may seem like a waste, leaving at least 6 in/15 cm of thread to tie your knots will make all the difference.

Always make sure that the knot you've made will hold. Depending on the project, the stringing material, and the placement, you may want to secure the knot with glue. There are pros and cons to consider. Materials like silk cord, thread, ribbon, suede, and leather are absorbent and will change color, even after the glue dries. Therefore, always test your glue on a scrap piece of stringing material first. There is no reason not to use glue on a knot at the end of a strand; it provides extra security, and any discoloration of the stringing material can be concealed by a finding. But adding glue to the very visible knots in between beads on a knotted necklace can detract from the final product. The knots on a continuous strand necklace are hidden inside the bead holes, so using glue will not pose a problem. If you do decide to add glue for extra protection, cyanoacrylate, crystal cement, and clear nail polish are all good choices.

how to MAKE A SINGLE OVERHAND KNOT

Single overhand knots, used frequently in beading, are knots on a single strand. Use this technique to make the knots between the beads in a knotted necklace. Single overhand knots, all made in the same direction, lend a beautiful drape to stringing material.

DIRECTIONS

1 :: Cross the left thread over the right. Bring it around the back and through the center of the loop.

2 :: Pull the ends of the thread to secure the knot in place. If applicable, add glue to the knot and trim away excess or weave the ends of the thread back into the beads to hide them.

how to MAKE A DOUBLE OVERHAND KNOT

Double overhand knots, also frequently used in beading, are used to make knots on a single strand. A second single overhand knot is tied after the first one, thus making the knot more secure.

DIRECTIONS

1 :: Cross the left thread over the right. Bring it around the back and through the center of the loop. Bring it around to the back a second time and through the center of the loop.

2 :: The thread should look as shown in image 2, right.

3 :: Pull the ends of the threads to secure the knot in place. If applicable, add glue to the knot and trim away excess or weave the ends of the thread back into the beads to hide them.

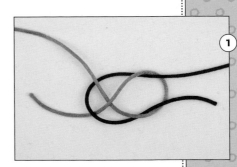

how to **MAKE A WEAVER'S KNOT**

Weaver's knots are used to secure two strands together. They are just as strong as square knots, but they lie flatter and are less bulky. I found this knot helpful in making the Hard Candy Cocktail Rings, www.chroniclebooks.com/beading, for these very reasons.

DIRECTIONS

1 :: Loop the thread on the right back on itself. Position the thread on the left across the bottom of the loop, around the back of the loop, and around to the front. Cross the thread over itself and under the bottom of the original loop.

2 :: Pull the ends of the threads to secure the knot in place. If applicable, add glue to the knot and trim away excess or weave the ends of the threads back into the beads to hide them.

how to MAKE A SQUARE KNOT

A square knot is an all-around good knot used to secure two strands together. Such knots hold well and are strong.

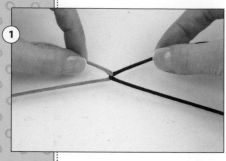

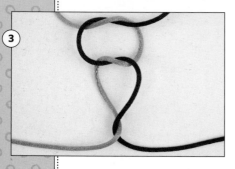

DIRECTIONS

1 :: Cross the right thread over the left. Then bring both threads back in the direction they came from, as shown at left.

2 :: Make a single overhand knot by crossing the left thread over the right.

3 :: Make another single overhand knot by crossing the thread now on the left over the right.

4 :: Pull the ends of the threads to secure the knot in place. If applicable, add glue to the knot and trim away excess or weave the ends of the threads back into the beads to hide them.

how to **MAKE A SLIP KNOT**

Slip knots are made on a single strand and are adjustable. They create a loop that can be enlarged or reduced. They are also temporary, and can be used to keep beads from falling off stringing materials or for other short-term purposes. Afterward, simply pull the short end and the knot disappears. You will notice that the first two steps below are the same as the wire crochet stitches used in the Wildfire bracelet, page 141.

DIRECTIONS

1 :: Cross the left thread over the right. Bring it around the back.

2 :: Reach through the loop from the front and grasp the thread. Pull it through the center and out to the right to create a second loop.

3 :: Pull the loop to tighten the knot. Note: To untie the knot, pull the short thread.

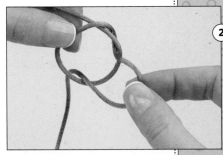

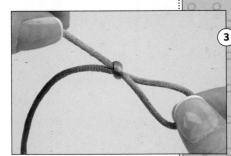

Beaded lace, chain, netting, and off-loom bead weaving stitches can all be made with only a few tools. Simple beads, a needle, and thread can be used to create almost anything you can imagine—open-weave designs such as the Byzantine Lace necklace (www.chroniclebooks.com/beading), tight weaves of flexible fabric such as the Lots of Luxe bracelet (page 125) and the Moonlit Night necklace (page 93), and even an elaborate beaded garden, as in the Hothouse Flowers bracelet (page 147). Sometimes bead weaving doesn't even require a needle. The Hard Candy Cocktail Rings (www.chroniclebooks.com/beading) are woven using transite, transforming seed beads and crystals into wearable woven art.

how to PREPARE BEADS FOR BEAD WEAVING

Anytime you work on a project with many small beads, such as seed beads or crystals, set up your work area so you can work efficiently.

Use beading mats: Since small beads roll, bounce, and get lost easily, place a piece of fabric, a dish towel, or a beading mat on your work surface to keep the ones you drop contained.

Use bead dishes: Shallow dishes are convenient for beads, allowing you to easily pick up one bead at a time on your needle. Be sure to anchor the dish to your work surface. You only need to knock it over once to always remember to secure it. Place clay adhesive, such as Fun-Tak, underneath the dish. Place only one type or color of bead in each dish. This will make putting away any beads you don't use easy, and you won't have to separate mixed seed beads.

Pour beads: Pour seed beads slowly, with the package opening touching the bottom of the dish. If you pour them a few inches above the dish, the beads will likely bounce out. Don't put all the beads into the dish at once; you'll be more likely to spill them. It's easiest to fill the dish partway, work until you're out of beads, and then replenish them.

Pick up one bead at a time: Find a bead with its hole facing up. Place the point of the needle in the hole. Tip the bead over with the needle and quickly lift the tip. The bead will "jump" onto the end of your needle. Then slide the bead down the needle. Jostle the bead dish to position other beads with hole side up.

how to PREPARE BEADING THREAD

There are four important things you need to do to prepare your thread: pre-stretch it, condition it, choose to use a single or double thread, and add a bead stopper. Review all of the next four sections before you begin a project so you can make the best choices.

how to PRESTRETCH BEADING THREAD

Beading thread stretches out over time in finished pieces. It can even stretch while you're working, causing gaps or drooping strands in your beadwork. To prevent this, always prestretch your thread. This is especially important when you are using a thread, such as Nymo, that is prone to stretching.

DIRECTIONS

1 :: Cut the amount of thread you want to use.

2 :: Begin at one end of the thread. Grasp a small section in both hands and tug on it at opposite ends until you feel it give.

3 :: Continue to stretch the thread in sections until the entire length has been stretched.

4 :: Condition the thread, thread your needle, and add a bead stopper (page 348).

how to CONDITION THREAD

Applying beeswax or thread conditioner to your beading threads prior to starting your beadwork will make the threads less prone to tangling and knotting while you work and will help to prevent weakening, fraying, and break-ing after the piece is finished. Some threads, such as Nymo, are sold unwaxed, but others, such as Silamide, are prewaxed.

Beeswax tends to be sticky and will stiffen the thread more than conditioner; it also keeps strands stuck together. This can work to your advantage depending on the project. Beeswax is also inexpensive but can bother people with allergies to bee products. Thread conditioner, while pricier, is hypoallergenic. Try both to determine which you prefer to work with.

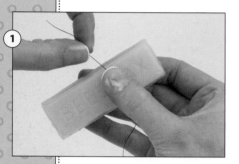

DIRECTIONS

1 :: With one hand, hold the beeswax or thread conditioner. Use the thumb on the same hand to hold the end of the thread against the wax or conditioner. Use the opposite hand to pull the thread up to coat the entire length. Now run the thread between your thumb and forefinger to coat the threads thoroughly and remove any wax or conditioner "crumbs" that may have been left behind.

IMPORTANT :: Chunks of beeswax are often left behind on your thread after you've conditioned it. The wax will clog up your bead holes and your needle. Be sure to remove it prior to starting. (This is not much of a problem with conditioner.)

how to START A SINGLE-THREADED STRAND WITH A BEAD STOPPER

There are many advantages to doing your bead weaving with a single-threaded strand. You must pass the needle and thread multiple times through the same beads, and a single thread won't fill up the bead holes as quickly as a double-threaded strand will. This leaves

you lots of room to stitch, weave in any loose ends, and begin new threads in the middle of a project. For the same reason, a single strand doesn't limit the size of the thread you use as much as a double-threaded strand does.

Single-threaded strands are also useful when you make a mistake (as I do all the time) and have to remove some stitches. You can simply slide the needle off the thread, use the end of the needle to loosen the stitches, and pull them out. Rethread the needle on the same thread and start again. The only downside: you must hold on to the needle and thread while you work. (See step 5 below.)

I used a single-threaded strand to make the netting and peyote projects—see the Lots of Luxe bracelet (page 125), the Byzantine Lace necklace (www.chroniclebooks.com/beading), and the Moonlit Night necklace (page 93).

DIRECTIONS

1 :: Cut a 16-in/40.5-cm length of prestretched and preconditioned thread. Thread one end through the eye of the needle. Fold over a 3-in/7.5-cm tail.

2 :: Thread on a bead that is a different size and color than the beads for the project. This will be the bead stopper.

3 :: Slide the bead stopper down to the opposite end, stopping it 4 in/10 cm before the end of the thread. Bring the needle around and insert it into the bottom of the bead stopper without piercing or sewing through the existing thread. Pull the thread through.

4 :: Repeat step 3 one or two more times to secure it. The bead should stay in place, but you should still be able to move it along the thread, and later remove it, if you loosen the stitches.

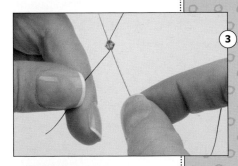

5 :: To work with a single-threaded strand, secure the thread and tail between your fingers while you work to keep the thread from slipping off the needle.

how to START A DOUBLE-THREADED STRAND WITH A BEAD STOPPER

The main advantage to working with a double-threaded strand is the support it provides the beads. You also never have to worry about the needle falling off the thread. You can use a double-threaded strand to do your bead weaving, but I find it easier to use a single thread, particularly if you make a mistake. (See "How to Start a Single-Threaded Strand with a Bead Stopper," page 348, for more information.)

In the Hothouse Flowers bracelet (page 147), the individual beaded flowers are assembled from multiple beads and seem to "grow" out from the core of the bracelet. The double thread gives the beads extra support.

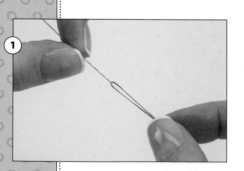

DIRECTIONS

1 :: Cut a 36-in/91.5-cm length of prestretched and preconditioned thread. Thread one end through the eye of the needle. Bring the needle to its midpoint, drawing the cut thread ends together.

2 :: Thread on a bead that is a different size and color than the beads for the project. This will be the bead stopper.

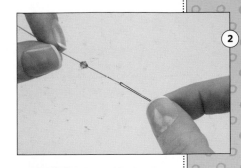

3 :: Slide the bead stopper down to the opposite end, stopping it 4 in/10 cm before the end of the thread. Bring the needle around and insert into the bottom of the bead stopper without piercing or sewing through the existing thread. Pull the thread through.

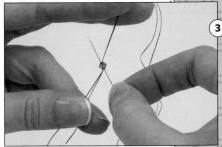

4 :: Repeat step 3 one or two more times to secure the bead stopper. The bead should stay in place, but you should still be able to move it along the thread, and later remove it, if you loosen the stitches.

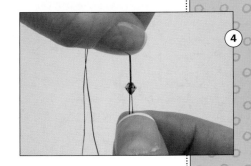

THE PEYOTE STITCH

The following sections are an introduction to the most popular off-loom bead weaving stitch, the peyote stitch. It creates a flat, flexible fabric using only beads, a needle, and thread.

The peyote stitch is characterized by a tight weave of beads in which each row is one half-step higher than the row before. There are a number of variations: even-count peyote, odd-count peyote, two-drop and three-drop peyote, circular peyote, and tubular peyote. Each is made using the same simple principle: add a new bead, skip the next bead, and insert the needle into the bead after that. Here I'll introduce you to the even, odd, and tubular peyote stitches.

Using seed beads that are uniform in size yield the best results. I prefer to use Miyuki Delica seed beads. They are made in Japan, have a consistent cylindrical shape and large bead holes, and come in a variety of colors, finishes, and metals, including sterling silver and 24K gold plated. They are more expensive than other seed beads, but I think the result is worth it.

The most challenging thing about bead weaving is maintaining the proper amount of tension on the thread. If your thread is too loose, the outside edges can be misshapen, loops of thread may stick out, and gaps may appear between beads. If your thread is too tight, the beads may pucker in some places (making the piece prone to breakage) and will not lie flat. These problems can be solved with practice.

The first few rows are the most difficult because the recognizable pattern doesn't take shape right away. To make this process easier, tighten up your threads after each bead is added and follow the instructional photos. Once the peyote pattern starts to form, your beading will go much more quickly.

Most bead-weaving projects are made in sections, so you must learn how to start a new thread in the middle of your project, weave sections together, and end a thread. You may be tempted to use an extra-long thread to avoid such work, but it would undoubtedly tangle or knot, forcing you to cut it off and start a new one. As you get better at bead weaving and develop some of your own tricks, you'll be able to use longer threads. In general, you should work with about 18 in/46 cm of thread. (If you're using a double thread, cut 36 in/91.5 cm so you're still working with 18 inches.) And always leave *at least* a 6-in/15-cm tail.

how to ANCHOR THREAD ENDS USING A KNOT

This technique is used to anchor the end of an old thread or the beginning of a new thread to an existing bead project. First, choose the point on the project where you want to secure the thread. It should be a space between two adjacent beads. Use your stringing material to tie an overhand knot (page 342) around the base thread that runs between the beads, trapping it inside the knot.

You will need this knotting technique to secure the stringing materials in the Pink Champagne necklace (page 101), Moonlit Night necklace (page 93), the Byzantine Lace necklace (www.chroniclebooks.com/beading), the Lots of Luxe bracelet (page 125), the Hothouse Flowers bracelet (page 147), and the Hard Candy Cocktail Rings (www.chronicle books.com/beading).

DIRECTIONS

1 :: Bring the thread underneath the base thread and back up to the starting point. Tie an overhand knot. Weave the long thread through a few more beads and make another knot. Repeat this step as many times as necessary to secure the thread. Hide the short thread end in the adjacent beads.

You'll need to start a new thread on your project whenever the old thread runs out and your beaded section isn't complete. It involves reweaving the last few rows, following the same path as the first thread and tying overhand knots along the way.

If you are doing any type of flat peyote, you'll want to begin a new thread on the same side that the last thread ended, and weave the thread to the opposite side and back again, anchoring the thread with knots as you go. *You should end up with the new thread in the same position that you ended the old thread.* Now you're ready to continue weaving. After a few rows, set the new thread down, pull the old thread taut, and follow the directions for "How to End a Thread by Weaving In," page 355.

The directions below illustrate this technique on a flat peyote project. If you're working with tubular peyote, begin a new thread between the first two beads on the row you just completed. Weave the thread through the row again, tying knots in between every few beads and pick up where you left off. After adding a few new rows, set the new thread down, pull the old thread taut, and follow the directions for "How to End a Thread by Weaving In," page 355.

Instead of beginning a new thread, you can also set your beaded section aside, start from scratch, and weave a second section. Then follow "How to Weave Two Peyote Sections Together," page 354, to secure them together.

DIRECTIONS

1 :: When you begin to run out of thread, finish weaving the last row of beads on your section, making sure to leave at least a 6-in/15-cm tail. Thread another needle with a new prestretched and preconditioned 18-in/46-cm thread. Insert the needle one column in from the edge a few rows away from the old thread. With the end of the thread, tie an overhand knot around the base thread that runs between the beads, trapping it inside the knot.

2 :: Weave the thread to the opposite side, following the original path and tying overhand knots to anchor it between the beads on every few columns along the way.

Old Thread

New Thread

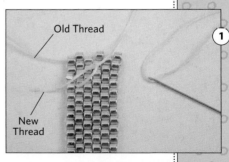

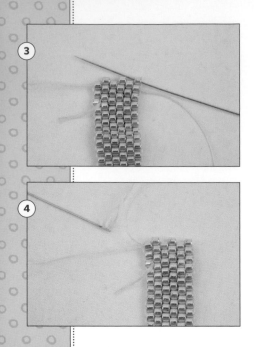

3 :: Move one row up and weave the thread, following the original path to the opposite side, tying knots along the way. Repeat step 2, finishing with the needle in position to reweave the last row that was added.

4 :: Reweave this last row of beads, exiting the thread through the same bead as the original thread tail. Turn the beaded section over and continue to add rows. Follow "How to End a Thread by Weaving In," facing page, to weave the old thread tail into the beads.

> **••• TIP •••**
>
> See "How to Anchor Thread Ends Using a Knot," page 352, for a more detailed explanation of the knot you need to tie between the beads.

how to WEAVE TWO PEYOTE SECTIONS TOGETHER

If you prefer to do your off-loom bead weaving in sections, as I do, you'll need to know how to weave two sections together. Weave one thread tail between the two sections in the same direction the thread was originally woven. Then weave the remaining thread tail between the two sections in the same direction it was originally woven, which will be in the opposite direction from the first thread. Pull both thread tails taut and anchor them with knots, following the directions for "How to End a Thread by Weaving In," facing page. The directions on the opposite page illustrate this technique on a flat peyote project, but if you're working with tubular peyote, the principle is the same.

An alternative to this technique is "How to Start a New Thread Midproject," page 353, to continue weaving on the section you're now creating.

DIRECTIONS

1 :: Place a peyote beaded section on a flat work surface, with the thread tail exiting the top row of beads to the right.

2 :: Position a second peyote beaded section above the first, with the thread tail exiting the bottom row of beads to the left. Make sure the bead patterns line up. If necessary, add or remove a row of beads from one section.

3 :: Thread the needle with the thread tail from step 1. Insert the needle into the bead directly above it (from the second section). Working from right to left, insert the needle into the adjacent bead on section 1. Then insert the needle into the adjacent bead on section 2.

4 :: Weave the thread between the two sections, alternating between picking up one bead on section 1 and one bead on section 2 until the opposite side is reached. Pull the threads taut. Set the needle down. Thread a second needle with the thread tail from step 2. Insert the needle into the bead directly below it (from the first section). Working left to right, weave the thread between the two sections as before until the opposite side is reached. Pull the threads taut. Now hide and secure the thread end by following "How to End a Thread by Weaving In," below.

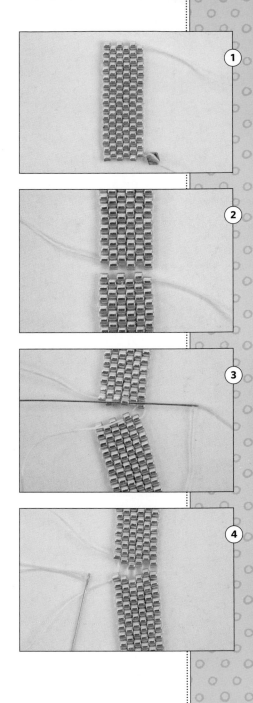

how to END A THREAD BY WEAVING IN

This technique is used to secure and hide your thread ends within your beaded section.

DIRECTIONS

1 :: Thread the needle with the thread tail. Insert the needle into the bead directly above it. Pull the thread taut.

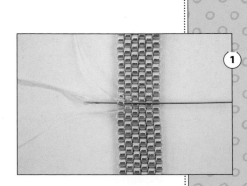

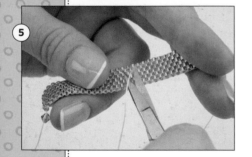

2 :: Tie an overhand knot around the base thread that runs between the beads, trapping it inside the knot.

3 :: Insert the needle through a few more beads, following the path of the weave.

4 :: Tie a single overhand knot around the base thread that runs between the beads, trapping it inside the knot.

5 :: Repeat steps 3–4 as many times as necessary to secure the thread end. Tie a double overhand knot (page 342). Insert the needle through the nearest bead and pull the thread taut. Trim away excess thread using sharp scissors.

● ● ● **TIP** ● ● ●
....

See "How to Anchor Thread Ends Using a Knot," page 356, for a detailed explanation of the knot you need to tie between the beads.

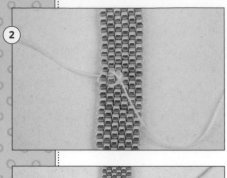

how to MAKE THE EVEN-COUNT FLAT PEYOTE STITCH

Even-count flat peyote is one of the easiest bead-weaving techniques to perfect, and it is a good one to start with if you are new to off-loom beading. Even-count flat peyote, as its name indicates, uses an even number of beads.

DIRECTIONS

1 :: Thread a needle with a prestretched and preconditioned single strand of thread.

2 :: At the opposite end, secure a bead stopper.

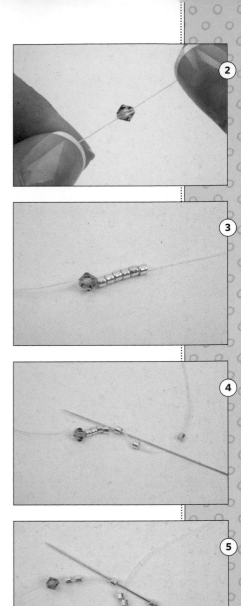

3 :: Thread on an even number of seed beads. In this example, use six beads. These six beads make up row 1.

4 :: Thread on one seed bead (#7). Skip over the bead (#6) closest to it and insert the needle into the following bead (#5) from row 1. Pull the needle through and make the threads taut.

5 :: Thread on a seed bead (#8). Skip over the next bead (#4) and insert the needle into the following bead (#3) from row 1. Pull the needle through and make the thread taut.

6 :: To finish the row, thread on a seed bead (#9). Skip over the next bead (#2) and insert the needle into the following bead (#1) from row 1. Pull the needle through and make the thread taut.

7 :: The beads should be locked in place and look as shown in image 7. Note that there are three rows. Row 1: #2, #4, #6; row 2: #1, #3, #5; row 3: #9, #8, #7.

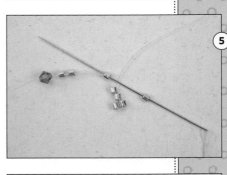

EVEN-COUNT FLAT PEYOTE STITCH

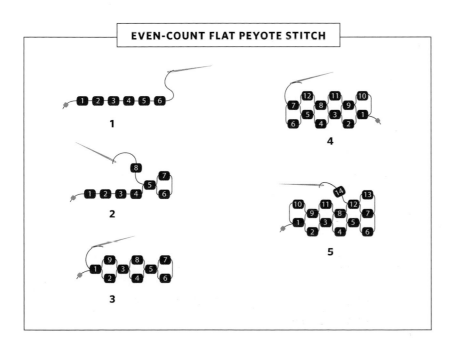

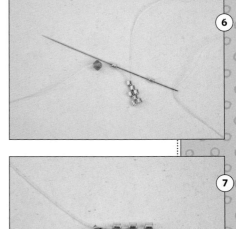

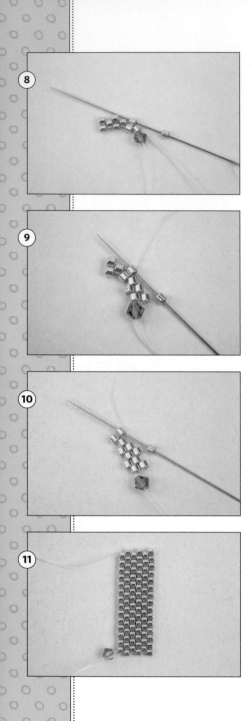

8 :: Turn the beaded section over so that the bead stopper and threaded needle are on the right-hand side. To begin row 4, thread on a seed bead (#10), skip over the next bead (#1), and insert the needle into the following bead (#9) from the previous row. Pull the needle through and make the threads taut.

9 :: Thread on a seed bead (#11). Skip over the next bead (#3) and insert the needle into the following bead (#8) from the previous row. Pull the needle through and make the threads taut.

10 :: Thread on another seed bead (#12). Skip over the next bead (#5) and insert the needle into the following bead (#7) from the previous row. Pull the needle through and make the threads taut. This completes row 4.

11 :: Repeat these steps to add rows until the sufficient length is achieved.

IMPORTANT :: The following information may sound confusing, but it is important to know. It will make much more sense after you start beading yourself.

• String on an even number of beads to make row 1.

• As you add more beads, row 2 and row 3 actually will be created simultaneously.

• Each row that is added, beginning with row 2, will have half the number of beads of row 1.

• The new bead you thread on will end up sitting directly above the bead you skip.

• When you thread your needle through a bead that has already been stitched, be careful not to pierce or sew through the existing thread; that could tear it. If you've made a few passes through the bead and you feel some resistance on the needle, pull it out and reinsert it in a different place in the bead hole.

· · · · TIP · · · ·

These directions are for someone who is right-handed. If you are left-handed, begin with the bead stopper on the right-hand side. You can then weave from left to right. At the end of the row, turn the beaded section over so you can weave from left to right again.

MASTERING THE ART *of* BEADING

how to MAKE THE ODD-COUNT FLAT PEYOTE STITCH
USING FIVE OR MORE BEADS

In order to do the odd-count flat peyote stitch, it is necessary to first understand and have experience with the even-count flat peyote stitch (see page 357). Odd-count flat peyote, as its name indicates, uses an odd number of beads. These directions can be used when you begin with five or more beads.

Odd-count flat peyote is slightly more difficult than even-count flat peyote. On one side, you can start a new row exactly as you would in even-count peyote. On the opposite side, you make more passes through the beads to bring the needle back into the proper position. This means that every other new row you add requires these extra steps.

DIRECTIONS

1 :: Thread on an odd number of seed beads, in this case nine. Begin the next row and thread on four more beads just as you would in even-count peyote. Thread on the last bead (#14) and insert the needle into the bead directly below it (#1) to begin making the figure eight. Pull the threads taut.

2 :: Continue making the figure eight by inserting the needle through the center bead (#2) and the bead (#3) diagonally below it.

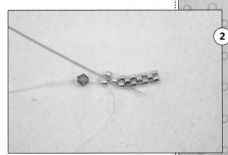

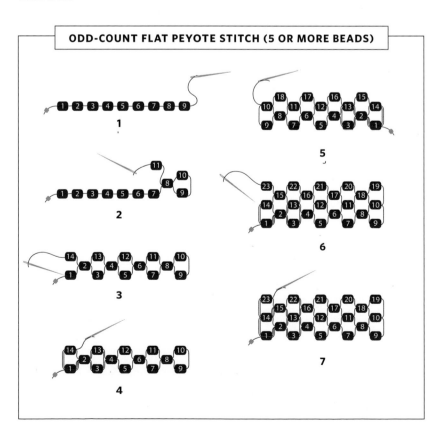

ODD-COUNT FLAT PEYOTE STITCH (5 OR MORE BEADS)

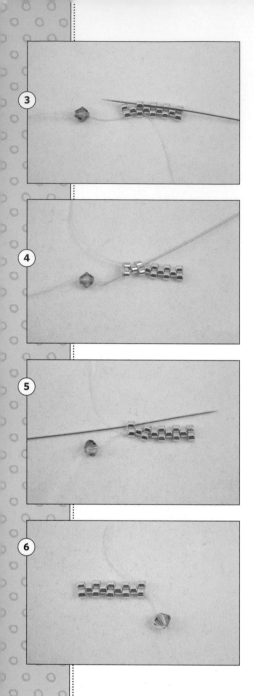

3 :: Working toward the unfinished end, insert the needle through the bead directly above the last bead (#13) in step 2. The thread will run vertically in the middle of the beaded section but will slip between and be hidden by the two columns of beads.

4 :: Continue making the figure eight by inserting the needle through the center bead (#2) and bead #1. Pull the threads taut.

5 :: Finish the figure eight by inserting the needle into the bead (#14) that ended the row in step 1. Pull the threads taut.

6 :: Turn the beaded section over. You are now in position to begin the next row by threading on a new bead. It will be necessary to secure this side of the beaded section with a figure-eight turn with every other row you add.

IMPORTANT :: Be sure to read the notes labeled "Important" and "Tip" from "How to Make the Even-Count Flat Peyote Stitch," page 356, for more important information before you begin, but take note of this critical difference:

In odd-count flat peyote you:

• String on an odd number of beads to make row 1.

• Each row that is added, beginning with row 2, will have one bead less, or one bead more than half the number of beads strung in row 1.

how to **MAKE THE ODD-COUNT FLAT PEYOTE STITCH USING THREE BEADS**

These directions are specifically for the Lots of Luxe bracelet (page 125). Doing this stitch with only three beads requires you to make a few adjustments to the directions listed in "How to Make the Odd-Count Flat Peyote Stitch Using Five or More Beads" (page 359). Be sure to review that technique before following the directions on the opposite page.

As described in that technique, you can start a new row on one side exactly as you would in even-count peyote. On the opposite side, you have to make more passes through the beads to bring the needle back into the proper position. Every other new row you add requires these extra steps. If you begin with five beads, you can use the last three columns to make your figure-eight turn. If you begin with three beads, you have only three columns and therefore can make only a partial figure-eight turn to get your needle into the proper position.

DIRECTIONS

1 :: Thread the needle with a prestretched and preconditioned single strand of thread.

2 :: At the opposite end, secure a bead stopper.

3 :: Thread on three seed beads.

4 :: Thread on one more seed bead (#4). Skip over bead (#3). Insert the needle into the following bead (#2) in row 1, which in this case is the middle bead. Pull the needle through and make the threads taut.

5 :: To secure this side and properly position the needle for the next row, make a partial figure eight. To begin, thread on a seed bead (#5). Insert the needle through bead #1. Pull the needle through and make the threads taut.

6 :: Continue the partial figure eight by inserting the needle through bead #2 and then bead #3.

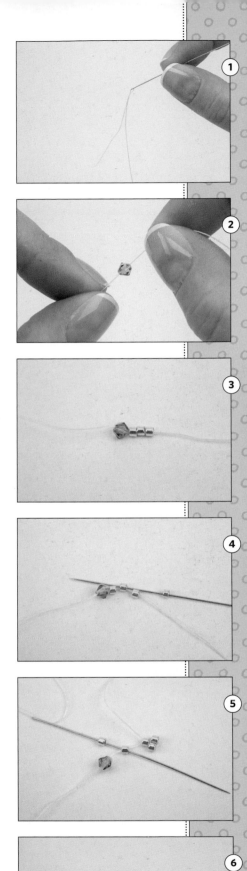

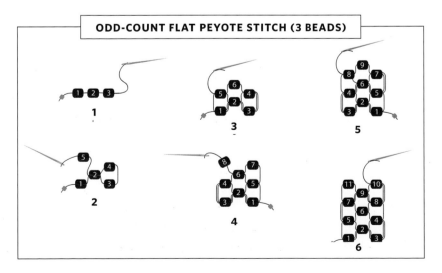

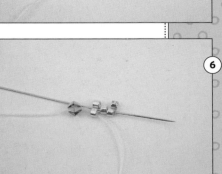

ODD-COUNT FLAT PEYOTE STITCH (3 BEADS)

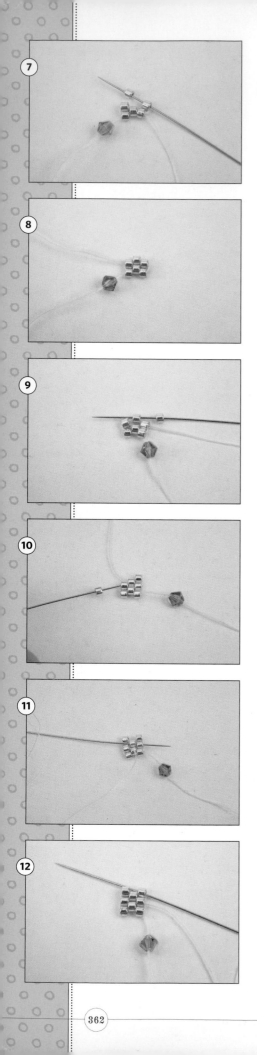

7 :: To complete the partial figure eight, insert the needle through bead #4. Now the needle is in position to start a new row (row 4). Thread on another seed bead (#6). Skip over the next bead (#2) and insert the needle into the following bead (#5) from the previous row.

8 :: Pull the needle through and make the threads taut so that the beads take shape and look like those shown in image 8, left.

9 :: Turn the beaded section over so that the needle is on the right-hand side. Thread on another seed bead (#7). Skip over the next bead (#5) and insert the needle into the following bead (#6) in the previous row. Pull the needle through and make the threads taut.

10 :: Thread on another seed bead (#8) and secure the side by making a partial figure eight. Insert the needle into the bead directly below it (#4).

11 :: Continue making the partial figure eight by inserting the needle through beads #6 and #5.

12 :: Insert the needle into bead #7. Pull the needle through and make the threads taut. Now the needle is in position to start a new row.

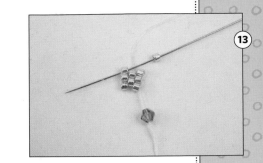

13 :: Thread on a new seed bead (#9). Skip over the next bead (#6) and insert the needle into the following bead (#8). Pull the needle through and make the threads taut. Repeat these steps to add as many rows as needed.

IMPORTANT :: Be sure to read the notes labeled "Important" and "Tip" from "How to Make the Even-Count Flat Peyote Stitch," page 356, for more important information before you begin, but take note of this critical difference:

In odd-count flat peyote using three beads you:

• String on three beads to make row 1.

• Each row that is added will only have one or two beads in the entire row.

how to MAKE THE EVEN-COUNT TUBULAR PEYOTE STITCH

In my quest to learn the tubular peyote stitch, every set of directions I found recommended that after you complete the foundation circle of beads (step 2, page 364), you either tie a knot or run the thread through the circle two more times to secure it. I concluded that this was why my tubular peyote stitches looked nothing like they were supposed to.

In order for the beads to shift into position, there has to be an appropriate amount of slack in the thread. If you secure the foundation circle with a knot or run the threads through the circle a few times, the beads can't move. So I tried to leave some slack in the thread before tying the knot. But what's the right amount of slack? When there's too much slack, the beads don't align properly. The knot prevents you from pulling on the thread and tightening up the beads, as does running the thread through extra times. I was most successful not securing the foundation circle. You can always reinforce the beaded end later if you like.

I use different-colored seed beads to visually explain this technique: a different color for each new row. However, these are not the kinds of beads you would use to do the peyote stitch. They are too round and are not uniform. See "The Peyote Stitch," page 351, for more information about choosing beads. You are also looking at an aerial view here. When you actually do this stitch, the beads will look like this photo for only the first three or four rows. The beads will then begin to take shape. Tighten the threads up and the bare threads will disappear and the beads will lock into place and form a tube.

DIRECTIONS

1 :: Thread the needle with a prestretched and preconditioned single strand of thread. At the opposite end, secure a bead stopper. Thread on an even number of seed beads. This example uses twelve beads, which make up row 1. Bring the needle around and insert it into the first bead.

2 :: Pull the needle through and pull the threads taut to form a circle.

3 :: Thread on one bead. Skip over the next bead and insert the needle into the following bead. Pull the thread taut.

4 :: Repeat step 3 until you have threaded on half the number of beads you started with (in this case, six beads) and have gone all the way around the circle. Note: Just as in flat peyote, the orange beads displace every other red bead, so there are now three completed rows.

5 :: Do not thread on another new bead. Instead, insert the needle into the first (orange) bead you threaded on after the original (red) circle. Pull the thread taut. This is called stepping up. The needle is now in position to start row 4.

6 :: Thread on one new (light blue) bead. Skip over the next (red) bead and insert the needle into the following (orange) bead. Pull the thread taut.

7 :: Repeat step 6 until you have threaded on half the number of beads you started with (in this case, six beads) and have gone all the way around the circle.

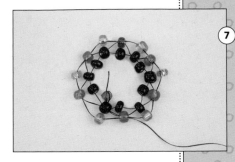

8 :: Do not thread on another new bead. Instead, insert the needle into the first (light blue) bead that began the row. Pull the thread taut. The needle is now in position to start row 5.

9 :: Repeat steps 6–8 as many times as necessary to add additional rows.

IMPORTANT :: What makes the tubular peyote stitch different from the even- and odd-count flat peyote stitches is that it requires a technique called stepping up. Look at step 4. Remember that the new bead you thread on will sit directly on top of the bead you skip. If you leave the thread where it is, coming out of the first red bead, and add a row of new beads, they will pile on top of the row you just added. The goal is to add beads to the spaces between the beads in the previous row. Now look at step 5. Each time you finish a row (the orange row was just finished, and the thread is exiting the first red bead), the next bead will be in the "up" position. Insert the needle, without a new bead, into the bead in the up position. This will always be the first bead of the row you just completed. The needle is now in the proper position to start the next row. You will know that you are doing the stitch correctly, and stepping up, if with each new row the first bead always shifts over one position to create a diagonal.

how to **MAKE THE ODD-COUNT TUBULAR PEYOTE STITCH**

To make the odd-count tubular peyote stitch, see "How to Make the Even-Count Tubular Peyote Stitch," above. Simply eliminate the instructions for stepping up. After finishing one row, your needle will already be in the proper position to string on a new bead, and you can begin the next row immediately.

There are lots of ways to finish your peyote jewelry. Here are some suggestions.

To finish flat peyote:

Add a woven loop and button clasp. (See the Lots of Luxe bracelet, page 125.)

Attach clamp ends to both ends; attach a clasp. (See "How to Use a Clamp End with Ribbon," page 288.)

Weave in two thread tails on each short end. Secure them to clamshells, bead tips, or knot cups and a clasp. Or cover the tails with coordinating seed beads or French bullion wire to protect the thread. Then secure the threads to jump rings, end bars, or multistrand clasps. Weave the thread ends back into the beaded piece. (See the Byzantine Lace necklace, www.chroniclebooks.com/beading.)

To finish tubular peyote:

Attach end bars and a clasp. (See the Moonlit Night necklace, page 93.)

Stitch both ends closed, leaving thread tails. Make a loop strung with coordinating beads on one end and add a button or bead clasp to the other. (See the Hothouse Flowers bracelet, page 147.)

Stitch both ends closed, leaving thread tails. Add a bead cap, bullet end, or cone end to each end and attach a clasp. (See the Lorelei Lee earrings, page 189.)

EMBELLISHING

There are many techniques for adding decorative elements, embellishments, and finishing details to your jewelry. See the following sections to learn how to make and use ribbon bows, rhinestones, buttons, charms, and pendants.

how to **MAKE A DOUBLE BOW**

Bows are a lovely addition to jewelry. They can be added to pendants, placed on chains, or used as clasps. Bow-making is also a handy skill when you're wrapping up your jewelry to present as gifts.

Once you understand the ribbon-tying technique on the following page, you can expand it to make a bow with as many loops as you like. The number of loops your bow has, and how full it looks, is determined by how many folds you make in step 1. If you want more than four loops, two on each side, continue to overlap the ribbon, always folding it over itself in the opposite direction from the previous fold. As you do this, line up the folded edges of the ribbon; they should all be of equal length. But no matter how many loops you want, before you tie the bow you should always have the original short ribbon end and an odd number of loops on the right-hand side and an even number of loops on the left-hand side. Then you can proceed with steps 2–8.

Multiloop bows are easiest to make with wire-edged and grosgrain ribbon. Wire-edged ribbon allows the bow to hold its shape, and grosgrain's texture helps it to grip. Satin ribbon is the most difficult type to use because it is so slippery—the knot tends to loosen quickly after being tied. If you really love the look of satin ribbon, use a needle and thread and a few tiny stitches to secure it in the center. Glue is a little harder to use because it tends to seep through the fabric. I have been pretty successful using permanent adhesive on satin ribbon, though. (See "Glues and Adhesives" in the glossary, page 59, for more information.)

DIRECTIONS

1 :: Place the ribbon horizontally on a clean, flat work surface. Measure 5 in/12 cm of ribbon. At the 5 in/12 cm mark, fold the ribbon over itself for 4 in/10 cm from the folded end. At the 4 in/10 cm mark, fold the ribbon over itself in the opposite direction for 4 in/10 cm from the last folded end. At the 4 in/10 cm mark, fold the ribbon over itself again in the opposite direction. Do not cut away any excess ribbon.

2 :: Pick up the folds of ribbon in the center. There should be two loops on the left and one loop on the right. The two ribbon ends should be on the right as well. While still holding the ribbon center with your left hand, pick up the top, long ribbon end with your right hand.

3 :: Reposition your left fingers while maintaining your grasp on the center as shown. Place your thumb and index finger on top and your middle finger on the bottom. Wrap the long ribbon end over your index finger and around to the back.

4 :: Continue wrapping the long ribbon end by bringing it around to the front and back up to the center. Slip the ribbon under your thumb as shown. Move the long ribbon end off to the left.

5 :: Without altering your grip on the ribbon, carefully set it down on the work surface. You should be able to identify the loop in the center, made in steps 3–4.

6 :: Again, do not move your left hand. With your right hand, reach through the center loop with your thumb and index finger. Grasp the long ribbon end and pull it back through the center loop to make the second and final loop on the right side. Note: You are making a loop, or "bunny ear." Do not pull the long ribbon end all the way through.

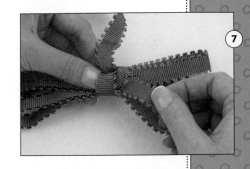

7 :: Firmly grasp the two loops on the left. Gently pull the loop on the right. Determine which side of the loop, the front or the back, tightens the loop in the center. Continue pulling the loop to tighten and secure the center. Pull the loop out to the right until it is the same length as the other loop on the same side.

8 :: Turn the entire bow over. This is the front side, where the center knot is flat. (See step 7 and look at the center knot. The ribbons cross. This is how you recognize the back side of the bow.) Trim the ribbon ends to the desired length.

> **• • • TIP • • •**
>
> You can change the measurements above to make larger or smaller bows.

how to USE RHINESTONES

Bead stores sell rhinestones in many sizes, settings, colors, and forms. They are available in different qualities, plastic and glass, as well as Austrian crystals. Flat-back rhinestones, rhinestone chain, and rhinestone-accented findings, beads, and buttons add lots of drama and sparkle to your jewelry pieces.

Rhinestone costume jewelry can also be an excellent source for your beaded jewelry. Check out thrift stores, flea markets, yard sales, and your own jewelry box, as well as any store that carries teen accessories. Often you can find this junk jewelry for very little money. Learn to assess even unattractive pieces for harvestable parts—manufactured jewelry can have gorgeous rhinestone elements that can be incorporated into your designs.

Take a look at the following projects that use rhinestones.

FLAT-BACK RHINESTONES:

LORELEI LEE EARRINGS page 189

TORCH SONG HEADBAND page 259

RHINESTONE CHAINS:

RENAISSANCE BRACELET page 121

CARNAVALE EARRINGS page 161

GREEK GODDESS HEADBAND page 245

STARDUST HAIR COMBS www. chroniclebooks.com/beading

how to USE BUTTONS IN BEADING

Buttons can be easily incorporated into your jewelry designs and are just as beautiful as beads. Many have rhinestone and pearl accents, which are my favorites. I also love to use vintage buttons. (See "Sources and Resources" for vendors.) Buttons may be shaped like flowers, fruit, hearts, or stars and may be made from shell, glass, metal, enamel, bone, horn, or wood. Use them as clasps or charms or in place of (or in addition to) beads when designing your jewelry. Refer to the following projects for inspiration:

Charms are a great addition to any piece. Add multiple ready-made charms to necklaces and bracelets or just one to make simple earrings. You can also fashion your own charms from beads or buttons.

how to MAKE DOUBLE-SIDED CHARMS

Part of the allure of a charm bracelet is that it moves. Charms flip around when the bracelet is worn, so make charms double-sided if possible. This will ensure that your jewelry looks great all the time.

See the Storybook bracelet (www.chronicle books.com/beading) for more examples of double-sided charms.

DIRECTIONS

1 :: Begin with two charms of equal size.

2 :: Apply cyanoacrylate gel to the back side of one charm.

3 :: Position the second charm on top of the first, back sides together, aligning the hanging loops. Let dry.

how to TRANSFORM FLAT-BACK BEADS INTO CHARMS

Any bead or button with a flat back can be transformed into a double-sided charm or connector when you glue two of them together with a length of wire in between— even if they have shanks. When finished, use the wire to make a wrapped-wire loop on one end to make a charm, or on both ends to make a connector.

See steps 16–21 of the Bisou bracelet, page 131, for more-detailed instructions.

how to MAKE COLLAGE PENDANT CHARMS

Any jewelry finding that has a flat, inset surface area can be used to make a collage. Place paper, beads, or glitter into the inset— even colored nail polish can be poured in to mimic enamel. You can turn findings with loops for hanging into pendants or charms. Pendant findings with open spaces, such as filigree findings, can be hung from a chain or turned into brooches when you add a pin back, or into rings when you attach it to a ring form.

See steps 3–8 of the Bisou bracelet, page 131, for detailed instructions on how to make a collage pendant charm using paper decorations.

See steps 2–4 of the Victoria ring, page 227, for detailed instructions on how to make a collage pendant charm using beads.

how to MAKE BEADED WIRE LETTERS

Wire letters make great charms or pendants. By shaping wire strung with seed beads, you can embellish your jewelry with words, phrases, an initial, or a monogram. See steps 9–15 of the Bisou bracelet, page 131, for detailed instructions.

how to ATTACH A PENDANT

There are many ways and materials you can use to attach a pendant to a necklace. Review steps 14–17 of the Café au Lait necklace, page 109, to see how to attach a pendant using silk cord and a bead cap secured with a knot. If you want to add the pendant to a strand of beads, you'll need to adapt the directions slightly. On step 16, instead of threading the strands through the loop on the rose connector, you would wrap both ends around the center bead, one strand to the right of the bead and one strand to the left. Then follow the remainder of steps 16–17 to finish.

Instead of using soft stringing material, you can also use this technique with beading wire or transite that you secure with a crimp bead. Hide the crimp bead under the bead cap, just as you hid the knot.

Another option is to string a ring on the center of your beaded strand instead of a center bead, as shown in step 7 of the Snow Queen necklace, page 105. Then use a jump ring to attach the pendant to the ring. You can also string on a bail in the strand's center to add a pendant. See step 10 of the Watercolors necklace, www.chroniclebooks.com/beading.

You can also use wire or a headpin to attach a pendant. See "How to Join Wrapped-Wire Loops without Using a Connector," page 320, to begin to make a wrapped-wire loop. Then slip the loop over the center point of the necklace and finish the wrapped-wire loop, securing the pendant to your beaded strand.

SOURCES AND RESOURCES

ARTBEADS.COM

11901 137th Avenue Ct. KPN
Gig Harbor, WA 98329
253-857-3433
866-715-BEAD (2323) toll free
www.artbeads.com

Beads, semiprecious stones, Swarovski crystals, Czech pressed-glass and fire-polished beads, pearls, findings, tools and supplies

BAZAAR STAR BEADERY

216 East Ridgewood Avenue
Ridgewood, NJ 07450
201-444-5144
www.bazaarstarbeadery.com

Loose and strung beads and findings

Aqua blue beads (Ladies Who Lunch); lime green beads (Hothouse Flowers); sterling-silver hoop earrings (Mint Julep)

BEADS WORLD, INC.

1384 Broadway
New York, NY 10018
212-302-1199
www.beadsworldusa.com

Beads, semiprecious stones, Swarovski crystals, pearls, chains, rhinestone chain, findings, tools, and supplies

Rhinestone ball clasp (Ladies Who Lunch); coral stick beads and chips (Bali Ha'i); pink Chinese crystal beads (Pink Champagne); rhinestone three-part clasp (Moonlit Night); midnight blue Chinese crystal rondelles (L'Heure Bleue); red glass pearls (Wildfire); light green pearls (Romantic Notions); blue goldstone beads (Starry Night); pink pearls (Hampton Classic)

BLUE MOON BEADS

7855 Hayvenhurst Avenue
Van Nuys, CA 91406
800-377-6715
www.bluemoonbeads.com

Beads, findings, and tools (also available in Michaels Stores)

Watermelon pink pearls (Country Garden); light sapphire three-sided beads, sapphire blue pearls, light sapphire faceted rondelles (L'Heure Bleue); leverback ear wires (Firefly)

CINDERELLA CLUB

242 West 36th Street
New York, NY 10018
212-629-6772
(No Web site, but definitely worth visiting)

Rhinestone costume jewelry

Crystal rhinestone flowers with shanks were harvested from one bracelet (Bisou); amber rhinestone flowers with shanks were harvested from another (Aria)

COSTUME JEWELRY SUPPLIES

1377 Dodson Road
Blairs, VA 24527
434-836-0099
www.costumejewelrysupplies.com

Rhinestones and settings

FIRE MOUNTAIN GEMS AND BEADS

One Fire Mountain Way
Grants Pass, OR 97526
800-423-2319 toll free
www.firemountaingems.com

Beads, semiprecious stones, Swarovski crystals, Czech crystals, pressed-glass and fire-polished beads, pearls, chains, findings, Smart Beads, tools, and supplies

Rose quartz and jade heart-shaped beads (Country Garden)

FUN 2 BEAD

1028 Sixth Avenue
New York, NY 10018
212-302-3488
www.fun2bead.com

Loose and strung beads, semiprecious stones,
Swarovski crystals, pearls, chain, findings, tools, and
supplies

Enamel flower charm (Bisou)

FUSION BEADS

3830 Stone Way North
Seattle, WA 98103
206-782-4595
www.fusionbeads.com

Beads, semiprecious stones, Swarovski crystals, Czech
pressed-glass and fire-polished beads, pearls, chains,
findings, tools, and supplies

24K gold plated Delica beads (Byzantine Lace); hematite and galvanized silver Delica beads (Moonlit Night);
Eiffel Tower, open-heart, and puffed-heart charms,
circle collage pendants, Amazing Glaze, pink and black
cane beads (sold as Mademoiselle Cane Glass Bead
Mix), fuchsia and amethyst beads with black polka
dots (Bisou); galvanized silver Delica beads (Lots of
Luxe); all Czech pressed-glass flowers and leaves
(Hothouse Flowers)

GENUINE TEN TEN

1010 Sixth Avenue
New York, NY 10018
212-221-1173
www.j-genuine.com

Semiprecious loose and strung beads, findings, tools,
and supplies

GOODY BEADS

15105 Minnetonka Industrial Road, Suite 111
Minnetonka, MN 55345
952-938-2324
www.goodybeads.com

Beads, semiprecious stones, Swarovski crystals, Czech
fire-polished beads, pearls, Venetian-style blown glass
beads, chains, findings, and supplies

GRACE LAMPWORK BEADS

1551 McCarthy Boulevard, Suite 111
Milpitas, CA 95035
866-965-9966
www.gracebeads.com

High-quality handmade lampwork beads of Italian and
German glass

JOLEE'S JEWELS

EK Success
100 Delawanna Avenue
Clifton, NJ 07014
973-458-0092
www.eksuccess.com

Swarovski crystal beads; components and findings with
Swarovski crystals (also available in Michaels Stores)

Rhinestone rondelles: Jolee's Jewels Fancy Crystal Ball
Sliders (Ladies Who Lunch); rhinestone circle pendant:
Jolee's Jewels Double Crystal Ring December Light
Azore (Snow Queen); gold cubes with Austrian crystal
accents: Jolee's Jewels Dangle Cube Leaf Mix (Water-
colors); gold rose connector: Jolee's Jewels Luscious
Rose Gold (Café au Lait); pink pavé rhinestone star
charms: Jolee's Jewels Assorted Pavé Stars Crystal
Violet (Bisou); silver post earrings with aquamarine
crystals: Jolee's Jewels Earring Posts Crystal Ribbon
Swirl Aquamarine (Caribbean Sea); Austrian crys-
tal bicones in smoke, crystal, pink, and champagne:
Jolee's Jewels Crystal Bicone Bead Star Mix (Frosting);
Austrian crystal bicones in plum, violet, light amethyst,
and lilac: Jolee's Jewels Crystal Bicone Bead Purple Mix
(Plum Delicious)

MANNY'S MILLINERY SUPPLY COMPANY

26 West 38th Street
New York, NY 10018
212-840-2235
www.mannys-millinery.com

Silk and velvet flowers and exotic feathers

Velvet flower pin with eyelash feathers (Torch Song)

METALLIFEROUS

34 West 46th Street, 2nd Floor
New York, NY 10036
212-944-0909
www.metalliferous.com

Metal findings, wire, chain, and bangles; good source for tools and supplies

Fruit and leaf stamped-brass charm (Café au Lait); copper beads (Gold Digger)

MICHAELS STORES, INC.

8000 Bent Branch Drive
Irving, TX 75063
800-642-4235
www.michaels.com

National craft-supply store with comprehensive beading section with semiprecious stones and pearls, tools, and supplies including Scrimp Beads, Smart Beads, Jolee's Jewels, and Petals a Plenty.

Transite (Pink Champagne/Bee Mine/Hard Candy cocktail rings/Raspberry barrette); lime green wire (Lime Wire); gold filigree heart charm, polka dot paper, clear and alphabet sticker sheets, heat gun (Bisou); rose gold beads (Starry Night); filigree oval connectors (The Nile); super-sticky double-sided tape (Stardust hair combs)

M&J TRIMMING

1008 Sixth Avenue
New York, NY 10018
212-204-9595
800-965-8746
www.mjtrim.com

Ribbons, trim, buttons, beads, feathers, and Swarovski flat-back rhinestones and pointed-back jewels with sew-on settings

All rhinestone buttons (Wildfire/Lots of Luxe/Hothouse Flowers/Bee Mine/Dew Drop/Orange Blossom); flat-back rhinestones (Lorelei Lee/Torch Song); purple square rhinestone and crystal square rhinestone, pointed-back Swarovski jewels with sew-on settings (Plum Delicious/Stardust); Indian peacock-eye feathers and feather pads (Torch Song)

NEW YORK BEADS

1026 Sixth Avenue
New York, NY 10018
212-382-2994
www.beadson5th.com

Loose and strung beads, semiprecious stones, Swarovski crystals, pearls, chains, findings, tools, and supplies

PETALS A PLENTY

Plaid Enterprises, Inc.
3225 Westech Drive
Norcross, GA 30092
800-842-4197
www.plaidonline.com

Beads, chain, findings, and charms (also available in Michaels Stores)

Double-sided metal connectors with floral detail, double-sided flower connectors with green enamel centers, robin's-egg blue beads, red beads, rectangular cable-link chain, blue feather charms, yellow flower charms, metal flower charms, red metal roses, green beads, metal beads, yellow flower-shaped charms, blue flower-shaped charms (Storybook); blue metal roses (Desert Sky); yellow and green metal roses, antique copper ring form (Primrose Path)

SHIPWRECK BEADS

8560 Commerce Place Drive NE
Lacey, WA 98516
800-950-4232
www.shipwreckbeads.com

Large supply of Czech crystal, pressed-glass beads and fire-polished beads, semiprecious stones, Swarovski crystals, pearls, chains, findings, tools, and supplies

All Czech pressed-glass flowers and leaves (Hothouse Flowers)

STAR'S CLASPS

139 A Church Street NW
Vienna, VA 22180
800-207-2805
www.starsclasps.com

Wide variety of clasps

STRUNG OUT ON BEADS

33735 Essendene Avenue
Abbotsford, B.C.
Canada V25 2G7
604-852-8677
www.strungoutonbeads.ca

Wide variety of Czech beads and Austrian and Chinese crystals

TINSEL TRADING

47 West 38th Street
New York, NY 10018
212-730-1030
www.tinseltrading.com

Cords, ribbons, trims, buttons, beads, and flowers

TOHO SHOJI

990 Sixth Avenue
New York, NY 10018
212-868-7466
www.tohoshojiny.com

Loose and strung beads, semiprecious stones, Swarovski crystals, pearls, shell beads, chains, findings, and wide variety of hair findings

Faceted, smooth and filigree gold beads (Gold Digger); silver filigree oval pendant setting (Victoria); two-part barrette with beading oval (Raspberry barrette); gold hair comb (Orange Blossom)

TRINKETS BY T VINTAGE BEADS

Kirkland, WA 98033
206-399-3319
425-827-6615
www.trinketsbyt.com

Vintage crystal and vintage Lucite flower beads

Lucite trumpet, large and small flowers (Country Garden); green ceramic rose beads (Romantic Notions)

VENETIAN BEAD SHOP

1010 Stewart Drive
Sunnyvale, CA 94085
800-439-3551
www.venetianbeadshop.com

Venetian glass beads

THE WHOLE BEAD SHOP

PO Box 1100
Nevada City, CA 95959
800-796-5350
www.wholebeadshop.com

Unique foil-lined lampwork beads, German metal beads and findings, vintage buttons, and pendants

Celadon frosted-glass leaves (Country Garden/Mint Julep); gold twisted coins, gold oval jump rings, gold floral clasp (Sun-Kissed); pale yellow pressed-glass flower beads (Watercolors); pink birds pendant (Bisou); yellow foil-lined lampwork beads (Hothouse Flowers); gold headpins and gold fishhook (French) earring wires (Hampton Classic); gold ring form (La Vie en Rose); frosted crystal briolettes, crystal AB quilted discs (Stardust)

WONDER SOURCES, INC.

48 West 38th Street, Ground Floor
New York, NY 10018
212-563-4990
www.wondersources.com

Wide variety of semiprecious loose and strung beads

Rose quartz nuggets (Coco); carnelian nuggets (Sun-Kissed); light teal dyed quartz beads (Watercolors); turquoise beads (Oasis)

INDEX

MASTERING THE ART of BEADING

ACKNOWLEDGMENTS

····· IT TAKES A VILLAGE. ·····
THIS BOOK TOOK TWO.

Thank you to everyone at Chronicle Books who made this book possible, but most especially to Laura Lee Mattingly for her incredible patience and tireless hard work and Andrew Schapiro for his vision and gorgeous design work. Thank you also to Michelle Clair, Claire Fletcher, Laura Harger, Molly Jones, Nancy Deane, Christina Loff, Brenda Modliszewski, and Jodi Warshaw.

I would also like to thank my team in New York for their talent and dedication. Steven Mays, my wonderful friend, who knows that wine and music make all things better; Joe Pequigney, for patience which passeth all understanding; Marina Malchin, my miracle worker; Frank Santopadre for all your support; Gabrielle Sterbenz, who was a huge help and a whiz with the calipers; John Sterbenz, my personal bead-shopping chauffeur; Carol Sterbenz who dropped everything and came running at a moment's notice; Anne Newgarden for her turn of phrase and Maureen Mulligan—a twisted wire genius. I could not have done this without each and every one of you.

ABOUT THE AUTHOR

GENEVIEVE A. STERBENZ is a lifestyle expert and author of ten craft and home decorating books. She has won several awards for her work and has been featured on national television programs on networks such as CBS, the Discovery Channel, and HGTV. She lives in New York, NY. Visit her online at www.genevievesterbenz.com.

STEVEN MAYS has shot for Time Life Books, the Meredith Corporation, Abrams, Rizzoli, Hyperion, and Hearst Publications. He has a long and happy history of working with his friend Genevieve A. Sterbenz on craft and beading books. He lives in New York, NY.